SEX

with

PRESIDENTS

ALSO BY ELEANOR HERMAN

Nonfiction

The Royal Art of Poison

King Peggy *(with Peggielene Bartels)*

Mistress of the Vatican

Sex with the Queen

Sex with Kings

Murder in the Garden of God

Blood of Gods and Royals Series

Dawn of Legends

Reign of Serpents

Empire of Dust

Legacy of Kings

Voice of Gods

Queen of Ashes

SEX

with

PRESIDENTS

The Ins and Outs of
Love and Lust

in the White House

ELEANOR HERMAN

WILLIAM MORROW
An Imprint of HarperCollinsPublishers

HarperCollins books may be purchased for educational, business, or sales promotional use. For information, please email the Special Markets Department at SPsales@harpercollins.com.

FIRST EDITION

Designed by Nancy Singer

Interior images @ Amili/Shutterstock (historical costume); @ Varlamova Lydmila/Shutterstock (wedding rings); @ Morphart Creation/Shutterstock (White House); @ Vkilikov/Shutterstock (Thomas Jefferson); @ Christophe BOISSON/Shutterstock (American postcard); @ ullstein bild Dtl./Getty Images (White House photo)

Library of Congress Cataloging-in-Publication Data has been applied for.

ISBN 978-0-06-297056-5

20 21 22 23 24   LSC   10 9 8 7 6 5 4 3 2 1

To Mary Frances Manning, who eased for me the loss of my mother. You are family.

CONTENTS

There is no one whose sexual life, if it were broadcast, would not fill the world at large with surprise and horror.

—W. SOMERSET MAUGHAM

SEX

with

PRESIDENTS

INTRODUCTION

$\mathcal{I}$t is a truth universally acknowledged that the Achilles' heel is located nowhere near a person's foot but rather higher up. It has always been this way with humankind. In the beginning, Eve gave Adam an apple and, let's face it, he probably gave her a banana in return. They suddenly realized what those strange body parts were for and as a result got kicked out of Paradise. Fast-forward to the 1490s, when a new plague swept Europe, rotting private parts, bones, and noses with excruciating pain, followed by madness and death. Spread by sexual contact, syphilis, as one sixteenth-century apothecary put it, "Comes from choosing beds unknown and plugging holes best left alone." Few, alas, could bring themselves to stop plugging those unknown holes.

Who among us hasn't had at least one sexual encounter that was unwise, unsafe, or unethical? We risk losing marriages, friends, and even our lives for a sweet coupling that lasts minutes and the soaring exultation of an orgasm measured in seconds. The sex drive mocks logic and is resistant to common sense. This primeval instinct overpowers us, causing us to lose all self-control. Such loss of control never has more explosive consequences than when played out in the bedrooms of world leaders. Those dalliances affect not just an individual, a marriage, or a family. They affect entire nations.

Of course, some political leaders lose their self-control more often than others. "You know, I get a migraine headache if I don't get a strange piece of ass every day," President John F. Kennedy told British prime minister Harold Macmillan in 1962. Kennedy used sex with strangers not just as aspirin, but also to project a presidential image. On September 26, 1960, an hour and a half before the first-ever televised live presidential debate, Democratic nominee Kennedy cavorted with a prostitute in his Chicago hotel room for fifteen minutes. During the debate, he appeared relaxed, radiant, and confident. The Republican nominee, Richard M. Nixon—tense, sweating, and gray-skinned—looked as if he hadn't been laid in years. Chicago mayor Richard J. Daley said, "My God, they've embalmed him before he even died." Kennedy won the debate by a large margin among the seventy million television viewers. He was so pleased with his performance that he arranged to bed prostitutes right before every debate after that.

Donald Trump follows in a historic tradition of scandalous presidential sex. Weeks before the 2016 presidential election, his lawyer and fixer Michael Cohen paid porn star Stormy Daniels $130,000 for her silence about a one-night stand she had allegedly had with Trump ten years earlier. The resulting lies, cover-ups, shifting narratives, denials, and eventual admissions have resulted in Cohen sitting in the slammer for three years for campaign finance violations and the possibility that the president himself might be indicted after leaving office. And all because of—according to Stormy Daniels—two minutes of really bad sex.

Despite the American reputation for prudery, many of our leaders have had a colorful sexual past. One beloved president suffered a fatal stroke in his mistress's presence. Another was gay.

At least two first ladies were so fed up with their husband's phi-landering that they almost certainly had affairs of their own, one with a woman. Three presidents have been accused of rape. An-other had a thirty-year affair and seven children with his enslaved woman, and a leading presidential hopeful had a love child with his mistress while his wife was dying.

Why have so many national leaders been adulterers? Henry Kissinger, the secretary of state and national security advisor un-der presidents Nixon and Ford, had an explanation: "Power is the ultimate aphrodisiac." And he should know. With his Coke-bottle glasses, unprepossessing features, and a German accent thick as blutwurst, Kissinger was known as "Dr. Strangelove" in Wash-ington circles. Still, as one of the nation's most influential men, Kissinger bedded Hollywood's sexiest sirens.

Edgar Faure, prime minister of France twice in the 1950s, said, "When I was minister, some women resisted me." This is not surprising, as he was balding and bespectacled with thick lips and ears like Dumbo. "Once I became prime minister," he added, "not even one."

In the course of exploring the sex scandals of U.S. presidents and European leaders, we will discover the answers to several burning questions. For instance, what is sex like with the presi-dent of a nation? Does the man's charisma, his passion and zest for power make it better than with an average Joe—Donald Trump aside? Fortunately, letters and biographies illuminate both the delights and disappointments of presidential passion. More im-portantly, we will explore the issue of whether a strong sex drive has any relevance to political success or failure. Does rampant adultery show a lack of character, the stamina needed to run the country, or a bit of both?

And why have first ladies stayed married to such disgraceful philanderers—with the exception of one Italian who notified her husband of her intention to divorce by publishing her grievances in a major daily newspaper? Do these women make a Faustian bargain? They accept a life of luxury and fame as the price for humiliation and betrayal that everyone in the world knows about? Why did Hillary stick to Bill like glue—rambling on about a vast right-wing conspiracy—instead of throwing his gasoline-soaked clothes out the White House bedroom window, running downstairs, and setting them on fire? Why does Melania stay with Donald, giving vent to her fury in passive-aggressive fits of wearing inappropriate jackets and slapping his hand away on the red carpet? What kind of woman would make such a deal? Is any amount of money worth it?

What about presidential girlfriends? What's in it for them? Centuries ago, royal mistresses bedding smelly old kings received premium pay packages: titles, lands, castles, and jewels. But presidential mistresses would be more likely to receive rewards along the lines of an official White House paperweight. Is it the excitement that attracts these women? Being, for a few minutes, at the epicenter of the universe? Do some of them set out to bag a powerful man, like JFK's countless girlfriends who gleefully disported themselves on the first lady's sheets? Is getting the president in bed a kind of trophy?

We will examine the differences between the American reaction to such love affairs and people of other nations. When Americans have caught their leaders with their pants down around their ankles, they have often reacted with shock and outrage. Astonishingly, the founding strain of puritanism brought to Plymouth, Massachusetts, by a few dozen bleak souls in 1620 existed until quite recently in the American character—even four centuries and 330 million citizens of all nationalities later, a kind of virus from hell, resistant to time, genetic dilution, and common sense.

Lyndon Johnson once raged to his mistress, "If a man can't do a little of what he's not supposed to, he ain't much of a man. Hell, our country is so outdated. Why can't we do like the Chinese and fuck all the women we want and populate the world like the good Lord wanted us to? What is so goddamned wrong with that? In this fucking Victorian society, we've become stalemated by fucking only one woman."

Many Europeans would agree. From time immemorial, their reaction to such behavior has been a slow smile followed by a wink. Perhaps it should come as no surprise that France has the unique distinction of being the only nation where a president is known to have died while receiving oral sex from a mistress in the presidential palace, a fact that swells some Gallic breasts with pride.

We will also investigate the changing role of the press in such scandals. Since the 1790s, the American press has, at times, formed a barricade of complicit silence, maintaining the fiction of presidential dignity in the face of adultery, orgies, abortions, and sweaty grappling in White House closets. At other times, reporters scenting a sex story have resembled sharks in a feeding frenzy.

Lastly, we will examine the recent death of American puritanism. Because the truth is no one even pretends to care about political sex scandals anymore, not even evangelical Christians, who hold their nose when they vote for Donald Trump.

ARTICLE I
SOURCES

*N*ational leaders are, by their very nature, the subjects of copious written material. Most such material focuses on policy issues, with love affairs, if they are mentioned at all, a mere footnote. In some cases, the absence of juicy sex stories is not due to the unsullied conduct of the president, but because of a dearth of detailed information in the form of love letters, autobiographies, and newspaper reports.

For instance, James Garfield, who was president for only six months in 1881 before being felled by an assassin's bullet, had an affair in 1862 with an eighteen-year-old *New York Times* correspondent named Lucia Calhoun. His passionless wife, Lucretia, found the girl's love letters and convinced him to give up the relationship. What wouldn't we give to read those letters from a sex-obsessed teenager to the thirty-one-year-old future president. But, alas, thin-lipped Lucretia most probably poured whale oil on them and burned them.

James Buchanan (served 1857–1861)—often ranked as the worst U.S. president ever for his bungling of events leading up to the Civil War—had a thirteen-year affair with a man, William Rufus King, who was vice president for six weeks in 1853 as he fought a losing battle against consumption. Buchanan was the only U.S. president who never married, but he and King often lived together. In political circles, they were known as Mr. and Mrs. Buchanan, or Miss Nancy and Aunt Fancy, terms at the time used to denote gay men. When King served as ambassador to France in 1844, Buchanan wrote to a friend, "I am so solitary and alone having no companion with me. I have gone wooing to several gentlemen but have not succeeded with any of them."

Many in political circles understood the nature of their relationship, but the press never reported a word about it, even in a time of fevered yellow journalism. Historians believe this was because the press couldn't begin to grapple with the concept of homosexuality. Considered unnatural and unspeakable, it was also unwritable. Ironically, this morbid prejudice against homosexuality served at times to protect gay individuals. Though there were no newspaper articles on the relationship, we might have hoped to have some of the hundreds of letters Buchanan and King wrote each other as their political duties often separated them. These letters were evidently consigned to the flames by prim relatives who had cleaned out the desks of the deceased and, as they read hot and steamy gay love letters, felt their heads explode. And so almost nothing is known of the love affair of President Buchanan and Vice President King.

We have, alas, only the broadest outlines of another unusual affair. Richard Mentor Johnson of Kentucky, who served as Martin Van Buren's vice president from 1837 to 1841, called his enslaved woman Julia Chinn his wife, even though mixed-race marriages were illegal. He installed her as the mistress of his plantation, where they raised their two daughters as ladies, both of whom married rich white gentlemen. Newspapers excoriated him. One wrote, "He has endeavored often to force his daughters into society, that the mother in her lifetime, and they now, rode in carriages, and claimed equality. The idea of voting for him is loathed beyond anything that has occurred with us."

After Julia Chinn died, he took a second enslaved woman as his mistress but sold her at auction when he discovered she had been unfaithful. He brought his third African American mistress to Washington, D.C., and took her to social gatherings as his wife. It was not Johnson's choice of sex partners that caused the furor. He was, after all, only following in the footsteps of Thomas Jefferson. His insistence that his mistresses be recognized as social equals, though enslaved African Americans, created the resentment.

Nor is much known about Richard Nixon's affair with Hong Kong cocktail hostess Marianna Liu, whom the FBI believed was a spy for the Communist Chinese. They had met in 1966 at the bar where she worked in the Hilton Hotel, enjoyed a fling, and saw each other periodically. When Nixon announced his candidacy for the presidency in 1968, the FBI grew concerned. The Chinese government often placed gorgeous spies in Hong Kong cocktail lounges to seduce Western businessmen and politicians. Liu mysteriously owned extensive real estate in Hong Kong, far beyond the means of her modest salary, and the father of one of her closest friends was a general in the Red Army. Agents feared Liu could blackmail a future U.S. president. Undeterred, Nixon invited her to the White House and arranged for her to become a permanent U.S. resident.

Fortunately for us, most high-level U.S. political sex scandals are well documented. Some of the leaders themselves have written about their romances. Founding Father Alexander Hamilton published a hundred-page booklet about his illicit love affair. The rapturously pornographic love letters of Warren G. Harding speak for themselves, as do Woodrow Wilson's more discreet missives. Newspapers covered in graphic detail Thomas Jefferson's relationship with his enslaved woman Sally Hemings, Grover Cleveland's illegitimate child with a seamstress, Gary Hart's weekend with a blonde, and Bill Clinton's affairs with a lounge singer and an intern.

Warren Harding's young lover Nan Britton, mother of his child, was the first presidential mistress to write a kiss-and-tell book, in 1927. *The President's Daughter* was so graphic for the time that no publisher would touch it; she self-published and made herself a fortune. Dwight Eisenhower's lover, Kay Summersby, wrote of their wartime romance as she lay dying in 1975.

Several of John F. Kennedy's mistresses have written memoirs: "Mafia Moll" Judith Campbell, Swedish aristocrat Gunilla von Post, and White House intern Mimi Beardsley. Retired White House servants also published recollections of presidential misbehavior. In her memoirs, seamstress Lillian Parks saw Franklin Roosevelt's secretary Missy LeHand wandering in and out of his bedroom in her nightgown and Eleanor Roosevelt's girlfriend Lorena Hickock sleeping on the daybed in the first lady's bedroom. Dog keeper Traphes Bryant wrote of Kennedy's nude swimming parties in the White House pool. President Trump's one-night stand, porn star Stormy Daniels, not only wrote a book but also tweets about her liaison.

We even know the names some U.S. presidents called their penises. Warren Harding dubbed his appendage "Jerry." Lyndon Johnson named his "Jumbo" and sometimes waved it around when he was mad about Vietnam, showing off its impressive eight-and-a-half-inch length to envious male staff and admiring journalists. Bill Clinton dubbed his "Willard." It is tempting to believe that Richard Nixon called his "Tricky Dick," but we can't be sure.

THE CHANGING WHITE HOUSE

*T*he presidential residence at 1600 Pennsylvania Avenue in Washington, D.C., has had various names since John Adams moved into a smoky, partially finished shell in 1800: the President's House, the Executive Mansion, and the White House. According to a popular myth, the building wasn't called the White House until after it was whitewashed in 1814 to cover the scorch marks left by British arsonists. The fact is that the building has been white since its first paint job in 1798, and it was referred to as the White House in several newspapers before the Brits burned it. In 1901, President Theodore Roosevelt officially dubbed it the White House.

In 1902, Roosevelt built the West Wing after his wife complained about the presidential offices just down the hall from her bedroom—most presidents used the Lincoln Bedroom as their office until that time. She wanted a completely domestic space for the family, a cocoon of privacy, where she could walk out of her bedroom in curlers and a bathrobe without running into visiting dignitaries. Roosevelt razed a collection of ghastly mid-Victorian greenhouses to the west of the residence to build office space for himself and his staff, though his office was rectangular. His successor, William Taft, expanded the West Wing and created the first Oval Office to mirror the oval rooms on the south side of the White House. In 1933, Franklin Roosevelt, unhappy with the West Wing, redesigned it, creating the current Oval Office on the old laundry drying yard, in part because a room without corners made it easier for a wheelchair-bound individual to navigate. It was a bit larger than the first Oval Office and had more private access to the residence, useful for a handicapped president who pretended to the American people that he was not disabled. The same year, FDR built the White House swimming pool between the main building and the West Wing, as he found swimming an enjoyable form of physical therapy.

By the time of the Truman presidency, the White House was falling apart, its great age exacerbated by other factors. In the late nineteenth century, the building had been updated with modern amenities: running water, radiator heating, and electricity, with heavy pipes and wires run throughout the walls and floors. Further updates included an elevator, along with several bathrooms with marble fixtures, yet no braces were inserted to support the additional weight. Worse, in 1927 an entire third floor was added, providing fourteen much-needed new guest rooms, bathrooms, and storage areas, but causing tremendous structural strain. The building periodically shook, as if in a minor earthquake, and enormous cracks appeared in the walls. In the summer of 1948, the leg of first daughter Margaret Truman's baby grand piano sank through the decayed floor of her upstairs sitting room, causing plaster to crash down in the Family Dining Room below. She wrote, "For most of 1948, we lived in a forest of steel pipes in our bedrooms and sitting rooms. They were supposed to hold up the ceilings, but they could do nothing about the rot that was destroying the old timber."

Experts agreed that the White House was standing "purely from habit" and was in danger of imminent collapse, sending the president, his family, his staff, and all those historic antiques into a mushroom cloud of splinters and pilasters. Architects came up with three proposals: tear down the White House and build a new one on the site; build a new presidential residence elsewhere in the District of Columbia; or restore the existing structure. Fortunately, the third option was chosen. Truman and his family moved across the street to Blair House, which had been used as guest quarters for visiting dignitaries, while the White House was gutted down to the original bare stone walls. These were shored up from below by a new concrete foundation, and from within they were braced by a steel skeleton, which would support the weight of the rebuilt interior.

FDR's swimming pool, outside the main White House structure, survived the renovation. John F. Kennedy used it to treat his appallingly bad back, heating it up to 100 degrees. Richard Nixon, on the other hand, didn't like to swim. In 1970, he covered over the pool—it's still down there somewhere—beneath a new press briefing room. Before that, presidents gave press conferences in various rooms of the White House itself, which allowed journalists to traipse through and nose about. Nixon, secretive and paranoid with good reason, as it turned out, exiled reporters to the West Wing and out of his dark, Brylcreem-slicked hair. Or so he thought.

1

THE MEN WHO BECOME PRESIDENT: RISK-TAKING NARCISSISM

*I*t is a logical assumption that most sane people would not want to become president of a nation. Who in their right mind would want the unceasing stress, the death threats, the vicious criticism, and the constant chaos? The majority of those in possession of good mental health would choose peaceful, middle-class anonymity hands down over bone-grinding torture in an impressive palace.

When George Washington's vice president, John Adams, considered running for president in 1796, his wife, Abigail, warned, "You know what is before you—the whips, the scorpions, the thorns without roses, the dangers, anxieties, the weight of empire." Yes, yes he did. And he wanted it anyway.

And, indeed, there is a dark side to the dazzling confidence, the charm, and the talent to persuade and inspire possessed in such stunning quantities by many world leaders. In 2009, a team of psychologists identified a disorder they called "hubris syndrome." This illness is not genetic or inherent; it does not appear by early adulthood as most personality disorders do, including its evil twin, narcissistic personality disorder. Hubris syndrome *is acquired by wielding power over a period of time*. In other words, power *triggers* the illness. And when the power is gone, the illness subsides.

Characteristics include impulsivity, restlessness, recklessness, contempt for the advice of others, and overweening pride. Those who have it see the world as an arena in which to wield power and seek glory. They focus obsessively on their personal image, lose contact with reality, and see themselves as omnipotent messiahs. Unable to admit they have made a mistake, they find themselves increasingly isolated. No matter what horrors occur on their watch, they believe that history will vindicate them.

Long before the 2009 study, nineteenth-century American suffragist Elizabeth Cady Stanton noticed the correlation between imprudence and power. She wrote, "I have known statesmen, soldiers, scientists, men trusted with interests and empires devoted to the public good, whose patriotism no one doubted, yet reckless of their business and family affairs."

Lillian Parks, a White House seamstress who observed presidents from 1909 to 1960, said, "Maybe you're a lot better off married to an average American. As far as I can see, no average man ever became President . . . The White House uses people up like soap."

Some of the characteristics of world leaders are also the manic symptoms of bipolar disorder: increased energy and restlessness, euphoria, irritability, wild mood swings, unrealistic beliefs in one's abilities, poor judgment, increased sex drive, the need for little sleep, and a denial that anything is wrong.

Lyndon Johnson exhibited clear symptoms of both bipolar

and narcissistic personality disorders. As president, he had an obsessive need for secrecy and labeled anyone who disagreed with
him a Communist, a traitor, or a spy in the pay of the Kennedy
family. Refusing to take any personal responsibility for poor
choices—such as sinking the country ever deeper into the Vietnam conflict—he blamed all his failures on a conspiracy of his
enemies. For days on end, he would lie in bed with the covers
pulled over his head, then jump up and make a hundred phone
calls in a row. Johnson's press secretary George Reedy said that
he walked "on air" one minute and then was ready to "slash his
wrists" the next. Worried about Johnson's behavior, his special
assistant Richard Goodwin consulted psychiatrists, who provided
him some comfort. Johnson's personality type, they said, in its in-
spirational, indefatigable expression, could achieve great things
like leading "a Senate or even an entire country." Which was
true. On the domestic front—with Medicare, Head Start, and
the Voting Rights Act—Johnson accomplished as much as Franklin D. Roosevelt. In other words, some leaders are successful *because* they are crazy.

While not all politically ambitious men have hubris syndrome
or bipolar disorder in their full-blown expression, many are narcissistic risk-takers with feelings of invincibility. Seekers of high
sensation, risk-takers feed upon the thrill of knowing they could
get caught doing something they shouldn't. Afterward, they triumph in knowing they didn't get caught. They outsmarted everyone. And they are, primarily, in love with themselves.

Easily sexually aroused, they are always searching for the
next burst of excitement. On his trips abroad, French president
François Mitterrand, in his sixties, often disappeared with young
women for a couple of hours after his speeches. A friend of his

once remarked that he already had a wife and a mistress of many years, and a revolving harem of other lovers. "You are no longer twenty," she chided. "What's the point?"

Mitterrand replied solemnly, "You cannot understand. When I descend the tribunal, after the effervescence of the speech, I need to end in the arms of a woman."

There appears to be little difference between the thrills of seeking public power, with crowds of adoring fans, to seeking pubic power, with an adoring audience of one. The same compulsions that send a man hurtling toward the White House can also send him into a foolhardy tryst with a woman. High political office and dangerous sex are, in fact, all about hubris and power.

Research has shown that the severity of hubris syndrome, bipolar disorder, and narcissistic personality disorder spikes with increased power, resulting in ever riskier behavior. Warren G. Harding routinely had sex in a closet in the Oval Office, in one case when his wife was pounding angrily on the office door. As governor of New York, Franklin Roosevelt assigned his secretary and mistress, Missy LeHand, the bedroom next to his so that she could take dictation at any hour of the night, he said. In the White House, she lived a floor above Roosevelt but still wandered into his bedroom in her nightgown with no steno pad in hand, shocking the servants.

John F. Kennedy had sex with secretaries and prostitutes in the White House swimming pool and in his wife, Jackie's, bed. Lyndon Johnson's wife, Lady Bird, once walked into the Oval Office to find him in flagrante delicto with one of his secretaries on a sofa. A furious Johnson ordered the Secret Service to install a buzzer system. "If we saw Lady Bird heading for the elevator or stairs," an agent recalled, "we were to ring the buzzer."

As governor of Arkansas in the 1980s, Bill Clinton suggested he and his mistress, nightclub singer Gennifer Flowers, have sex during a party at the governor's mansion in the first-floor bathroom—with Hillary in the next room. According to Flowers, she turned him down. He also wanted to have sex with her in the state capitol building. "He liked the idea of having sex on his desk or on the floor with all his staffers right outside," she recalled in her 1995 memoir, *Passion and Betrayal.* "Bill felt an enormous sense of power from leading me into sexual adventures. He thought he was bulletproof in his relationship with me . . . He seemed to think nothing could ever touch him in an adverse way."

Donald Trump's risk-taking surprised former *Playboy* Playmate Karen McDougal, with whom he reputedly had an affair from 2006 to 2007. She told CNN's Anderson Cooper that Trump didn't care whether people saw them together and didn't seem to feel at all guilty about cheating on his wife. She said they made love in his home in New Jersey and once in his gilded Trump Tower apartment in New York City, where he lived with his wife and their young son, Barron. According to Karen, she asked, "Aren't you afraid to bring me here?"

Trump replied, "They won't say anything."

Porn star Stormy Daniels has a similar Donald Trump story. In an interview with *In Touch* magazine, she said, "He didn't seem worried about [anyone finding out about their tryst]. He was kind of arrogant. It did occur to me, 'That's a really stupid move on your part.'"

In 1912, the charismatic British politician David Lloyd George, who became prime minister in 1916, began a lifelong relationship with his secretary, Frances Stevenson, eventually fathering her child. It was an affair that could have ruined him politically had it come to public attention.

Italian prime minister Silvio Berlusconi went a tad further in his narcissism than his political colleagues, hanging up placards in all his palaces that read "Long Live Silvio!" He had private orgies, one of which featured twenty young women in naughty nun costumes dancing around an eight-foot-tall phallus, singing, "Thank God for Silvio!" In 2009, a psychiatrist said he suffered from "a personality with unlimited egocentricity."

"I am, far and away, the best prime minister that Italy has ever had in its one-hundred-and-fifty-year history," he said as he prepared to step down from office after a scandal involving sex with an underaged prostitute. He seemed to have forgotten that under him the Italian economy had tanked, unemployment had skyrocketed, and government services had ground to a halt.

According to their lovers, the risky behavior of Harding, Johnson, Kennedy, Clinton, Trump, Lloyd George, Mitterrand, and Berlusconi involved unprotected sex. In at least three cases (Lloyd George, Kennedy, and Clinton) this resulted in unwanted pregnancies and abortions. Not only did Lloyd George father a child with his mistress, but Harding, Mitterrand, and possibly Johnson did, too. Kennedy suffered from chronic chlamydia, a venereal disease, which may have caused Jackie's difficulty in having healthy children; out of a total of five pregnancies, she had one miscarriage, one stillbirth, and one infant who lived thirty-nine hours. There is a clear pattern among these men of recklessness, feelings of invincibility, and little concern for the collateral damage they caused to their wives and lovers.

Perhaps Michigan representative Candice Miller summed it up best in 2011, when she responded to a question about New York congressman Anthony Weiner tweeting photos of his wiener. "What is it with these guys?" she asked. "Don't they think they're going to get caught?"

Sadly, the answer is no. Or worse: they don't even care.

2

ALEXANDER HAMILTON AND THE IMPULSE OF PASSION

*A*merica's first political sex scandal began just fifteen years after the signing of the Declaration of Independence. A Founding Father, Alexander Hamilton never became president, yet his influence on the nation's history was far greater than that of many who did. His handling of the scandal has offered lessons to philandering politicians right up to President Trump, lessons most have unwisely chosen to ignore.

★ ★ ★

On a sizzling summer day in 1791, twenty-three-year-old Maria Reynolds called on the handsome, thirty-six-year-old Alexander Hamilton, then serving as the first U.S. treasury secretary, at his redbrick house in Philadelphia, ostensibly to ask for help. They had never met, but it was common for men of wealth and importance to accept visits from strangers seeking assistance. Hamilton must have been delighted that this particular stranger was so attractive.

Though we have no description of Maria's appearance, men seemed to go weak in the knees in her presence. Given the written records about her, and her own impassioned letters, we can paint a picture of this Drama Queen Sex Siren. She has huge breasts that she flaunts in her low-cut gowns, and a tiny waist. Her thick hair, which she leaves unpowdered, is the cascading wild tumble so fashionable at the time. Her big eyes are framed by long, dark lashes that she bats, but only at men. She is always ready to smile—let us give her dimples. Her voice is low and throaty, redolent of jazz and cigarettes, even though they haven't been invented yet. She positively radiates sex.

She told Hamilton that her husband, James Reynolds, had abandoned her for another woman, and she needed funds to return to her family in New York. She had turned to Hamilton as he was from New York and might be sympathetic to a fellow citizen in trouble. Perhaps Maria was also aware that the chivalrous Hamilton often assisted damsels in distress and had heard of his reputation as a ladies' man.

As Hamilton listened to her pathetic tale of abuse by James Reynolds—probably accompanied by a torrent of tears—he must have sized her up. The delectable young woman was offering herself to him in return for travel expenses. The temptation was irresistible. But Hamilton's wife, Eliza, and their four young children were just yards away from him. He told Maria that he wanted to help her, but she had come at an "inopportune time," as he later wrote. He got her address—a local boardinghouse—and promised to bring her thirty dollars, a substantial sum, about $800 in today's money. Clearly, he was intending to pay for more than stagecoach fare to New York.

"In the evening I put a bank-bill in my pocket and went to the house," he later confessed. "I inquired for Mrs. Reynolds and was shewn upstairs, at the head of which she met me and conducted me into a bedroom. I took the bill out of my pocket and gave it to her. Some conversation ensued from which it was quickly apparent that other than pecuniary consolation would be acceptable."

And so began the lurid affair that would trumpet Hamilton's sins in the tabloid press, tarnish his reputation, and humiliate his wife. Because Maria Reynolds didn't get dressed and take the next stagecoach home. She stayed in Philadelphia, enjoying an impassioned relationship with the treasury secretary. When, soon after the affair began, Eliza Hamilton took the children on a long visit to her father in Albany, Hamilton entertained Maria in the marital home and had sex with her on the marital bed. And when James Reynolds returned and reconciled with his wife, Hamilton continued seeing her. Soon, Alexander Hamilton, the second most important man in the country, and the brightest mind in that time of exceptionally bright minds, found himself the dim-witted victim of a tawdry extortion scheme that had targeted him in advance.

It was a strange, dark, and stupid detour in Hamilton's extraordinary life that, until this point, had arced ever upward. His was a rags-to-riches story, the stuff of an adventure novel. He had been born out of wedlock, a stain, in his time and place, that branded him as less-than, as if God himself had marked the boy as a moral misfit. His illegitimacy made him combative, ambitious, insecure, and swaggering, eager to prove he was the smartest guy in the room, and usually succeeding.

In 1772, community leaders in St. Croix, in the British West Indies, wanted to provide Hamilton—who was either sixteen or eighteen, records are unclear—with a brighter future. His mother was dead, his father had abandoned him years earlier, and he subsisted as a lowly clerk, reading every book he could get his hands on. Talented, personable, and brilliant, Hamilton's potential could never be realized on the sleepy little island. Benefactors raised funds to send him to New York to receive a sterling education.

In 1773, he entered King's College, now Columbia University, in New York City, where he impressed his professors and bolted through his studies, devouring legal and philosophical books in the library. He became an avid supporter of the Revolutionary cause, writing pamphlets and giving fiery speeches. When the university closed during the British occupation of New York, Hamilton put down his books, picked up his musket, and joined a militia, now reading every book he could on military strategy and history. Commissioned in February 1776 as a captain of artillery, he impressed his commanding officers with his precision drills of men in immaculate military dress, his profound military knowledge, and his valor in the Battle of Princeton on January 3, 1777.

Two weeks after the battle, George Washington, commander in chief of the Continental Army, invited Hamilton to join his staff as aide-de-camp, and soon relied on his administrative abilities and wide-ranging knowledge from all that reading. Though immensely popular with most, Hamilton's frankness insulted some, for his razor-sharp words could cut and slice just as efficiently as his razor-sharp bayonet. His friend William Sullivan said, "He was capable of inspiring the most affectionate attachment, but he could make those whom he opposed fear and hate him cordially." In fact, Hamilton loved being hated, dueling with words, and never-ending controversy.

Hamilton also loved women, with whom he flirted outrageously, and women loved him back. A slight figure at five foot seven, Hamilton had something delicate about him, almost feminine. With wavy chestnut hair and alert blue eyes, he had a face of elegant and surprising angles: a broad forehead, high cheekbones, beautifully molded thin lips, and a perfectly curved jaw. Hamilton's most distinguishing feature was his nose: high-bridged, bony, and irregular, thrust out impudently into the world, a metaphor in cartilage for its owner.

In 1780, he married Elizabeth Schuyler, daughter of General Philip Schuyler, one of New York's richest men, a true love match. Elizabeth—called Eliza and sometimes Betsey or Bess—was a pretty woman with dark brown hair, usually powdered white, with a little snub nose, full chin, and petite and shapely figure. But it was her charm that won the most admiration. Tench Tilghman, another one of George Washington's aides, described her as "a brunette with the most good-natured, lively, dark eyes that I ever saw, which threw a beam of good temper and benevolence over her whole countenance." In 1788, a French visitor, Brissot de Warville, said Eliza was "a delightful woman who combines both the charms and attractions and the candor and simplicity typical of American womanhood."

The first rumors of Hamilton's adultery came not long after his marriage and were disturbing indeed, as they concerned Eliza's sister, the vivacious, flirtatious Angelica. Only eighteen months older than Eliza, in 1777 Angelica had married the fabulously wealthy John Church. If she had been single three years later, it is quite possible that Hamilton would have married Angelica instead. Angelica was as different from Eliza in personality as she was in looks. She was taller and blond, with a long nose, and looked rather like an attractive collie in heat. A sophisticated fashion diva who would, in coming years, charm the elite of London and Paris, Angelica was, in short, more like Hamilton himself.

Those who saw Hamilton and Angelica—and sensed the crackling sexual energy between them—assumed they were lovers. Angelica never concealed her admiration for Hamilton, not even from Eliza. One missive in particular raises eyebrows. "I love him very much," she wrote her sister, "and if you were as generous as the old Romans, you would lend him to me for a little while . . . Ah! Bess! You were a lucky girl to get so clever and so good a companion." Hamilton wrote to Angelica in an equally flirtatious tone. Eliza never showed any sign of jealousy but seemed flattered that her older, more worldly sister thought so highly of Hamilton. She must have believed there was no physical relationship between the two. Maybe she was right. Or maybe not.

Prudish John Adams believed Hamilton and Angelica were having an affair, and it wasn't his only one. "His fornications, adulteries and his incests [an apparent insinuation that he had slept with his sister-in-law] were propagated far and wide," Adams wrote.

Most of Hamilton's substantial energy, however, would be directed not at fornications, adulteries, and incests, but at forming a new, sustainable U.S. government. The unity of the thirteen states fractured after the Redcoats sailed home. Each state—with its distinct personality, economy, boisterous hopes, and thundering fears—had its own ideas about governance. The Articles of Confederation, enacted in 1777, loosely regulated thirteen mini-kingdoms, granting states great power and severely limiting the central government. There was no provision for a chief executive and no federal taxing power. Indeed, no one wanted to mention the "t" word. Weren't taxes the reason they had rebelled against Great Britain to begin with? Many Americans felt that, with the Brits gone, now was the time to truly enjoy themselves in some kind of giant national frat party with limitless kegs.

Freedom is a wonderful concept, bankruptcy less so. The combined total loans from European banks to the thirteen states and the Continental Congress was some $79 million (more than

$2 billion in today's money), and the U.S. had no way to repay it. Welching on loans meant the young nation wouldn't be able to borrow more. Due to the lack of funds, soldiers had gone unpaid for years. Some had lost farms; others feared they would be thrown into debtors' prison upon leaving the army. Many soldiers marched on Congress demanding their pay.

Clearly, Hamilton believed, what was needed was a federal government collecting taxes, paying back old loans, negotiating new ones, and regulating trade, and an army run by the federal government rather than a hodgepodge of state militias with different uniforms, training, equipment, and regulations. But to do so, the Articles of Confederation had to be replaced with a Constitution. In 1787, Hamilton, who had been practicing as a lawyer, was named a delegate to what we know as the Constitutional Convention in Philadelphia. Many other delegates, particularly from the South, feared strong federal power, as it reminded them of the heavy-handed overreach of Great Britain they had so recently shaken off.

After four months of blistering debate and quite a few compromises on both sides, the Constitution was completed in September and ratified the following June. Hamilton's push for a strong central government had become law, and the basic elements of our present system of government—three equal branches of government and two legislative houses—came into effect. George Washington was chosen as the nation's first president to great acclaim. Given the fractious politics of the time, only a man of his superhuman dignity could preside over the squabbling sure to ensue.

Washington knew he would need a Cabinet, even though the Constitution didn't mention one. He appointed Hamilton as secretary of the treasury, Thomas Jefferson as secretary of state, and a Revolutionary War hero, Henry Knox, as secretary of war. Hamilton's department started off with thirty-nine employees. State had only five. War—which had no war to run—had two, Knox and a clerk.

Hamilton had to create a customs service on the spot, which would account for 90 percent of government revenue, and pushed Congress to form what would become the U.S. Coast Guard to prevent smuggling. By late 1790, he had already amassed a sizable government surplus. Loans were being paid back, government securities had tripled in value, and the country was enjoying high economic growth. In 1792, Hamilton created a national mint: most coins in circulation at the time were Spanish doubloons, British pounds, and French guineas.

The Constitution does not mention political parties and George Washington did not belong to one. But almost immediately, politicians fell into one of two categories. Those like Hamilton who wanted a strong central government became known as Federalists. Those like Jefferson who wanted states to have the dominant power called themselves anti-Federalists, though they soon became known as Democratic-Republicans, naming themselves after the ancient Roman republic which had thrown off the tyranny of kings. Confusingly, they soon became known as Republicans, and by the 1820s, Democrats.

The feud of the early 1790s is still with us today. Today's Republicans generally support a smaller government, greater states' rights, less federal control, and reduced taxation and regulation. Today's Democrats support greater regulation and federal control, greater government debt, and higher taxation.

The American press, which had gleefully lampooned King George III, his taxes, and his soldiers, now turned to partisan politics, an eighteenth-century version of Fox News and MSNBC.

Each paper was either Republican or Federalist and spent much of its ink skewering the other side with little regard to facts, gleefully spreading fear and hate. Americans devoured the vitriol. Then, as now, citizens loved good stories that gripped the heart and stirred up righteous anger. They enjoyed booing the villains, cheering the heroes, and shedding tears for victims. It was easier to see the world in clear, comforting black and white, rather than in fifty shades of confusing, morally ambiguous gray. Moreover, the news they chose confirmed the beliefs they held already, helping them avoid the discomfort of realizing they may, in fact, be wrong.

In his countless newspaper columns eviscerating Republicans, Hamilton presented himself as a paragon of virtue—a tactic that would later come back to haunt him. Writing of himself in the third person, he issued this challenge to his opponents: "Mr. Hamilton can, however, defy all their malevolent ingenuity to produce a single instance of his conduct, public or private, inconsistent with the strict rules of integrity and honor." In September 1791, when his affair with Maria raged at a fever pitch, he boasted to a Federalist politician that he was a man whose character was above reproach. "I pledge myself to you and to every friend of mine," he wrote, "that the strictest scrutiny into every part of my conduct, whether as a private citizen or as a public officer, can only serve to establish the perfect purity of it."

It is almost inconceivable that a genius like Hamilton, knowing he had powerful enemies, would allow himself to have a year-long affair with a trollop like Maria Reynolds and subject himself to the threat of blackmail. When Maria's now-reconciled husband asked Hamilton for a cushy government job, that should have been the first clue something was wrong. Sensing Reynolds was a sleaze, Hamilton politely demurred—he would never compromise the public trust by placing this man in government—but he didn't cease contact. Maria, he later explained, wouldn't let him. "She employed every effort to keep up my attention and visits," he recalled. "Her pen was freely employed, and her letters were filled with those tender and pathetic effusions which would have been natural to a woman truly fond and neglected."

"I have kept my Bed those tow days," Maria wrote in one such illiterate effusion, "and now rise from My pillow wich your Neglect has filled with the sharpest thorns I no longer doubt what I hae Dreaded to no but stop I do not wish to se you to say any thing about my Late disappointments No I only do it to Ease a heart wich is ready Burst with Greef I can neither Eate or sleep I have been on the point of doing the moast horrid acts at I shudder to think where I might been what will Become of me."

As if her letters weren't disturbing enough, Maria's past was darker than Hamilton knew. She had married the much older Reynolds when she was fifteen, and he soon began pimping her. The son of her first landlady in Philadelphia, Richard Folwell, later wrote, "She told me, so infamous was the perfidy of Reynolds, that he had frequently enjoined and insisted that she should insinuate herself on certain high and influential characters— endeavor to make assignations with them and actually prostitute herself to gull money from them." For a time, Maria dabbled in outright prostitution. Gentlemen hoping for an assignation left letters in her entryway and "at night she would fly off as was supposed to answer their contents."

Unaware of her sordid past, Hamilton believed Maria was truly in love with him, and it must have flattered his vanity. This exotic, oversexed woman—we can picture her leaving scorch marks on the sheets—was quite different from his honest, reliable wife of eleven years. His obsession for Maria led him to persuade

Eliza to stay in Albany for as long as possible. Worried that his wife might return home to find Maria in her bed, he wrote, "Let me know beforehand your determination that I may meet you at New York." When, in late August, she seemed on the point of returning home, he wrote, "Much as I long for this happy moment, my extreme anxiety for the restoration of your health will reconcile me to your staying longer where you are . . . Think of me—dream of me—and love me my Betsey as I do you." In September, when Eliza started for home, he advised her, "Don't alarm yourself nor hurry so as to injure either yourself or the children."

Was Maria Reynolds his only love affair? We don't know of any others for certain, but probably not. The fact that hours after he first met her, he hotfooted it to her rooms with money in his pocket indicates he did not suffer the hesitation and pangs of conscience of a first adultery. John Adams traced Hamilton's libertine ways back to his time as aide to George Washington during the Revolution, after which Hamilton committed "debaucheries in New York and Philadelphia," where he had made "his audacious and unblushing attempts upon ladies of the highest rank and purest virtue." Adams's wife, Abigail, concurred. "Oh, I have read his heart in his wicked eyes," she wrote. "The very devil is in them. They are lasciviousness itself."

Even with both spouses back home, Maria and Hamilton continued the affair, Hamilton under a pretense of friendship with the oily James Reynolds. Then, on December 15, 1791, Reynolds informed Hamilton that his wife had confessed her affair to him. "I am very sorry to find out that I have been cruelly trated by a person that I took to be my best friend instead of that my greatest Enimy. You have deprived me of every thing that's near and dear to me," he wrote.

"Instead of being a Friend, you have acted the part of the

most Cruelist man in existence, you have made a whole family miserable. She ses there is no other man that she Care for in this world. Now Sir you have bin the Cause of Cooling her affections for me. She was a woman. I should as soon suspect an angiel from heven and one where all my happiness was depending. And I would Sacrefise almost my life to make her Happy. but now I am determed to have satisfaction."

Maria, too, sent a letter, stating that if Hamilton didn't reply to James, he would write Mrs. Hamilton of the affair. "O my God," Maria wrote, "I feel more for you than myself and wish I had never been born to giv you so mutch unhappisness do not rite to him no not a Line but come here soon do not send or leave any thing in his power Maria."

And so, Hamilton found himself charged with ruining a marriage by alienating the wife's affections, a serious legal predicament at the time. The threat of informing Eliza must have been much more frightening, especially since she was then pregnant with their fifth child. He explained, "No man tender of the happiness of an excellent wife could, without extreme pain, look forward to the affliction which she might endure from the disclosure, especially a public disclosure, of the fact. Those best acquainted with the interior of my domestic life will best appreciate the force of such a consideration upon me. The truth was that . . . I dreaded extremely a disclosure—and was willing to make large sacrifices to avoid it."

Large sacrifices indeed. Reynolds began squeezing Hamilton for blackmail money—some $1,100 (about $30,000 in today's money)—over the course of several months. Even then, Hamilton continued to bed Maria, often with James's acquiescence. He must have been sexually obsessed by the woman, needing her as an addict does a drug that sweeps him to heights of euphoria and then, as it wears off, dashes him into hell. At those moments when he found the strength to try to break up with her, she wept, implored, and sent impassioned misspelled letters laced with vague threats.

It was an unfortunate stroke of fate when James Reynolds's friend, Jacob Clingman, ran into Hamilton at the Reynolds home in April 1792. Clingman had impressive political connections; he had served as a clerk of the first speaker of the House of Representatives, Republican Frederick Muhlenberg of Pennsylvania. Why, Clingman wondered, would the second most important man in the country be on such intimate terms with his lowlife friend? Reynolds—unwilling to admit he had been pimping his wife—explained that Hamilton, far from being the epitome of virtue he bragged about, was giving him money to speculate in government securities on his behalf. Hamilton, who had enacted laws preventing government officials from dealing in government securities, had been breaking his own ethical regulations and had secretly made $30,000 ($830,000 today) from this criminal activity, Reynolds said. When Clingman doubted this story, Reynolds had him wait outside Hamilton's office while he went in. Minutes later, he came out with $100 (the equivalent of $2,800 in 2020).

Hamilton, horrified to have run into Jacob Clingman at Reynolds's home, finally understood the threat to his career and refused to see Maria again. He ignored her wailing pleas and gave her husband a final payment of $50 ($1,400 today). He must have felt intense relief when the annoying pair stopped contacting him, and his life returned to normal. It was over, he thought. But he was wrong.

The Reynolds affair might never have come to light if James Reynolds and Jacob Clingman had not been charged in November 1792 with defrauding old Revolutionary War soldiers, just six months after Hamilton's affair with Maria ended. Stewing in a cell, Reynolds asked Hamilton to spring him, and Hamilton refused. Whatever threat Reynolds posed, Hamilton was certainly not going to use his political position to free a vile criminal.

Unlike Reynolds, Clingman was no hard-core scoundrel and soon found himself out on bail. He told his former boss, Congressman Muhlenberg, that Reynolds possessed evidence of Hamilton's illegally amassing a fortune from speculation. Clingman gave the congressman several letters from Hamilton to Reynolds that seemed to back up his claim. Horrified, Muhlenberg invited two other Republicans, Senator James Monroe and Representative Abraham B. Venable, both of Virginia, to join in the investigation. They were delighted to be in a position to crucify the obnoxious, swashbuckling leader of the Federalist Party.

The delegation first visited Reynolds in jail, where he dropped threatening hints but refused to say another word until he was freed. But as soon as he got out, he briefly visited Hamilton and disappeared. When the trio called on Maria, she said Hamilton had instructed Reynolds to "leave the parts, not to be seen here again," because her husband "could tell them something that would make some of the heads of departments tremble."

Hamilton's guilt seemed clear. But before sending a report to President Washington, the investigators felt it gentlemanly to at least give Hamilton a chance to explain himself. On December 15, they met with the treasury secretary and showed him his own handwritten letters to James Reynolds. Hamilton immediately acknowledged he had written them and told the entire Maria Reynolds saga in such exquisitely painful detail that one of his visitors—we can picture him wildly waving his hands—begged him to stop. But Hamilton couldn't put the brakes on his cathartic confession. He showed them Maria's poorly spelled love letters and her husband's sulky demands for money. Blushing furiously, the trio promised the matter would remain confidential. Hamilton asked for copies of the correspondence they had shown him for his records.

His request proved a mistake. James Monroe tasked John Beckley, a clerk of the House of Representatives who hated Hamilton, to copy them. Beckley made another set of copies for himself and, it seems, gave them to Hamilton's political nemesis, Thomas Jefferson.

For years, Hamilton had torn Jefferson and the Republicans to shreds in his newspaper columns. Now, on January 5, 1793, in Monroe's column on the "Vindication of Mr. Jefferson," he sent a thinly veiled warning to Hamilton. "I shall conclude this paper by observing how much it is to be wished that this writer [Hamilton] would exhibit himself to the public view, that we might behold in him a living monument of that immaculate purity to which he pretends and which ought to distinguish so bold and arrogant a censor of others."

Hamilton got the message. His enemies had the power to humiliate him. Perhaps that is why he never made a bid to become president. Even though he had been born on the Caribbean island of Nevis, the Constitution, realizing that no contenders for the presidency for decades to come would have been born as American citizens, stipulated that anyone holding U.S. citizenship on or before the 1787 adoption of the Constitution could run for office, no matter what their citizenship at birth. Surely, he must have wanted to be president.

Though Hamilton's enemies knew of the affair, Eliza did not. She lived in ignorant bliss, thinking she had the best husband in

the world. Maria Reynolds's marriage, however, was not so resil-
ient. In 1793 she divorced James—oddly enough, for adultery—
and married Jacob Clingman the day her divorce was finalized.

In January 1795, Hamilton resigned his treasury post. Ironically for someone accused of venality, Hamilton left his government office much poorer than he had entered it, with only $500
(some $10,200 today) to his name. He went back to his profitable
law practice, which netted him several times his government salary, to repair the damage.

In the fall of 1796, during the presidential election to replace
George Washington, Hamilton wrote twenty-five articles over
five weeks in the *Gazette of the United States* disparaging Thomas
Jefferson. Perhaps, because it had been four years since Jefferson
and his other enemies had learned about Maria Reynolds, Hamilton thought they would never use the information. Perhaps he
just couldn't help inserting himself in a provocative way into the
election. The result was predictable, especially once the calming
force of George Washington had vanished from the presidency,
replaced by the irascible John Adams. The Republicans were
ready to take down Hamilton.

In June 1797, they hired a tabloid journalist named James
Callender to write a series of pamphlets innocuously titled *The
History of the United States for 1796*, reporting on Hamilton's tenure as treasury secretary. Callender, a hack writer who dipped his
pen in venom, had fled to the U.S. from his native Edinburgh,
Scotland, to evade a sedition charge by the British government. In
his pamphlets, Callender promised to cut Hamilton down to size
and reveal his rank hypocrisy. "We shall presently see this great
master of morality, although himself the father of a family, con-
fessing that he had an illicit correspondence with another man's
wife," he wrote. But that wasn't all. Callender accused Hamilton

of having made a fortune by speculating in government securities and stated the money he had paid Reynolds wasn't for blackmail related to adultery, but for speculation. He published all the letters Clingman had given to the trio of investigators.

"So much correspondence could not refer exclusively to wenching," Callender pointed out. "No man of common sense will believe that it did . . . Reynolds and his wife affirm that it respected certain speculations." Callender accused Hamilton of writing Maria's misspelled love letters himself to make his illegal activity look like an ordinary love affair.

Hamilton realized a dignified silence would only encourage speculation about his speculation, a smear that would tarnish his reputation as a government official forever. He would be remembered for rumors of corruption rather than all his numerous public acts and the institutions he'd built from nothing. He decided to accept public humiliation for the affair while proving the allegations of corruption false.

Hamilton rage-wrote a detailed hundred-page booklet he titled *Observations on Certain Documents Contained in No. V and No. VI of "The History of the United States for the Year 1796," in Which the Charge of Speculation Against Alexander Hamilton, Late Secretary of the Treasury, Is Full Refuted. Written by Himself.* In it, Himself explained his relationship with Maria and James Reynolds in squirm-inducing detail. The first thirty-seven pages were purgative confession mingled with self-examination; the remaining fifty-eight pages comprised the misspelled letters of the Reynoldses. In no way, he insisted, did this tawdry affair have anything to do with compromising the public trust. He maintained his honor as an incorrupt and incorruptible public official by sacrificing his honor as a husband.

"The charge against me," he wrote, "is a connection with one

James Reynolds for purposes of improper pecuniary speculation. My real crime is an amorous connection with his wife, for a considerable time with his privity and connivance, if not originally brought on by a combination between the husband and wife with the design to extort money from me." If he had been a corrupt official, he pointed out, he certainly would have chosen a worthier accomplice than the sleazebag James Reynolds. "It is very extraordinary, if the head of the money department of a country, being unprincipled enough to sacrifice his trust and his integrity, could not have contrived profit sufficiently large to have engaged the cooperation of men of far greater importance than Reynolds," he wrote. And the paltry sums he gave Reynolds—usually thirty or fifty dollars at a time—would hardly have amassed the fortune he had supposedly stashed somewhere.

Hamilton's main concern in publishing the pamphlet was how it would affect his wife.

With such men, nothing is sacred. Even the peace of an unoffending and amiable wife is a welcome repast to their insatiate fury against the husband . . . This confession is not made without a blush . . . I can never cease to condemn myself for the pang which it may inflict on a bosom eminently entitled to all my gratitude, fidelity, and love. But that bosom will approve that even at so great an expense, I should effectually wipe away a more serious stain from a name which it cherishes with no less elevation than tenderness.

He concluded, "Thus has my desire to destroy this slander, completely, led me to a more copious and particular examination of it, than I am sure was necessary. The bare perusal of the letters from Reynolds and his wife is sufficient to convince my greatest enemy that there is nothing worse in the affair than an irregular and indelicate amour. For this, I bow to the just censure which it merits. I have paid pretty severely for the folly and can never recollect it without disgust and self condemnation."

Initially, it seemed as if his self-vindication had been a mistake. His supporters were aghast, his enemies delighted. "Humiliating in the extreme," said Henry Knox. Hamilton's old friend Robert Troup observed that Hamilton's "ill-judged pamphlet has done him inconceivable injury."

The Republican press had a field day with the pamphlet. Callender summed up Hamilton's defense: "I am a rake and for that reason I cannot be a swindler." Similarly, the Republican newspaper the *Aurora* mocked Hamilton's defense as "I have been grossly . . . charged with . . . being a speculator, whereas I am only an adulterer. I have not broken the eighth commandment . . . It is only the seventh which I have violated."

While Hamilton's affair remained the butt of Republican jokes, his reputation for public integrity remained undiminished. His embarrassing pamphlet dispelled any notions of impropriety in office. Perhaps David Cobb, a Federalist judge from Massachusetts, summed it up best in a letter to Henry Knox: "Hamilton is fallen for the present, but even if he fornicates with every female in the cities of New York and Philadelphia, he will rise again, for purity of character after a period of political existence is not necessary for public patronage."

Eliza never publicly commented on the Reynolds affair, though it surely must have mortified her to learn not only of her husband's adultery, but that the partner of his choice was an uneducated prostitute, rolling around with him in Eliza's own bed. She must have recalled Hamilton's letters to her that summer of 1791, urging her to stay in Albany for as long as possible. Later events proved that she wholeheartedly forgave him. As for Hamilton, he became more attentive than ever to his wife and children. He wrote her, "In proportion as I discover the worthlessness of other pursuits, the value of my Eliza and of domestic happiness rises in my estimation."

Though in private practice as a lawyer, Hamilton remained an influential mover and shaker, frequently advising members of President John Adams's Cabinet and serving as inspector general for the army. Once his bitter enemy Thomas Jefferson became president in 1800, however, Hamilton's influence in government decreased. His handsome nineteen-year-old son, Philip, died in a duel in 1801, so devastating his sister that she sank into mental illness. Hamilton found solace in religion and sat mostly on the sidelines, philosophizing. In an 1802 letter to a friend, he wrote, "Men are rather reasoning than reasonable animals, for the most part governed by the impulse of passion." Though he was discussing the heated political controversies of the day, he was probably also speaking about himself.

For his part, Thomas Jefferson was finally in a position to examine Hamilton's old treasury files for proof of theft. Licking his chops, he asked his new treasury secretary, Albert Gallatin, to find him "the blunders and frauds of Hamilton." Gallatin, who also disliked Hamilton, dived in "with a very good appetite," as he later recalled. "Well, Gallatin, what have you found?" Jefferson asked hopefully. Gallatin replied despondently, "I have found the most perfect system ever formed. Any change that should be made in it would injure it. Hamilton made no blunders, committed no frauds. He did nothing wrong." He added, "I think Mr. Jefferson was disappointed."

Jefferson's vice president, Aaron Burr, an unpopular individual, knew Jefferson did not want him as his running mate in the 1804 election and made a heated bid to become governor of New York. Burr lost, but he could not accept that his defeat was due to his terrible reputation in both public and private life: deflowering virgins, seducing wives, raping slaves, taking bribes, and stealing from the estates of his legal clients. He turned his beady eyes on Alexander Hamilton, who had spoken and written against him, and challenged him to a duel. Prickly Hamilton, still the impoverished, orphaned bastard boy at heart despite all his accomplishments, felt he needed to defend his honor.

None of Hamilton's family members had any idea of his dueling plans. He told his friends he would waste his shot, sending it into a tree or the air. Burr, however, spent his days in target practice. At seven o'clock in the morning of July 11, 1804, the two men, their seconds, and a doctor met at the infamous Weehawken Dueling Grounds across the Hudson River from New York City. Though details are unclear, it seems Hamilton did indeed waste his shot, while Burr shot to kill. The bullet sliced through Hamilton's spine, paralyzing him, and damaging his liver and diaphragm. Though Hamilton did not die instantly, it was clearly a mortal wound.

He was rowed back across the river to the home of a friend and put to bed. When Eliza arrived, she was frantic with grief and horror. Though suffering intense pain and heavy blood loss, Hamilton wanted to see his children one last time. Eliza lined all seven of them up at the foot of his bed, from twenty-year-old Angelica to two-year-old Philip, named after his deceased brother. Thirty-one hours after the duel, Alexander Hamilton died at the age of forty-nine.

Hamilton's untimely death devastated his wife. God, Eliza said, had given her all her life's joy in her first decades, and now the remainder would be filled with sorrow. "I have remarked to you that I have had a double share of blessing and I must now look forward to grief," she told a friend. "For such a husband, his spirit is in heaven and his form in the earth and I am nowhere any part of him is." She read his letters so often they eventually crumbled in her hands. She wore decayed bits of a love sonnet he had written her in a little bag around her neck.

Eliza devoted her remaining years—there were to be fifty of them—to burnishing Hamilton's rather tarnished reputation. His death had not stopped Jefferson and Adams from heaping slander on him, and Hamilton, for once, was in no position to defend himself with a flood of accusing newspaper columns. She employed thirty assistants to organize his voluminous papers into a biography.

In 1802, Hamilton had built a beautiful family home in Harlem, the Grange, in what was then a rural area of Manhattan, and planned to pay off his debts of more than $50,000 (some $1.2 million in today's money) over the next few years with his lucrative legal fees. To keep the family from destitution, Hamilton's good friends solicited donations from more than a hundred people, raising more than $80,000. Still, with seven children to raise and educate, Eliza was often reduced to begging friends for small loans to stay afloat. Two years after Hamilton's death, she and two other women founded the New York Orphan Asylum Society, the first private orphanage in New York. Eliza poured herself into helping children who, as her husband had been as a child on St. Croix, were alone, destitute, frightened, and dreaming of a life that didn't seem possible.

Eliza's rival for Hamilton's love, Maria Reynolds, also had some tough times. With the publication of Hamilton's 1797 pamphlet, she was known throughout the United States as a whore, happy to be pimped by her own husband, and even worse, a woman with very bad grammar and spelling. She and her second husband, Jacob Clingman, soon hightailed it out of the U.S. and moved to Great Britain. In 1806, she returned to Philadelphia using the name Maria Clement, with no Clingman in sight. No record exists of a divorce, so perhaps Clingman died, or maybe she just dumped him.

She found employment as the housekeeper of a Dr. Mathew, who became enamored of her—naturally—and married her in 1808. For the first time in her turbulent life, Maria, now in her forties, became respectable and respected. No longer a sexpot proudly sporting a ripped bodice, she found God and became active in the Methodist Church, proving Benjamin Franklin's observation that "when women cease to be handsome, they study to be good." A friend of Maria's in her later years said, "She enjoyed . . . the love and good will of all who knew her." Well into middle age Maria was described as "highly amiable and handsome." She died at the age of sixty in 1828.

Eliza's undiminished, rude good health shocked those who saw her climbing over fences in her eighties. In 1848, at the age of ninety-one, she moved to Washington, D.C., to live in her daughter's home near the White House, where she was often entertained. In the years leading up to the Civil War—which Hamilton's extraordinary vision had foreseen—everyone wanted to meet the woman who, seventy years earlier, had danced the minuet with George Washington.

Despite her unabated vigor and constant activity, Eliza suffered the loss of her husband every day during those long years. A visitor to her house recalled her playing a game of backgammon by the fire. "When the game was done," he said, "she leaned back in her chair a long time with closed eyes, as if lost to all around her. There was a long silence, broken by the murmured words, 'I am so tired. It is so long. I want to see Hamilton.'"

She died at ninety-seven on November 8, 1854.

3

THOMAS JEFFERSON'S
PURSUIT OF HAPPINESS

*E*veryone with an ounce of sense knows that karma is a bitch. Certainly, that is what President Thomas Jefferson discovered in 1802. Five years earlier, he had employed the scandal-rag journalist James Callender to trumpet Alexander Hamilton's adulterous affair with Maria Reynolds. Now Jefferson found himself hoist with his own petard when his hired gun, feeling under-rewarded for his efforts, turned on Jefferson, exposing in his trademark shrill, nasty prose a scandalous amour of the president's own.

★ ★ ★

On June 26, 1787, Abigail Adams, wife of John Adams, the first American ambassador to Great Britain, greeted a special visitor in London: Thomas Jefferson's younger daughter, just arrived on the *Robert*, commanded by Captain Ramsey. Nine-year-old Polly hadn't seen her father since 1784 when he went to France to conduct commercial negotiations, leaving Polly in the care of her aunt. Now she would recuperate with the Adamses from the five-week trip across the Atlantic, and then journey on to her father in Paris. Little Polly did not arrive in England unaccompanied, of course. She had a traveling companion to look after her.

Jefferson had hoped to find a "careful English woman" traveling on the *Robert* who would agree to look after Polly. Unable to do so, he wanted one of his mature enslaved women to undertake the task, but that woman was recuperating from childbirth. Polly's companion ended up being another of Jefferson's slaves: fourteen-year-old Sally Hemings, the half-sister of his deceased wife, Martha. (Sally's enslaved mother, Elizabeth Hemings, daughter of an African woman and a white man, had had six children with John Wayles, Martha's father.) The result of what developed in Paris—and what would continue for many decades afterward—would shake the 1804 presidential election, cause Jefferson's family to craft a carefully purged history, and tear apart families until the present day.

Immediately after retrieving Polly, Abigail wrote Jefferson, "The old Nurse whom you expected to have attended her was sick and unable to come. She has a Girl about 15 or 16 with her . . ." But within twenty-four hours of observing Sally, Abigail seemed to have had a frisson of foreboding. Perhaps it would be better to send Sally back to Virginia immediately. "The Girl who is with her is quite a child," she wrote, "and Captain Ramsey is of the opinion will be of so little service that he had better carry her back with him. But of this you will be a judge." On July 6, Abigail wrote even more disparagingly, "The Girl she has with her wants more care than the child, and is wholly incapable of looking properly after her, without some superior to direct her." The Girl, evidently, didn't even warrant the use of her name.

It is hard to imagine why Abigail ridiculed Sally for irresponsibility. At the time, a fourteen-year-old enslaved individual stood at the cusp of adulthood and would have been accustomed to working long hours quite efficiently. The Hemingses' light skin—Sally was three-quarters white—and their family relationship with Jefferson gave them privileged status among his slaves. Instead of breaking their backs in the fields, the boys were taught trades, and the girls worked in the house. It is likely that Sally had looked after other enslaved children at Monticello, sewed, and worked in the kitchen and laundry. How then could she have been "wholly incapable" of looking after Polly?

Could it be that the prudish Abigail disliked Sally because she showed too much spunk and not enough deference? Perhaps Sally had a confidence the prim northerner did not like in a servant. Was Sally too familiar with little Polly who was, in fact, her niece? Was she just bubbling over with excitement to leave the plantation for the first time in her life, cross the Atlantic Ocean, and arrive in sprawling, bustling London?

Or had Abigail Adams heard rumors that Jefferson had an eye for young mulatto girls, as mixed-raced people were called at the time? Puritanical in outlook and scrupulously faithful to each other, Abigail and John Adams enjoyed sneering at the immoral sexual behavior of others. It may be significant that Abigail thought that Sally was older than she was—fifteen or sixteen—indicating she was well developed for her age. Additionally, Sally was reported to be "very handsome," according to her son with Jefferson, Madison. Jefferson's white grandson, Thomas Jefferson Randolph, described Sally as "light colored and decidedly good looking." According to Isaac Jefferson, an enslaved man who became overseer of Monticello in 1797, Sally was "mighty near white" with "straight hair down her back." In his 1781 book, *Notes on the State of Virginia*, Jefferson wrote that white skin was more aesthetically pleasing than black because it enabled whites to blush, displaying their emotions and "the expression of every passion," which he found quite charming. He added that "flowing hair" was a particularly important attribute of Caucasian beauty, and that mulattoes had "superior intellect" to those of fully African descent.

The Adamses had spent a great deal of time with Jefferson while he and John negotiated the commercial treaties in Paris two years earlier. They must have seen that Jefferson, in his forties, still radiated virility, turning the ladies' heads. His astonishing height alone—he was almost six foot three in an age when the average man was five foot seven—would have made him stand out in a crowd. In addition, he was trim and handsome, with hazel eyes, reddish hair, a sensuous mouth, and a strong jaw. Perhaps, too, Abigail noticed that Sally resembled Jefferson's beloved late wife, Martha, since they had the same father. If that were the case, Sally might prove an irresistible temptation to the lusty bachelor who owned her.

Lusty though he was, Thomas Jefferson would never truly get over his wife's untimely death. Indeed, the life path he had carefully designed in his youth had taken surprising turns both tragic and fortuitous. Born in rural Virginia in 1743, the son of a well-to-do planter, he had received a sterling education, entering the College of William & Mary in Williamsburg at sixteen and two years later commencing his studies in law. Blessed with an omnivorous appetite for learning, he studied Latin, Greek, French, philosophy, mathematics, history, ethics, politics, and agriculture. He was fascinated by the world around him and, over the years, collected mastodon bones, studied the stars, cultivated 330 types of vegetables and 170 kinds of fruit, designed buildings, tinkered with inventions, and analyzed the Bible and wrote his own version, which he thought made a lot more sense than the original. His ravenous curiosity compelled him to collect thousands of books.

Admitted to the Virginia bar in 1767, Jefferson practiced law and served as a delegate to the Virginia House of Burgesses from 1769 to 1775. In 1772, the twenty-nine-year-old married Martha Wayles Skelton, a twenty-three-year-old widow, with whom he was deeply in love. Like Jefferson, Martha was an avid reader. She played the piano beautifully, often accompanied by Jefferson on the violin. She kept his house and entertained his friends and birthed his babies. In addition to his law practice and political responsibilities, Jefferson ran his five-thousand-acre plantation and built his new house on a hill, which he called Monticello, "little mountain" in Italian. It was, for a short time, the life he had dreamed of. Farming. Raising a family with a beloved wife. Dabbling in local politics while working as a country lawyer.

And then, in 1775, the course of this calm, predictable life was swept up into the whirlwind of the Revolution. That year, aged thirty-two, he was one of the youngest delegates to the Continental Congress. There he became friends with John Adams, a delegate from Massachusetts. As Adams soon learned, while Jefferson could be witty and warm with friends, revealing the treasures of his encyclopedic knowledge, he shrank from strangers, often avoiding eye contact. Sitting amid the nation's most powerful, argumentative men in the Continental Congress, he was positively tongue-tied. Adams said, "I never heard him utter three sentences together" and compared him to "the great rivers, whose bottoms we cannot see and make no noise."

Perhaps because of his height, Jefferson slouched when standing up and when seated rolled onto one hip. Seeing himself as a farmer-spokesman for the common folk, he usually dressed casually, sometimes even sloppily. It was easy for the older, more experienced men at the Continental Congress to ignore him as a rather stupid country bumpkin. But Adams, aware of Jefferson's vast knowledge and abilities, especially his powerful writing style, pushed to have him write the initial draft of the Declaration of Independence. Though Congress made changes to his document, it is Jefferson's words that ring throughout history: *We hold these truths to be self-evident, that all men are created equal, that they are endowed by their Creator with certain unalienable Rights, that among these are Life, Liberty, and the pursuit of Happiness.*

After an unsuccessful stint as governor of Virginia from 1779 to 1781, Jefferson felt he was poorly suited to public service and just wanted to return home, continue building his house, and spend time with his family. His wife, Martha, was sickly. She had given birth to six children during their decade-long marriage—though only two would live more than a few years—and she seemed to become sicker with each pregnancy. She never recovered from the birth of her last child in 1782. A few months later, on her deathbed, Martha made Jefferson swear he would never remarry. Jefferson's overseer, Edmund Bacon, later recalled, "Holding her hand, Mr. Jefferson promised her solemnly that he would never marry again."

When Martha died, Jefferson fainted. For weeks, he was inconsolable, his grief frightening those around him. He stayed in his room, walking "incessantly night and day only lying down occasionally when nature was completely exhausted," according to an early biographer who interviewed members of Jefferson's immediate family. He must have been suffering from clinical depression, yet he managed to rouse himself enough to serve in Congress in 1783 to 1784.

Still, his friends believed he needed a change of scene. In the summer of 1784, he was sent to Paris to join John Adams and Benjamin Franklin to negotiate commercial treaties with several countries. He brought with him his twelve-year-old daughter, Martha, called Patsy as a child; and James Hemings, Sally's nineteen-year-old brother, with the object of training him as a French cook.

Upon landing, Jefferson cast his comfortable sloppiness immediately aside. Here in France he would be representing his country and meeting King Louis XVI, Queen Marie Antoinette, and other power brokers. He powdered his hair and dressed in pastel brocades with diamond buttons, embroidered waistcoats, silk stockings, and frothy lace cravats and cuffs. For formal events he buckled on a jeweled sword. He sent Patsy to board during the week at the Abbaye Royale de Panthemont, the most exclusive convent school in Paris, though she returned home on weekends.

In 1785, the commercial treaties ratified, Franklin returned to Philadelphia, Jefferson replaced him in Paris, and Adams took up the position as U.S. ambassador in London. Jefferson rented the opulent Hôtel de Langeac—a sprawling, gated estate abutting the Champs-Élysées with a courtyard, gardens, and outbuildings. Here he entertained in the grand style, often inviting thirty people to dinner at a time, and far outspending his government allowance. But one of Jefferson's weaknesses—and one which would have horrific consequences for his enslaved people at Monticello—was his need to play the role of Lord Bountiful, the world's most generous and elegant host, regardless of whether he could afford it or whom it might hurt.

Perhaps because of the constant round of entertaining, Jefferson didn't follow Abigail's advice and send Sally back to Virginia. Another pair of young, well-trained hands would come in handy. Moreover, Jefferson had known Sally from the time she was a small child, arriving with her family at Monticello as part of his wife's inheritance from her father. When Jefferson had left Virginia in 1784, Sally was eleven. Perhaps he remembered her as an industrious worker, helping around the house. He sent a servant to London to escort his daughter and Sally to the Hôtel de Langeac. And on July 15, Sally Hemings arrived in Paris, no longer a flat-chested child, but a nubile girl budding into womanhood.

Though it is not known exactly what work Sally did for Jefferson, we can assume that during the week she ran errands, sewed, and helped her brother prepare meals. Perhaps she took care of Jefferson's linen and clothing and bustled around his bedroom dusting and tidying. She must have looked after his daughters when they returned home on the weekends. She would have helped them dress, curl their hair, and keep their clothing clean and pressed. At fifteen, Patsy attended various social events. Sally would have stood back against the wall watching her mistress dance and play cards, brought her a cup of punch or plate of food, or assisted her on the chamber pot.

As the personal maid of the American ambassador's daughter, Sally, too, was expected to look fashionable, attired in silk and satin, though with less decoration than her niece. Jefferson's records show that he spent a good amount on her clothing, taking her around personally to milliners, apparently without Patsy in tow. It is curious that a man in his august position would have accompanied his slave to dress fittings, when his housekeeper would have been a more appropriate choice.

Sally might have loved not only the gorgeous French fashions, but the entire Paris experience. She had been used to the slow plantation rhythm of a few hundred people methodically feeding animals, pulling plows, and weeding tobacco. Now she was in a metropolis of seven hundred thousand people, the largest city in Europe. Right outside her door, princely carriages rattled past. Prostitutes and street vendors flaunted their wares. Actors set up impromptu street theaters. Beggars displayed maimed limbs and suppurating sores. For the first time in her life, Sally had her own money. Jefferson paid her sporadic wages, as he did her brother James and had done for her relatives back at Monticello. She could march into an upscale store and buy herself something lovely. Perhaps she and her brother visited museums or the theater, or sipped coffee at a café.

But for Sally and James Hemings, the most exciting thing about Paris could have been the Freedom Principle, which stated that enslaved individuals could claim their freedom at the Admiralty Court. It seems that James Hemings was intending to stay in Paris after Jefferson departed. He paid for French lessons with a tutor to perfect his knowledge of the French language. As a master chef in a noble household—an enviable and highly respected position—he could have commanded a high salary.

Meanwhile, in France the popular disgust with government mismanagement and overspending rose to a boil. Hail, floods, and drought destroyed crops, resulting in starvation across France even as the government raised taxes. On July 14, 1789, thousands of citizens unleashed their rage in Paris, storming the Bastille prison, that symbol of royal suppression. Jefferson was thrilled that France was following in America's footsteps. "My fortune has been singular to see in the course of fourteen years two such revolutions as were never seen before," he wrote.

Excited as he was by political events in France, Jefferson was itching to take his daughters back home and return a few months later without them. Enjoying her stay in the convent, Patsy told her Protestant father she wanted to become a nun. Jefferson, who had great difficulty telling anyone flat-out no, took her into society more, sometimes to as many as three balls a week, where she was such a success that he feared she would fall in love with a Frenchman and beg to marry him. In that case, Jefferson might never see her again. He was terribly afraid of losing those he loved—his father had died when Jefferson was thirteen, and he had lost not only his wife but four of their six children. "I am born to lose everything I love," he lamented to a friend in 1787.

Moreover, Jefferson was not entirely comfortable with the education his daughters were receiving. As America's ambassador, he had done what was expected by sending them to their prestigious convent school where they learned music, dancing, art, and languages. That was fine, in its way. Back in Virginia they would attend a dance now and then and amuse themselves at home playing the piano, painting, or reading a book in French. But, as he complained to his sister-in-law, nothing the girls learned there would make them particularly "useful in [their] own country." Better, Jefferson believed, that they know how to make a pudding and mend a shirt.

Jefferson found French women—with their sharp wit, fierce self-confidence, and devastating attractions—a bit frightening, perhaps even emasculating. These Gallic Amazons wore powdered hair a foot high, with ostrich feathers waving another two feet above that. They had white lead–painted faces with black beauty spots and bright red cheeks, and rustled in poofed satin gowns, trailing clouds of heady perfume in their wake.

It's not that he wasn't attracted to these bold women. In August 1786, Jefferson had had an intense affair with twenty-seven-year-old Maria Cosway, a talented portrait painter resident in London, who was visiting Paris with her husband, Richard, also an artist. She had a full face, wide blue eyes under dark brows, a straight little nose, and pouting lips. Her golden hair was piled high and tumbling down to her shoulders in the popular 1780s coiffeur of a whirlwind destroying a wig store. For a month, while Richard Cosway painted portraits, Jefferson and Maria visited châteaux, strolled in gardens, and took carriage rides in the countryside. They had fallen deeply in love. Jefferson wrote of being smitten with "a generous spasm of the heart," and we can imagine he experienced other generous spasms as well. He was overcome with grief when her husband took her away a month later, though he soon got over it.

In the winter of late 1787 and early 1788, the dazzling Angelica Church, who had been living in London with her husband, visited Paris. The sister-in-law of Alexander Hamilton—with whom he was presumed to have had an affair—captivated Jefferson as much as she had his political enemy. Theirs was, most likely, a gallant flirtation; effusive demonstrations of affection were fashionable at the time. But as far as a long-term relationship was concerned, Jefferson yearned for a more comfortable type of woman like his late wife, one who loved nothing so much as sitting in a rocking chair by the fire, knitting.

Someone, in fact, like Sally Hemings. By the time Jefferson prepared to return to Virginia, the lovely girl was sixteen. Here was a young woman who could never have emasculated him, never could have threatened him. Never could have *left* him. She could not demand marriage and try to make him break his promise to his late wife. A man could not marry his slave. Legally, she was required to do his bidding as long as she lived. Sally, for Jefferson, was the perfect solution.

And what about Sally? How did she feel about him? We know frustratingly little about her as a person, her thoughts and feelings, hopes and dreams and disappointments, and barely anything about her relationship with Jefferson. As an enslaved woman, she leaves us no portraits, no letters or diaries. We do not know if she was literate, though her brother James was. And we have no idea when the affair began. Did he set out immediately to seduce the pretty fourteen-year-old? Or did the daily contact over two years gradually result in feelings on both sides?

Our only source of information was her son with Jefferson, Madison Hemings, who, in 1873 at the age of sixty-eight, spoke with a journalist from an Ohio newspaper. Regarding Sally's tenure in Paris, Madison said, "During that time, my mother became Mr. Jefferson's concubine . . . When he was called back home she was enceinte [pregnant] by him. He desired to bring my mother back to Virginia with him, but she demurred. She was just beginning to understand the French language well, and in France she was free, while if she returned to Virginia she would be re-enslaved. So she refused to return with him." It was, for a time at least, Sally Hemings's own declaration of independence.

Again, Jefferson was in danger of losing someone he cared for, as well as his unborn child. In France, he could not force Sally to return with him. "To induce her to do so," Madison continued, "he promised her extraordinary privileges and made a solemn pledge that her children should be freed at the age of twenty-one years. In consequence of his promises, on which she implicitly relied, she returned with him to Virginia. She trusted Jefferson over French law, with her life and the lives of her children." Madison described their pact as a "treaty," a bargain on both their parts.

Did Sally Hemings love Thomas Jefferson more than freedom? Or did she merely tolerate him but longed to see her mother, brothers, and sisters in Virginia again? Did she believe that her relationship with the plantation master would raise her family's status even higher, obtaining greater comforts and privileges for them all? Was she afraid of remaining in Paris, pregnant and alone?

And why didn't her brother James, a master chef, fluent in French, stay and claim his freedom? It is likely that he planned to return to France with Jefferson in early 1790 and wanted to spend some time visiting his family at Monticello whom he hadn't seen in five years. Whatever the reason behind their extraordinary decisions to return to slavery, on October 22, 1789, Sally and James Hemings set sail for Virginia, looking back at France, as the freedom they could have had dwindled on the horizon and disappeared.

Just four months later, James's plan to return to France and freedom were ruined when President George Washington appointed Jefferson the first U.S. secretary of state. Jefferson—and James—would not be returning to Paris. They would be going to the interim U.S. capital, New York. James was stuck in slavery, though Jefferson would free him in 1796 once James had trained his brother Robert as a master chef to replace him.

After Jefferson's daughter Patsy married in February 1790, he gave her several slaves, but not Sally, who had been her lady's maid for two years in France and would have, under other circumstances, been the logical choice. Yet Jefferson ended up sending Sally's fourteen-year-old niece.

It is intriguing how every household slave at Monticello is mentioned in family correspondence *except* Sally Hemings, and her absence from the letters is a clue in itself. After Jefferson's death, Patsy sifted through his documents to prepare them for publication. Numerous letters that did not reflect well on Jefferson were not published. Let us imagine that Patsy found the following note she had written her father decades earlier: "Dear Father, I am in sore need of a lady's maid. It's a pity Sally can't be the new maid, but I understand she is big with child. Please send me someone else." Surely, she would have consigned such a missive to the flames, along with anything else mentioning Sally.

Jefferson's daughters must have understood the nature of his relationship with Sally Hemings, especially when she gave birth to several light-skinned children, at least some of whom resembled him. As awkward as the relationship must have been for his daughters, they likely appreciated the fact that Jefferson did not remarry and sire legitimate children who could draw off their expected inheritance. This kind of family upheaval happened quite frequently in an era when so many young women died in childbirth. Sally's children could never inherit for two reasons: they were illegitimate, and they were slaves. But Sally's baby, born most likely in the spring of 1790, seems to have died in infancy; Madison's mention of this pregnancy more than eighty years later is the only extant reference to it.

As secretary of state, Jefferson found himself increasingly at odds with Alexander Hamilton, the secretary of the treasury. The vastly differing views that had first become apparent while negotiating the Constitution continued to inflame their hatred for each other as the nation fell into two political parties. Jefferson found himself, along with James Madison, the leader of the Republican Party, Hamilton in charge of the Federalists. Jefferson rejected national debt, banks, and vibrant commerce. He believed the most virtuous life was farming, pulling your plow—or better yet, watching your slaves pull your plow—over the rich earth to bring forth food.

While Hamilton enjoyed fierce vocal debate, Jefferson could not bear to argue with anyone and disliked those who did. He saw disagreement as bad manners. In a letter to John Adams he wrote, "I do not love difficulties. I am fond of quiet, willing to do my duty, but made irritable by slander and apt to be forced by it to abandon my post." If Hamilton poked holes in his proposals, Jefferson, clearly passive-aggressive, would not jump up and respond angrily. He would sit quietly, plotting revenge in the form of nasty newspaper columns, using aliases.

At the end of 1793, Jefferson resigned from his position as secretary of state, feeling snubbed by President Washington, who mostly sided with Hamilton, and returned to Monticello. He ran for president in 1796 and came in second after John Adams, which, according to the electoral system of the time, meant the nation had a Federalist president, John Adams, and a Republican vice president, Jefferson, who labored to undermine everything the president did. He secretly worked with the French to thwart Adams's policies and wrote nasty anonymous newspaper articles about the irascible chief executive tearing off his wig and kicking it across the room in rage. Picture Hillary Clinton as Donald Trump's vice president, or vice versa, and you will understand the strange and horrible politics of the late 1790s.

When Jefferson won the presidential election of 1800, he sought to portray himself as a man of the people. For two weeks after his inauguration, he stayed at his boardinghouse near the Capitol and dined at the common table. Once ensconced in the White House, Jefferson often answered the door himself wearing an old robe and bedroom slippers. When William Plumer, a Federalist from New Hampshire, arrived at the White House and saw the slouching, slovenly Jefferson open the door, he naturally assumed he was a servant, and a poorly dressed one at that.

In one case, Jefferson's dress resulted in a diplomatic furor. On November 29, 1803, Anthony Merry, the new British ambassador to the U.S., arrived at the White House to present his credentials in a blue dress coat with gold braid, white breeches, white silk stockings, a feathered hat, and a dress sword. Jefferson ambled into the room wearing slippers "down at the heels," as a furious Merry wrote his superiors in London, woolen stockings, and old clothing of "utter slovenliness." Not only did Merry feel that he had been personally insulted, but he viewed Jefferson's appearance as an insult to King George III, whom he represented. And it probably was, when we consider how Jefferson had powdered and curled his hair and sported brocade suits with diamond buttons while serving in France. To make matters worse, while Jefferson and Merry were speaking, the president of the United States of America repeatedly kicked his rotten old slipper up in the air and caught it on his toe. Soon after, when Merry and his wife arrived for a White House dinner, they found that the traditional system of ranked seating had gone out the window, replaced by a kind of unseemly musical chairs as guests fought over the most honorable seats. The ambassador boycotted official functions.

And now, as president, Jefferson's bad karma came back to haunt him. James Callender, the hack journalist he had hired to publicize Alexander Hamilton's tawdry love affair with Maria Reynolds, became furious that Jefferson, as president, wasn't doing enough to reward him. He demanded that Jefferson appoint him postmaster of Richmond as payment for services rendered, a demand Jefferson refused. Callender decided to poke around Charlottesville and Richmond to see what dirt he could dig up on his former employer. And it wasn't very hard to learn of Sally Hemings. It seemed that her thirteen-year relationship with the president was the best-known secret in the commonwealth of Virginia.

A vicious racist, Callender was disgusted by the news. Jefferson, a man Callender had worked with and looked up to for several years, was a traitor to the white race. Callender would humiliate him publicly, as well as Sally Hemings and their children. "It is well known that the man, whom it delighteth the people to honor, keeps, and for many years has kept, as his concubine, one of his slaves," Callender wrote in the September 1, 1802, issue of the *Richmond Recorder*. "Her name is SALLY." It was just the first salvo in a cruel attack. The September 14, 1802, issue of another Richmond newspaper, the *Virginia Federalist*, reported that, according to multiple sources, "Mr. J," a man in a position of great power, had "a number of yellow children and that he is addicted to golden affections."

Though Callender was correct that Sally had given birth to five children by then, three of them had died. Either he didn't know that, or he didn't want to portray Sally as a figure worthy of sympathy. It served Callender's purpose to present Jefferson as populating the world with countless mixed-race bastards. He reported that Sally's oldest child, the one born soon after she returned from France, was still living and called "President Tom," bore "a striking resemblance to the President," and was "putting on airs."

Callender called Sally "the African Venus," "Dusky Sally," "Yellow Sally," and "Black Sal," and indicated she lived in the pigsty at Monticello. "A slut as common as the pavement," she had sex with thirty men of all colors. Learning that three teenaged enslaved girls worked in the White House kitchen, Callender crowed that Jefferson kept a "stable of mulatto girls" there for his sexual pleasure. Sally was caricatured in newspaper cartoons and ridiculed in ribald ballads. Newspapers in Europe commented on her.

Jefferson maintained a dignified silence about the accusations, which was easier to do in a time when there was no threat of a microphone being stuck in your face. Moreover, unlike Hamilton, he had not been falsely accused of financial crimes that he would have felt obligated to deny. There is no record in his family papers—of course not—about the reactions of Jefferson, his family, and Sally herself to Callender's vitriol. The one thing Sally had possessed was her privacy, her dignity. Now the entire world knew her name, her shame, her love—if love it was—and her bargain. Now millions of people saw her as the Black Whore of Babylon. We can assume her large, supportive family buoyed her up, as did Jefferson himself. Perhaps he sent her encouraging letters from Washington, which the family later burned.

Callender's last months were difficult ones. Though readers loved his florid, nasty prose, some of those who knew him personally were heartily sick of him. In December 1802, one of his former defense attorneys beat him on the head with his walking stick. In March 1803, a group of Republicans attacked his newspaper office. Another former friend in an open letter in the Richmond *Examiner* suggested that Callender, once he stopped drinking whiskey, should swallow a dose of James River water. A few months later, Callender did just that. He was found drowned in the James River in three feet of water, reportedly too drunk to stumble to shore. Either that, or one of his literary victims had murdered him.

While Callender had hoped his disreputable revelations would prevent Jefferson from enjoying a second term, his plan did not work. In November 1804, Jefferson won 162 out of 176 electoral votes, winning on a strong economy, low taxes, and the triumph of the Louisiana Purchase. In 1803, he had bought some 828,000 square miles of territory from France for $15 million (some $340 million in today's money), doubling the size of the United States with a pen stroke. Perhaps his best-known accomplishment in his second term was the return in 1806 of the two-year expedition led by Meriwether Lewis and William Clark to explore the new territory and beyond, all the way to the Pacific, mapping the land, initiating diplomatic relations with native peoples, and bringing back plants, seeds, and minerals.

In 1809, Jefferson left office and returned to Monticello to play the role of virtuous resplendent farmer. Soon after, his daughter Patsy—now going by her legal name of Martha—separated from her abusive, alcoholic husband and moved back to Monticello with her eight children. It must have been awkward having her father's enslaved mistress at the house, along with all those nearly white enslaved children who looked just like the author of the Declaration of Independence. Martha demanded that Jefferson send them all away to one of his other plantations, but he refused.

Jefferson, who always loved to entertain, providing countless guests with the finest food and wines, now reveled in hospitality so extreme it was almost pathological. Any stranger could knock on his front door and stay as an honored guest in Hotel Monticello, where no one ever paid a cent. Entire ravenous families arrived with their hungry servants and famished horses, sometimes staying weeks at a time. Jefferson, whose finances had always been precarious, had left the White House poorer than he had arrived because of his lavish entertaining. Now he was racking up more debts, and completely unconcerned by the work he was giving his enslaved people—changing bed linens, doing laundry, cooking, cleaning hearths, and emptying chamber pots. But there would be far worse consequences.

Sally Hemings kept out of the way of Monticello visitors, quietly going about her business. "It was her duty, all her life which I can remember, up to the time of father's death, to take care of his chamber and wardrobe, look after us children and do such light work as sewing," her son Madison recalled. Jefferson made sure that his private quarters were strictly off limits to the countless visitors wandering through the house. During his presidency, he had had "porticles" built, structures attached to the exterior of his private living area, with louvered blinds, which prevented people from peering into his bedchamber.

It was a good idea, because many of the visitors to Monticello had read about the African Venus and were keeping an eye out for her. In 1811, one visitor, Elijah Fletcher of Vermont, reported after his visit, "The story of black Sal is no farce. That he cohabits with her and has a number of children by her is a sacred truth and the worst of it is, he keeps the same children as slaves, an unnatural crime which is very common in these parts."

Of the seven children Sally had with Jefferson, only four survived to adulthood. The boys—Beverly, born in 1798, Madison in 1805, and Eston in 1808, when Jefferson was an impressive sixty-five—learned the craft of fine furniture making in the Monticello carpentry shop. His daughter Harriet, born in 1801, learned to weave and spin. Back in Paris in 1789, Jefferson had promised Sally that he would free their children when they turned twenty-one, a promise he did not fulfill. It is likely that he was afraid they would leave him if freed and, as we know, he had a deep-seated fear of losing those he loved.

In 1822, when Beverly was twenty-four, he was fed up enough to simply walk away from Monticello, and Jefferson did not pursue him. Soon after, twenty-one-year-old Harriet decided to leave, too. The Monticello overseer, Edmund Bacon, reported that he gave her $50 (more than $1,000 today) and put her on a stagecoach north, probably to join Beverly. Bacon described Harriet as "nearly as white as anybody, and very beautiful." Both Beverly and Harriet lived as white people in Washington, D.C., and married well-to-do whites. After several years, they changed their names so no one could trace them back to their black family and stopped writing home.

In a spectacular coincidence, eighty-three-year-old Thomas Jefferson died on July 4, 1826, the fiftieth anniversary of the founding of the United States, as did the only other signer to become president, John Adams. The two had started off as friends, became rabid enemies, and finally reconciled in their final years. Indeed, Adams's last words were, "Jefferson lives," but Jefferson had died a few hours before.

Jefferson's death had horrific consequences for his slaves. Six months after his death, his surviving daughter, who inherited his staggering debts, advertised "130 Valuable Negroes" to be auctioned off. How tragically ironic that Thomas Jefferson—who penned the most powerful words of liberty and equality in human history—ended up sending these people to the auction block, to have their lives uprooted, their families separated, to work for new and perhaps cruel masters. The laws for freeing slaves were complex and designed to make it difficult. Many whites feared that freed slaves would wreak revenge for their heinous treatment. They wanted them either to remain enslaved or go back to Africa. Yet Jefferson could have freed a good portion during his lifetime, and freed them all in his will, as George Washington had done in his. But doing so would have deprived his white family of valuable property at a time when they would be dealing with his massive debts.

Jefferson officially freed only two slaves during his lifetime, Sally Hemings's two brothers, James and Robert, in the 1790s, though they had to work for it. He had allowed two of his children with Sally to head north. In his will, he freed two more sons with Sally, twenty-one-year-old Madison and eighteen-year-old Eston, whom he called his "apprentices." His will did not free Sally; wills were recorded in the county courthouse where any nosy person could read them. Jefferson's daughter Martha informally gave Sally—who was her aunt—"her time," allowing her to live as a free person.

Sally moved into a rented house on Main Street in Charlottesville and later moved into her son Madison's house. Before she died in 1835 at the age of sixty-two, Sally gave her sons precious, carefully harbored mementos of Jefferson: a pair of eyeglasses, shoe buckles, and an inkwell, apparently all that she had left of him. Perhaps she had truly loved him after all.

In 2017, archeologists tore out a tourists' bathroom in Monticello's basement under the South Terrace and, based on the description of Sally's room by Jefferson's grandson, declared it to be Sally's. It is being restored and furnished, a tribute to the nation's most famous unknown African American woman.

Over the years, Thomas Jefferson's white descendants have not only bent over backward to deny his relationship with Sally Hemings but twisted themselves into pretzels. Not only were any references to Sally destroyed soon after his death, but in the 1850s, Thomas Jefferson Randolph, Martha's son, bruited it about that the late Peter Carr, one of Jefferson's nephews by his sister Martha, had fathered Sally's children. The story was published and generally accepted. The oral history of the Hemings family was ridiculed as a pack of lies, uppity black people desperately trying to latch on to the saintly Thomas Jefferson.

A 1998 DNA test on Jefferson's white descendants and a descendant of Eston Hemings, however, upset the applecart. It showed that Peter Carr could not have been the father. There were seven other male Jeffersons who could have been, including his younger brother Randolph. Although Randolph had never been mentioned as a possibility before the test, his name was put forward by people desperately grasping at DNA straws. Moreover, Randolph, though he lived only twenty miles from Monticello, had visited only four times as documented in Jefferson's obsessive-compulsive recordkeeping—in September 1802, September 1805, May 1808, and sometime in 1814—none of which coincided with the conception of Sally Hemings's children. Nor was he in Paris when Sally conceived her first child. However, since Madison Hemings's recollections of his mother's tales are the only indication of this child, some historians believe there is insufficient proof of its brief existence.

The fact is that during a period of nineteen years from her arrival home from Paris in 1789 until the birth of her seventh child in 1808, Sally Hemings never conceived when Jefferson was away from Monticello. This indicates she may never have had another sexual partner. One compelling detail is that on July 11, 1797, Jefferson arrived at Monticello after a long stay in Philadelphia, and thirty-eight weeks later Sally had a baby. Another is that Jefferson noted the fathers of all his female slaves' children in his farm book except for the children of Sally Hemings. He never listed their father. Nor were there any rumors in that gossipmongering era of Jefferson having any other lover. It seems the two of them stayed faithful to each other until death.

4

GROVER CLEVELAND'S HIGH CHARACTER

*P*erhaps Grover Cleveland learned a valuable lesson from Alexander Hamilton on how to deal with a political sex scandal: tell the truth. For his refusal to lie, spin, and shred the truth, he has been applauded in the history books. But there is a darker side to his story. Three U.S. presidents have been accused of rape. Grover Cleveland was the first. Unlike the two who followed him, he never denied it. And, despite the expected squawks of puritanical outrage, most voters didn't care.

★ ★ ★

On the evening of December 15, 1873, thirty-three-year-old Maria Halpin walked briskly down the freezing streets of Buffalo, New York, on her way to a friend's birthday party at a nearby hotel restaurant. She had no idea, as she saw a man coming toward her, his black broadcloth coat and top hat visible in the yellow gaslight, that her life was about to veer horribly off course in a scandal that would rock the nation.

As he approached, Maria recognized Grover Cleveland, a lawyer finishing up his term as county sheriff, and she greeted him in pleasant surprise. Cleveland, thirty-six, lived a block and a half from Maria's rooms in Mrs. Randall's boardinghouse and had been courting the stunning widow for several months now. We do not know how they first became acquainted. Perhaps it was at the nearby Episcopal church they both attended. Or maybe he had first seen her at the Flint & Kent department store, where she waited on him behind the counter in the lace and cloak section.

Cleveland had been immediately attracted to the elegant beauty with an hourglass figure. At five foot eight, Maria was nearly a head taller than most women and moved with a regal poise. She had jet-black hair, sky-blue eyes, full lips, and white skin set off by the mourning she still wore three years after the death of her husband from tuberculosis. With two young children to support, Maria left her daughter in the care of her father in New Jersey and took her son to Buffalo, where she accepted a job in a new department store. Graceful, charming, and beautiful, she soon become a top salesperson.

"He sought my acquaintance," Maria later recalled of Cleveland, "and obtained an introduction to me from a person in whom I had every confidence, and he paid me marked attention." Cleveland was "persistent," she said. Maria asked some of the other congregants in her church about Cleveland's character, which, "so far as I then knew, was good, and his intensions I believed were pure and honorable." It seemed the prosperous, popular Mr. Cleveland was finally looking to marry.

Cleveland wasn't a handsome man, but he had a jovial personality and a keen intelligence. Six feet tall, he was built like a bull, with brown hair, bright blue eyes, and a small hooked nose over a walrus mustache. An imposing individual, he radiated virility and power. He lived in a hotel, reveling in the bachelor life, eating in fine restaurants, smoking cigars, playing cards, and drinking with his friends.

The son of a Congregational minister, Cleveland had grown up in Central New York, studied law, and was admitted to the New York bar in 1859. His income was sizable, and he sent most of his earnings back to his widowed mother and younger sisters. He would, by any standards, be an excellent catch.

On that dark December street, Cleveland invited Maria to dinner. She declined, telling him about the birthday party. Her friend and other guests would be waiting for her, she said. But Cleveland kept urging her to accept his invitation until she finally agreed, and the two of them headed to the popular Ocean Dining Hall & Oyster House. After an enjoyable dinner, he walked her to her lodgings. He had done so before, Maria said, and knew that her ten-year-old son was living with her. Perhaps that is why, with her son in the next room, she always felt safe.

We only have Maria's account of what happened in her rooms that night. As soon as they were alone, she said, he got on top of her and "by use of force and violence and without my consent" had intercourse with her. "Up to that hour my life was as pure and spotless as that of any lady in the city of Buffalo. There was not the slightest shadow of suspicion over me." Now she knew she was a "ruined" woman.

We can picture her, bruised, torn, humiliated, miserably pulling down her skirt and wiping tears from her face. She told him she would report the rape to the authorities. "He told me that he was determined to ruin me if it cost him $10,000," she recalled, "if he was hanged by the neck for it. I then and there told him that I never wanted to see him again and would never see him and commanded him to leave my rooms, which he did."

Cleveland knew that Maria would have a hard time making any charges stick, and if by any chance she did, as the local sheriff, he would be in an excellent position to make them disappear. It was generally believed a woman could not be raped unless she was overpowered by more than one man. Every man knew that women could keep their legs closed if they really wanted to and, failing that, the self-welding mechanism on their vaginas would kick into action. Resistance was viewed as spirited foreplay. A "real" rape victim's injuries had to be substantial: broken bones and enormous bruises. Anything else was seen as consensual, after which the woman had second thoughts and made a false report of a crime. And pregnancy was a sure sign she had enjoyed the sex.

It didn't help Maria's case that she had led what was then considered a dubious lifestyle to begin with. For one thing, she was a woman living without a male relative or a female chaperone. For another, she walked the streets alone at night to attend events like birthday parties in hotel restaurants. She had accepted a man's invitation to dinner issued on the street. Even worse, she had invited a man up to her rooms. A virtuous woman would never have done any of those things. And, as far as we know, she suffered no broken bones or horrifying bruises from her struggle. The law would have assumed that, even if she had struggled briefly at the beginning of the attack, she consented to the sex by the end.

As bad as things stood, they got much worse. Six weeks after the assault, Maria realized she was pregnant. She had few options. She could try to induce an abortion by swallowing poison, or she could go to a backstreet abortionist, risking her life. If her pregnancy became known, she would lose her job and her reputation. She did not feel she could tell her father what had happened; he would have blamed her. The best path open, she decided, would be to marry her rapist. And so, she chose "to inform him of the consequences of his actions . . . he being the proper person to whom I could tell my trouble."

Maria wrote Cleveland a note demanding that he come see her at Mrs. Randall's. When he arrived at her rooms, in "despair" she told him of her pregnancy and insisted that he marry her. He was furious.

"What the devil are you blubbering about?" he cried. "You act like a baby without teeth." After a while, according to Maria, he calmed down, said he "would do everything which was honorable and righteous" and "promised that he would marry me."

Over the next several weeks, Cleveland gave Maria some money, raising her hopes that this nightmare might end up working out. But he never agreed to set a wedding date. When her pregnancy began to show, she left her job at the department store. She confided to her pastor what had happened, who reached out to Cleveland about his duty to marry her. Cleveland, though he "acknowledged his fault," said he was not certain that he was the father. He would, however, be willing to help support the child. Maria, realizing Cleveland would not marry her, fell into a deep depression.

Cleveland arranged for the top obstetrician in Buffalo, Dr. James E. King, to deliver the baby at the only hospital in town that served unwed mothers. There, on September 14, 1874, Maria gave birth to a boy, whom Cleveland named Oscar Folsom Cleveland for his best friend. Two days later, Dr. King took the baby from Maria and put him in the care of his sister, who was due to give birth any day. For the next year, Minnie Kendall raised her son and Maria's as twins. It is not known why Cleveland took the baby from his mother. Perhaps he was afraid of her showing up at his prestigious law office with a wailing baby, clamoring for money and marriage.

He allowed Maria to see her son briefly on two occasions. Both times she cried and begged to keep him. Perhaps Cleveland began to have some sympathy for her. Maybe, too, he finally realized she would not try to shame him publicly. Whatever the reason, after a year, he instructed Minnie Kendall to give Maria her son back. Overjoyed, Maria once again begged Cleveland to marry her. They could live as a family. It wasn't too late. "Marriage was the only step possible to even partially repair the wrong he had done," she explained. It would wipe clean the "stain on her honor." He again refused. And Maria, severely depressed, began to drink heavily.

Her supportive neighbor Mrs. Baker said, "She took to drink to drown the grief that was consuming her." Learning about her alcohol abuse, Cleveland grew concerned that his child might be in danger. He asked a friend of his, a judge, to visit Maria to persuade her that her drinking endangered her toddler. If she placed her son in the Buffalo Orphan Asylum, Cleveland would give her money to start her own dressmaking shop in Niagara Falls. It was all for the good of her son and herself. Exhausted, sick with grief and depression and liquor, Maria agreed to everything. She signed legal papers surrendering all claims to her son and giving him to the orphanage. On March 9, 1876, under the name of Oscar Halpin, the eighteen-month-old was officially placed in the Buffalo Orphan Asylum. Maria set off for Niagara Falls to begin a new life.

But within days she realized she had made a tremendous mistake. She returned to Buffalo and, on April 28, grabbed her son from the orphanage and fled. The police found her in an apartment on July 10, 1876, and tore a shrieking Oscar from her arms. Then they dragged her kicking and screaming into another waiting carriage.

When the carriage stopped less than an hour later, Maria looked out the window and saw she had arrived at the Providence Lunatic Asylum where she was committed against her will. The following morning, she was evaluated by Dr. William Ring, who could tell she had been drinking. Otherwise, he found her well-spoken and ladylike. He sat spellbound and horrified by her tale of rape, the loss of her child, and now her unjust imprisonment in an insane asylum. He told her she was free to leave whenever she wanted, but he advised her to rest there a few days. On July 21, somewhat recovered from her ordeal, she checked herself out.

Maria consulted a top Buffalo lawyer about getting her son back, who told her she also had grounds to sue for "assault and abduction." As he moved forward with the case, her brother-in-law Simeon Talbott said the family would not put up with a "public scandal." Her family—her old father, her two older children—would be "bowed down in an exposure of Maria's shame." Talbott handed her an agreement signed by Grover Cleveland stating he would pay her $500 (more than $12,000 today) if she agreed to give up Oscar and never make any claim against his father for anything. Totally defeated, Maria signed. On January 1, 1877, Dr. James E. King, who had delivered Oscar, and who had placed him with his sister for a year, removed the two-year-old from the orphanage and began formal adoption proceedings. His only child had died a couple years earlier at the age of ten, and his wife longed for another. Oscar Folsom Cleveland became James E. King Jr. No longer living in a rented room with an alcoholic mother, no longer one of dozens of unwanted children in the orphanage, now Maria's baby lived with prosperous parents in a large house with a wide front porch and fenced lawn.

When Grover Cleveland ran for mayor of Buffalo in 1881, he must have been delighted that Maria Halpin had left town years earlier for parts unknown, especially as he was running on a platform of honesty, responsibility, and clean government. A gang of crooks had been running city hall for years, the mayor and city council giving themselves commissions on all public works contracts. This meant that contracts were awarded to the highest bidder at taxpayer expense. Vowing to stop such corrupt practices, Cleveland, a Democrat, was swept into office in a Republican city on a wave of public disgust at the status quo. He took office January 1, 1882.

When the city council awarded an unscrupulous businessman a contract more than $100,000 ($2.5 million today) higher than the lowest bid to clean the city streets—and gave themselves generous kickbacks—Mayor Cleveland vetoed it, stating, "I regard it as the culmination of a most bare-faced, impudent, and shameless scheme to betray the interests of the people." The story made the newspapers across the state, and the people of Buffalo—Republican and Democrat alike—stood squarely behind their mayor. The contract was voided. Cleveland's new sewer system ended up costing $764,000, half the price of the $1.5 million estimate the previous council had received.

By August, only seven months into his job as mayor, Democratic Party leaders asked Cleveland to run for governor. He agreed and quickly won the nomination and then the governorship in a landslide. Now he started cleaning up the massive corruption in New York State. Newspaper articles praising Cleveland appeared across the U.S., and in early 1884 party power brokers asked him if he would consider running for president. Initially, Cleveland was hesitant. He had had "a woman scrape" a decade earlier, he explained. He could only pray that it would not come out. The party officials didn't mind, probably because most politicians had had "woman scrapes." Besides, Cleveland's battles with corrupt politicians were the talk of the nation. At the 1884 Democratic National Convention, General Edward S. Bragg of Wisconsin nominated Cleveland with the words "We love him for the enemies he has made."

Dr. George Lewis of Buffalo had watched Cleveland's meteoric political rise with increasing dismay. Back in 1876, a patient of his had brought her friend, Maria Halpin, to ask him for advice. She had related the whole sordid tale of her rape by Grover Cleveland, and while Lewis sympathized greatly, he told her he didn't see how he could help. He hadn't said a word to anyone about Maria's visit when Cleveland was elected mayor in 1881 and then governor a year later. But now, in July 1884, as the presidential conventions were quickly approaching, he told Maria's story to the Reverend George H. Ball, pastor of the Free Baptist Church.

Appalled, Ball started investigating. He went to the Buffalo department store where Maria had worked, and her supervisors confirmed she had left after becoming pregnant with Cleveland's child. Ball next interviewed Dr. William Ring at the lunatic asylum, who also corroborated Maria's story, as did her former landlady. But Ball could not find Maria herself. She had disappeared from Buffalo eight years earlier. Undeterred, Reverend Ball began writing to newspaper editors, accusing Cleveland of the "grossest licentiousness," though it was too late to stop his nomination as the Democratic presidential candidate on July 11. No paper printed his letter, but many journalists were certainly interested in learning more. They interviewed Ball, the landlady, the lunatic asylum doctor, and Maria's former colleagues at the department store.

On July 21, the *Evening Telegraph* broke the story of Cleveland's bad behavior, titled "A Terrible Tale." Part of the tale was a letter from Ball, who remained anonymous, accusing Cleveland of "habitual immoralities with women," "debauchery," and drunken, bloody bar fights, along with Maria's "seduction" and her involuntary commitment to an insane asylum. Meanwhile, Ball wrote, Cleveland pretends "before the great American public that he is a model of virtue, pre-eminently worthy of being honored by their votes and being exalted as an example of ambitious youth to imitate . . . It would be criminal to allow the virtuous to vote for so vile a man as this under a false impression that he is pure and honorable. It is painful to think of his offenses and shameful, infinitely shameful, to have such a man commended to the suffrages of a Christian nation. It is enough to alarm all decent people . . ." The *Evening Telegraph* described Maria as a woman of "culture, proud spirit and hitherto unblemished life," who had been "shamed," "disgraced," and "dishonored."

Though no word of rape had been uttered, even a seduction might have been enough to derail Cleveland's campaign, and his advisers were apoplectic. Desperate, they split up and ran around the city trying to buy up every copy of the offending newspaper from the newsstands. The paper gleefully printed more. Charles Goodyear, Cleveland's friend, telegraphed him in Albany asking for instructions on how to proceed with the scandal. Cleveland was celebrating the twentieth birthday of Frances Folsom, daughter of his deceased best friend, Oscar, along with her mother, Emma. For ten years, he had been nervously anticipating the other shoe to drop. Or, as the *Evening Telegraph* put it, "The mine that has long slumbered under the feet of Grover Cleveland has at last been exploded."

Without missing a heartbeat, Cleveland telegraphed back: "Whatever you do, tell the truth." Yes, he was the father of Maria's son. But his supporters, concerned that voters would reject him for not having been a virgin at the age of thirty-six, spun an exculpatory tale. The real father was Oscar Folsom who, being dead, was in a poor position to deny the charge. When Cleveland learned that newspapers were getting ready to carry the Folsom story, he was livid. He wrote to Daniel Lockwood, a Democratic congressman from Buffalo:

> I learned last night that McCune [Charles McCune, editor of the *Buffalo Courier*] had started the story and told it to newspapermen that I had nothing to do really with the subject of the Telegraph story—that is, that I am innocent—and that my silence was to shield my friend Oscar Folsom. Now is this man crazy or does he want to ruin anybody? Is he foolish enough to suppose for a moment that if such was the truth (which it is not, so far as the motive for silence is concerned) that I would permit my dead friend's memory to suffer for my sake? And Mrs. Folsom and her daughter at my house at this very time! I am afraid that I shall have occasion to pray to be delivered from my friends . . . This story of McCune's of course must be stopped. I have prevented its publication in one paper at least.

But Democratic Party leaders felt they had to fight back as the Maria Halpin story ran in more than one hundred newspapers across the country. Many editors noted that the governor hadn't denied the accusation. Horatio King, publisher of the *Christian Union* magazine, ignored Cleveland's instructions and wrote a particularly damning story about Maria Halpin for the *New York World*. A decade earlier, when Governor Cleveland was "sowing his wild oats" as every young man does, the story went, he began a relationship with Maria Halpin, who was "not a good woman by any means." Maria had been having affairs with three other men at the same time, all of them married. King described the real father in terms that make it clear he was referring to Oscar Folsom: "The man who in reality was the father of the infant had an interesting daughter whom he idolized. He was in constant dread lest his offense should reach his wife and child, and Cleveland, being the only unmarried man, relieved him of the embarrassment by shouldering all of the responsibility. That man is dead, and the child is his perfect image in manner and looks. Cleveland acted a heroic part, suffering the obloquy that his friends might not bring unpleasantness to their hearthsides." Cleveland was, in fact, not a vile seducer of innocent womanhood, but a self-sacrificing hero.

Maria, meanwhile, was living with her late aunt's husband, James Seacord, in the village of New Rochelle, New York, eighteen miles outside of New York City. She had lived quietly, keeping house for her uncle after her aunt's death, and making dresses to earn a little extra money. We can only imagine Maria's shame as she read the Terrible Tale. When a neighbor asked her whether the allegations against Cleveland were true, she replied, "They are, and God knows they are true, too."

Frantic Democratic political operatives tracked her down and attempted to persuade her to issue a statement "pronouncing the story of her alleged relations with the governor a base fabrication." She did not respond. Then her twenty-one-year-old son, Frederick, received a telegram from Cleveland's political adviser William Hudson, asking for a meeting in Manhattan. When Frederick arrived, Hudson told him it was in his mother's best interests to publicly deny a relationship with Cleveland. He then showed him a statement he wanted her to sign calling the Terrible Tale "false and malicious." It went on, "I received from Mr. Cleveland uniform kindness and courtesy. I have now and have always had a high esteem for Mr. Cleveland. I have not seen him in seven or eight years."

If Maria signed the statement, she would be paid $10,000 ($260,000 in today's money), and Frederick would receive a job with the commissioner of the New York State Board of Public Works. Maria didn't sign it, but she agreed to Hudson's suggestion to disappear from the media feeding frenzy for a time and went into hiding on the west side of Manhattan. Her Democratic handlers told her she could leave her refuge at any time, but if she did so, someone would probably try to kill her as many Cleveland supporters had been making death threats. While she was in hiding without access to newspapers, the pro-Cleveland press dragged her name through the mud.

One aspiring fiction writer from the *Boston Globe* pretended he had sat down with Maria in James Seacord's house for an interview. "Mrs. Halpin is evidently an epileptic," he wrote, "and she has every symptom of insanity. Her eyes are glassy; she cannot look her questioner in the face; she has the trembling twitching of the muscles and the sudden starts at every unexpected noise peculiar to insane persons."

"I have been very sick and am very sick now," she supposedly said. "I will not live six months I know. I hope that Mr. Cleveland will be elected, and I would not want to put anything in the way of his success. I do not wish Mr. Cleveland any harm. I have no quarrel with Mr. Cleveland. He is a good, plain, honest-hearted, nice man who has always been friendly to me and used me kindly. It is a shame that the newspapers should have issued such lies. I would not harm a hair on the head of Mr. Cleveland."

Maria's brother-in-law Simeon Talbott, who had negotiated

the $500 settlement years earlier, received a letter from Cleveland urging him to make a public statement declaring that Cleveland had always treated Maria with respect. If he did so, the governor promised him "anything I could wish for in case he was elected." Cleveland added that he had never authorized Horatio King to publish such lies about Maria. When Talbott discussed Cleveland's request with Maria, she said she would rather die than issue any public statement that would support Cleveland's candidacy.

The Democratic political machine was not just defending its candidate, it was seeking to take down his opponent with similar salacious tales. Operatives dug up dirt on Republican nominee James Blaine indicating that back in 1851 he had had a literal shotgun wedding, at which the bride's brother held a gun to his head during the entire ceremony, and the bride had a baby eleven weeks later. Presenting Cleveland with corroborating documents, his aides boasted that this would "more than" offset the Maria Halpin story. Cleveland took the papers, tore them to pieces over a trashcan, and then tossed them into the fire. "The other side can have a monopoly of all the dirt in this campaign," he said.

When the shotgun marriage story made its way into the *Indianapolis Sentinel*, Cleveland said he was "very sorry it was printed. I hope it will die out at once." It turned out the true story was not damning at all. Blaine and his wife had married a year before their son was born, but nine months after the ceremony they discovered the preacher had not possessed a proper license, so they married again.

But the scandalized Reverend George Ball wasn't finished yet with his own dirt. In a letter to the Buffalo *Evening Telegraph*, George Ball described Cleveland as a "champion libertine, an artful seducer, a foe to virtue, an enemy of the family, snare to youth, and hostile to true womanhood . . ." Ball thundered, "The issue is evidently not between the two great parties, but between the brothel and the family, between indecency and decency, between lust and law . . . between the degradation of women and due honor, protection and love to our mothers, sisters, and daughters."

For their part, Cleveland's allies did all they could to undo the damage of the Terrible Tale. If Ball could use the press to vilify their candidate, they could use it to defend him. On August 11, the *Buffalo Courier* defended Cleveland's forcible committal of Maria in an insane asylum. "There was no abduction. The authorities had acted in the best interests of the child. There was no cruelty. The mother was in a state of intoxication, and she was removed lawfully and with no more force than was necessary."

Cleveland found a defender in none other than Mark Twain, who scoffed, "To see grown men, apparently in their right mind, seriously arguing against a bachelor's fitness for President because he had private intercourse with a consenting widow! Isn't human nature the most consummate sham and lie that was ever invented?" Twain was assuming the relationship had been consensual.

It was fortunate for Cleveland that his opponent, James Blaine, though a faithful husband and family man, had a ghastly reputation for corruption. As speaker of the House in 1869, he had been accused of accepting $130,000 ($2.5 million today) in bribes to secure land grants for portions of the Transcontinental Railroad. Though he was never criminally charged, during the 1884 election some of his correspondence regarding the odiferous deal surfaced, ending with the instruction, "Burn this letter."

At a meeting where Cleveland supporters discussed the two scandals—Cleveland's illegitimate son and Blaine's corruption—a journalist summed it up. "Well," he said thoughtfully, "from what I hear, I gather that Mr. Cleveland has shown high character and great capacity in public life, but that in private life his conduct has been open to question, while, on the other hand, Mr. Blaine in public life has been weak and dishonest, while he seems to have been an admirable husband and father." Those gathered nodded in agreement. "The conclusion I draw from these facts," the journalist continued, "is that we should elect Mr. Cleveland to the public office which he is so admirably qualified to fill and remand Mr. Blaine to the private life which he is so eminently fitted to adorn."

In early September, having hidden for a solid month, Maria showed up at her uncle's house "crushed in spirit and broken in health." She had finally realized the Democratic Party wanted her out of sight until the November election. Now, with access to newspapers, she learned what they had been writing about her. She was a whore. A lunatic. A drunkard. Fury gave her strength. She decided to give an in-depth interview to a sympathetic newspaper, Manhattan's *Morning Journal*.

"Grover Cleveland is the father, and to say otherwise is infamous," she declared. "The attempt to connect the dead Oscar Folsom with me or my boy, of which I hear, is cruel and cowardly. I had but a very slight acquaintance with Oscar Folsom. It does not seem possible after all I suffered for Grover Cleveland and my boy's sake that an attempt will be made to further blacken me in the eyes of the world . . ."

She continued, "My sufferings, subsequently my fruitless efforts to have him fulfill his promise of marriage, his neglect of myself and my child, my abduction and violent treatment by his hired tools were truthfully but only partially told in the *Buffalo Telegraph* of July 21. It would be impossible to cover the events that made up those years of shame, suffering, and degradation forced upon me by Grover Cleveland."

The reporter asked Maria about a rumor going around that she was considering issuing a statement vindicating Cleveland. "Maria Halpin drew herself up," the reporter wrote, "as preparing for a supreme effort, and replied in a most impressive and earnest manner, 'Me, make a statement exonerating Grover Cleveland? Never! I would rather put a bullet through my heart.'"

The September 27 issue of *Judge* magazine blazoned on its cover a color cartoon called "Another Voice for Cleveland." It showed Maria, her face planted in a handkerchief, holding a squalling infant with "Where's my Pa?" coming out of his mouth, even though by this time their son was ten years old. A fat-bellied Cleveland—bearing a tag on the bottom of his coat that read "Grover the Good"—is so upset his top hat is falling off. Republicans roared with laughter at the cartoon, and "Where's my Pa?" became their rallying cry. When Cleveland spoke at campaign events across the country, hecklers in the audience jeered, "Where's my Pa?"

On October 22, Henry Ward Beecher—a popular clergyman and social reformer—spoke at a Cleveland rally in Brooklyn, New York, calling Maria Halpin a "harlot and a drunkard." Maria, reading the papers the following day, was so furious she decided to fight back in the press once more and invited Charles Banks, the owner of the *New Rochelle Pioneer*, to meet with her. Banks helped her write an affidavit, which he published. She began:

> I would gladly avoid further publicity of this terrible misfortune, if I could do so without appearing to admit the foul and false statements concerning my character and habits . . . I deny that there was anything in my actions or against my character at any time or place up to the hour I formed the acquaintance of Grover Cleveland

on account of which he or any other person can cast the slightest suspicion over me. My life was as pure and spotless as that of any lady in the City of Buffalo—a fact which Grover Cleveland should be man enough and just enough to admit, and I defy him or any of his friends to state a single fact or give a single incident or action of mine to which any one could take exception. I always felt that I had the confidence and esteem of my employers . . . and this I could not maintain if I had been the vile wretch his friends would have the world believe. He sought my acquaintance and obtained an introduction to me from a person in whom I have every confidence, and he paid me a very marked attention. His character, so far as I knew, was good, and his intentions I believed were pure and honorable.

The details of the night of her ruin were too "revolting" to be made public, Maria wrote. But "there is not and never was a doubt as to the paternity of our child, and the attempt of Grover Cleveland or his friends to couple the name of Oscar Folsom or anyone else with that of the boy, for that purpose, is simply infamous and false."

Republican papers picked up her story; Democratic ones ignored it or dismissed it as false. But the statement must have been cathartic for Maria who, unburdening herself of a decade of mute victimhood, wasn't done yet. She submitted to Banks another statement detailing the rape. She began with meeting Cleveland on the street, of his pressing her to accept his dinner invitation, and his accompanying her to her rooms afterward. "While in my rooms," she wrote, "he accomplished my ruin by the use of force and violence and without my consent." Finally, she had spoken of the rape. If Cleveland's supporters waited with bated breath for him to angrily dismiss the accusation of rape, they were sorely disappointed. He never addressed it, which many voters saw as an admission of guilt. The burning question was: Would they care?

When election day, November 4, came around, Cleveland lost his home county, Erie, because of Maria Halpin's story. He won big in Manhattan, which cared mostly about his reputation for low taxes and cutting bureaucratic red tape. In the national popular vote, however, he won by only 25,000 votes out of ten million cast. A difference of just 600 votes in strategic states would have lost Cleveland the election. His supporters didn't care that he won by a hair. They just cared that he won. Many of them ran out into the streets crying:

> Hooray for Maria! Hooray for the kid!
> We voted for Grover and damned glad we did!
> Ma, Ma, where's your pa?
> Gone to the White House, hahaha!

It is important to remember that only men could vote in the 1884 election. It is likely, given Cleveland's slim majority, that if women had voted he would not have been elected. While many readers criticized the *Telegraph* for breaking the sensational and highly indelicate story, a Mrs. O. K. Smith of West Eager Street in Buffalo wrote the editor shortly before the election, "All honor to the bravest paper in Buffalo! Women, if you have any influence, use it." Whatever influence they used, it wasn't quite enough.

The biggest takeaway from the 1884 election is that the majority of voters, forced to choose between a corrupt candidate and a rapist, chose the rapist. Whatever Grover Cleveland had done to Maria Halpin, it hadn't cost them a dime. He had never stolen from his constituents—indeed, quite the opposite; he had prevented others from doing so—and had kept taxes low. Then there was the matter of his honesty. Given that he never bothered to deny the rape, he certainly wouldn't lie to them about politics.

As president, Cleveland refused to fire government employees for the sin of being Republican and said anyone who was doing a good job could stay. He reduced the number of federal employees, feeling that government had become bloated. He was a president in the mold of the old Republicans—government should keep its stinking hands off as much as possible. Thomas Jefferson would have loved him.

Since the birth of Frances Folsom, Cleveland had served as a kind of godparent to her. After Oscar died in a carriage accident when Frances was eleven, Cleveland became the court-appointed administrator of his estate. He remained in close contact with Frances as she grew up, frequently visiting her and her mother, Emma, so much so that newspapers hinted he would propose to Emma, which she herself believed. "I don't see why the papers keep marrying me to old ladies," he groused to an assistant as Frances morphed into an elegant young woman. "I wonder why they don't say I am engaged to marry her daughter." They probably didn't say he was engaged to marry Frances because she was twenty-seven years younger, radiantly beautiful, and seemed more like the daughter of the old, gray, obese president. Tall for her time at five foot seven, with a slender but shapely figure, she had thick chestnut hair, violet eyes, and a pert, intelligent face.

Cleveland visited Frances at Wells College in Aurora, New York, a place where her mother, Emma, could not intrude on their rendezvous, and frequently sent flowers. Emma Folsom, realizing which way the wind was blowing, was not pleased to learn that all this time her daughter had been the object of his affections. On June 2, 1886, Cleveland became the first—and until now, the only—president to marry in the White House. Twenty-one-year-old Frances was the youngest first lady in history and soon became immensely popular. The Clevelands would have five children.

Cleveland lost the 1888 election to Republican nominee Benjamin Harrison. As Frances Cleveland left the White House, she told a servant, "Now, Jerry, I want you to take good care of all the furniture and ornaments in the house, for I want to find everything just as it is now, when we come back again." When asked when she would return, she responded, "We are coming back four years from today." The Clevelands moved to New York City, where Grover returned to the practice of law.

Frances Cleveland had been correct. Her husband bounced back into office in the next presidential election. Grover Cleveland is the only U.S. president to serve two nonconsecutive terms—1885–1889 and 1893–1897. His second term was marred by strikes and a depression. Even so, his reputation for probity and good character survived the troubles of his second term. Maria Halpin's accusations of rape were soon forgotten.

Her son with Cleveland, James E. King Jr., became a physician and a pioneer in the field of gynecology. He was married briefly, had no children, and died in 1947 at the age of seventy-two. He never reached out to his birth mother, nor did she try to contact him.

As for Maria, after the scandal died down, she married James Seacord, her uncle by marriage. Nearly seventy, he was sickly and fragile. Most likely, the marriage offered her a safe haven and a bit of financial security. In 1899, a widow for the second time, she married again, a man named Wallace Hunt. In 1902, Maria Halpin died of bronchial pneumonia at the age of sixty-two. "Do not let the funeral be too public," she told her husband in her final illness. "I do not want strangers to come and gaze on my face. Let everything be very quiet. Let me rest."

5

WOODROW WILSON'S THROBBING PULSES

*W*oodrow Wilson might have resembled a prim Sunday school teacher or, by his own description, "a rare bookworm . . . incapable of sentiment, smileless and given over to dead love." But underneath his bow tie and button-down shirt surged a raging libido.

★ ★ ★

In October 1915, Mary Allen Hulbert had every reason to hope that her life was going to change. At fifty-three, she was a faded beauty, though still slender. She had lost much of her substantial divorce settlement to bad investments and a wastrel son and now lived in a shabby apartment in Los Angeles.

But she had had two amazing strokes of luck in recent years. The first was that her lover of several years, Woodrow Wilson, had been elected president of the United States in 1912. The second was that his wife of thirty years, Ellen, had died of kidney disease in August 1914. Bereft, Wilson had written Mary soul-wrenching letters describing his loneliness. Now that the year-long mourning period was over, he was bound to remarry. More than any other man on the planet, Wilson needed the companionship of a lively, fun-loving woman. And though he had loved Ellen dearly, her bouts of depression had caused him to take the vivacious Mary as a lover in the first place. Because of her devotion to her husband, Ellen permitted it.

Surely, the time had come when Wilson would invite Mary to visit him in Washington again. Surely, he would propose to her, and they could be together the way she had always dreamed. No more financial difficulties. No more dreary little apartments. No more pulling her hair out over her alcoholic son starting one doomed business venture after another. Mary would be first lady of the United States, an international celebrity, living in wealth and style, married to the man she passionately loved.

But when Mary sat down to read the newspaper on that golden October day, she must have shrieked out loud. For there, on the front page, was the news that President Woodrow Wilson had announced his engagement to Mrs. Edith Galt, the wealthy widow of a Washington, D.C., jeweler. The bride-to-be, the paper announced, was thirty-eight—the writer had gallantly shaved off five years—and "a woman of unusual beauty" who was always "modishly gowned." The headline also trumpeted—in a sop to American women who might have resented the president for remarrying so soon after his mourning ended—that the president had finally come out for "woman suffrage." The happy couple would be married in December. "Gay Capital Season Sure," crowed the headline.

We can picture Mary staring at the words that shattered her hopes, destroyed her dreams, and broke her heart, words that swam on the page as her eyes filled with tears. And then, she let the pages flutter to the floor.

Mary Allen Hulbert Peck had met Wilson back in February 1907, when he was vacationing in Bermuda without his wife in the hopes of reducing his blood pressure. A few months earlier, he had gone temporarily blind in one eye due to a burst blood vessel and may have had a small stroke. While doctors of the time could diagnose high blood pressure, they had no way to treat it other than prescribing rest and relaxation. And Wilson sorely needed both. As president of Princeton University, he had been mired in constant bitter arguments with faculty and alumni over the school's future. If he did not reduce his stress, doctors warned, he could have a catastrophic—perhaps fatal—stroke. Ellen could not join him as she was caring for their sick daughter.

Wilson was immediately enchanted by the island, so "warm and soft and languid," where the daily tumult of Princeton seemed "remote and theoretical." He was eager to be "irresponsible"— and he was—"and so renew my youth"—and he did.

Since 1892, Mary had been spending her winters in Bermuda to get away from her overbearing husband. Mary Hulbert had been a widow with a young son when she married a wealthy widower, Thomas Peck, in 1890. The marriage was an almost immediate failure. Stressed and depressed at home in Pittsfield, Massachusetts, with her husband's annoying children and feuding parents, in Bermuda she was "joyous, with an almost pagan delight in basking in its beauty," as she later described it. She soon elbowed her way into the center of the island's social scene, entertaining the most famous visitors, including Mark Twain. Known for her "frank courting of susceptible males," Mary Peck was "a bewitching woman, and a snare for men folk," according to one Bermuda matron. Another mentioned "a little restless look of unfulfillment about her eyes and mouth that gave grounds for romantic speculation," a polite Edwardian description of a well-heeled tart.

With thick, dark hair piled high, large, pale blue-gray eyes, and pretty features, Mary Peck glided from luncheons to beach picnics to balls in large feathered hats and large feather boas. It was her confidence and engaging conversation that attracted most, her "absorbing way of listening to the words of wisdom uttered by a *man*," as Wilson's cousin later described her.

In February 1907, a friend of Mary's invited her to dinner to meet Woodrow Wilson, whom she had read about in the papers. There Mary was introduced to a prim-looking, silver-haired gentleman with a long face, a lantern jaw, calm gray eyes, and a pince-nez perched on the bridge of his aristocratic nose. At five foot eleven and 170 pounds, he was dapper in his high, starched collars and top hat. Despite his resemblance to a hanging judge, Wilson had an impish sense of humor and a love of playfulness.

Sparks flew between them that first night as they conversed animatedly about the nature of freedom. Wilson was enthralled. Here was a free spirit, a woman of wit and vivacity, all the things his wife, poor devoted Ellen, was not. He saw Mary again the next night and the following day wrote to her from the port just before he boarded his homeward-bound ship. "It is not often that I can have the privilege of meeting anyone whom I can so entirely admire and enjoy," he gushed. Back in Princeton, he sent her two books of essays, one of them authored by himself, so "that you may know me a little better."

Mary wrote back that she had hesitated to tell him "what knowing you has meant to me." A flurry of enthusiastic letters bounced from Bermuda to Princeton and back. Wilson told her that her letters served "to keep me in heart amidst much unrewarding toil."

Most men who embark on a love affair after more than twenty years of marriage have fallen out of love with their wives. Not so Woodrow Wilson. He was still deliriously in love with Ellen, whom he had met in 1883. The twenty-six-year-old Atlanta lawyer had gone to Rome, Georgia, on business and seen a pretty, twenty-three-year-old woman in church. She had apple cheeks, golden-brown hair, and large, velvety brown eyes that impressed him as "splendid, mischievous, laughing." Wilson thought to himself, "I'll lay a wager that this demure little lady has lots of life and fun in her!" She did not, in fact. Her father would soon die in an insane asylum, possibly from suicide, and her brother was repeatedly institutionalized throughout his life. Compared to them, Ellen had won the genetic lotto of the family with only moderate depression. Though she would never be the life of the party, she would prove herself highly intelligent and loyal.

A talented artist, Ellen had considered remaining single and devoting herself to her landscape painting, but Wilson pressed his suit so ardently she found resistance was futile. He peppered her with letters. "Never was a man more dependent than I am upon love and sympathy," he wrote, and it was true. Woodrow Wilson would love the three women in his life with an obsessive intensity. He and Ellen were engaged five months after their first meeting and married after he had finished his doctoral program at Johns Hopkins in 1885.

The Wilsons had three daughters in quick succession. Ellen not only raised his children and ran his home, she devoted herself to helping his career, organizing his papers, translating scholarly articles from German, and entertaining his business contacts, giving up her own dreams of being a professional artist. In 1890, he accepted the chair of political economy and jurisprudence at his alma mater, Princeton. He was immediately popular with his students and soon become a leader among the faculty.

The Wilsons seemed to have had a fulfilling sex life. Wilson wrote Ellen that she was not only "an intellectual man's close confidante, companion, counsellor, but also *Love's Playmate*, led on to all the sweet abandonments and utter intimacies of love."

But Ellen knew she disappointed in one regard. Her husband loved whimsy and laughter. After dinner, he romped with their daughters and danced wildly around the house. He rejoiced in spirited conversation, droll quips, and witty repartee, especially in the company of women. Without them, he seemed to wilt. Ellen, however, "considered herself a grave and sober person," according to her daughter Nell. She could not provide lightheartedness to a man who needed it nearly as much as he needed air. But she had a solution. "Since you have married someone who is not gay," she often told him, "I must provide for you friends who are." She found lively female friends whom she invited frequently to dinner and, when he traveled, encouraged him to "go to see some of those bright women."

In 1902, Wilson became Princeton's new president. A powerful speaker, he traveled the country lecturing on government issues. Ellen, raising children and nursing a conga line of sick relatives, rarely went with him. Their love letters after nearly two decades of marriage were intensely romantic. She wrote, "Surely there was never such a lover before, and even after all these years it seems almost too good to be true that you *are* my lover."

Ellen must have been leery of her husband's new best friend as letters from the ebullient Mrs. Peck arrived with irritating frequency, and when they did an overjoyed Wilson sat down immediately to pen his reply. In January 1908, Wilson returned to Bermuda once again to lower his blood pressure, though the trip surely raised Ellen's own because she couldn't go with him this time either; she was caring for her brother who had had a nervous breakdown. She must have worried about Wilson rejoining this middle-aged Circe of Bermuda, with a knack for turning men into drooling dogs. But she sent him off anyway, after issuing an "injunction," a warning of some sort.

It must have been challenging for Wilson to remember his wife's injunction once he had returned to the Land of the Lotus-Eaters. He and Mary saw each other every day, walking along the beach, picnicking, reading to each other, discussing life and people and politics. "I found him longing to make up as best he might for play long denied," Mary later wrote, in a cutting allusion to poor morose Ellen. They also discussed Wilson's political ambitions. Should he run for governor of New Jersey? Important men in the Democratic Party suggested he do so, and he had always wanted to enter politics. Mary encouraged him to follow his dream.

Wilson wrote long letters to Ellen describing the fun he was having with Mary, adding, "While she delights me, you enslave me." Surely this made his wife feel much better. He showed Mary a picture of Ellen, who must have examined the sad, dark eyes staring out of a plump face with a twinge of triumph. She told him she wanted to keep it.

He wrote Ellen, "I brought two pictures of you with me . . . and Mrs. Peck is so charmed with them that she insisted upon keeping one of them on the mantel-piece of her drawing room, so that it sometimes seems as if my darling were there." He wanted the three of them in that drawing room, all happy together. It seems he needed both women to complete himself and desperately hoped that Ellen and Mary, out of their love for him, would understand.

When Wilson returned to Ellen after his winter fling, the poor woman must have been more depressed than ever. She accused him of "emotional love" for Mary. Wilson denied it, though his protestations of innocence were belied by his letters to "his precious one, his beloved Mary," recalling their "delectable walks to the South Shore when you were like a gay child of nature, released into its native element, and I felt every quickened impulse of the blood communicated to me."

In the spring of 1909, Mary separated from her husband and moved to New York City. Wilson was overjoyed—not only was she single, she was living close by—and Ellen must have been less so. He visited Mary frequently, called her on the telephone, and thought of her with "admiration and longing," as he waited for her next letter. "I must keep in constant touch with you, if my spirits are to be steady and my tasks well done," he wrote.

In the winter of 1910, Wilson went to Bermuda again for his blood pressure. Ellen must have been thrilled that Mary was in New York taking care of her dying mother. On the island, Wilson dreamed of his two loves and wrote them frequently. He told Ellen that she was "so exactly what I want and need" and "I am very, very lonely without my love to sustain me." He informed Mary that she was "perfectly satisfying and delightful, so *delectable*" and "I am lonely wherever I go because you are not there!" Wilson informed her he could not go anywhere on the island without thinking of her. All his "pulses throbbed" as he entered the cottage that she had loaned him. "It seemed to me a mere romance to be in it, after all the thoughts I had had of it, and the peculiar associations. If you could have been there it would have been perfect . . ."

Mary replied saucily, "Does the bougainvillea fling itself over the cottages as of old? Why, why can I not be there—to fling myself where I would!"

Ellen, always more sedate, wrote her husband, "It is quite impossible to express my love. It is greater than ever, and I had thought that too was impossible!" Ten days later, she vowed, "I would give my life, ah! how freely to make life happier for you. I love you with all my heart and soul and strength and mind." Perhaps she was telling him she was permitting his affair so that he could be happy.

Ellen even called on Mary in New York when she took her daughter Nell to see a play there. She cheerfully wrote Wilson that she'd had "a delightful little visit" with his friend. We can only wonder how delightful the visit truly was. Clearly, Ellen was working hard to prevent Mary from becoming a scandal. Because if a man's wife called on his reputed mistress, she couldn't really be his mistress, could she? And if Wilson were going to have the political future he had long dreamed of, the scandal of Mary could not be permitted to derail it.

As the university squabbles resolved themselves to the satisfaction of Wilson's opponents, he decided that after twenty years at Princeton, it might be time for him to finally dive into politics. On September 25, 1910, he was nominated for New Jersey governor. He campaigned on a strong progressive platform and became known for his rousing speeches, easily beating his Republican opponent 54 to 43 percent.

Wilson was such a popular governor—enacting laws for workers' compensation and restricting child labor and public corruption—that many Democratic power brokers wanted him to run for president in 1912. Both Ellen and Mary encouraged him, yet both felt, too, that something would be irretrievably lost. As first lady of New Jersey, Ellen had already given up much of the stress-free home life she had so enjoyed and would lose it altogether if Wilson became president. Mary worried he might cease contact with her completely to avoid scandal. But it was too late for that. When Wilson campaigned in Chicago in early April 1912, burglars broke into his hotel room and stole a suitcase full of letters but no valuables. Clearly, it was a political hit job. Wilson must have waited with dread for the other proverbial shoe to fall.

The Democratic National Convention, which started on June 25 in Baltimore, was of particular interest as the Republican convention held a week earlier had resulted in two candidates who would, most likely, split the vote. Incumbent president William Howard Taft was nominated after a brutal contest with former president Theodore Roosevelt, who stormed off announcing he would form a third party. The Democrats had an excellent chance of capturing the White House, which had been Republican ever since Grover Cleveland left office in 1897.

On July 2, on the forty-sixth ballot, Woodrow Wilson was nominated as the Democratic candidate for president of the United States. He wrote Mary—who was now divorced and took the name of her first husband, Hulbert—that his feelings would never change, and she was always in his thoughts, "a noble, sweet, free, unspoiled inspiriting" woman, for whom "nature found a fit form." He complained that sixteen newspaper reporters had been assigned to follow him, "to know where I am, who is with me, and what I am doing at all times. They must move as I move, go where I go . . . All eyes are watchful of my slightest action." He would not be sneaking to New York to visit her anytime soon.

The October surprise was the surfacing of Woodrow's letters from Mary. Theodore Roosevelt's campaign heard that someone was "hawking" the letters, which were reported to be "salacious and incriminating." When Roosevelt's campaign managers suggested they obtain and publish them to tank Wilson's candidacy, Roosevelt replied they would be "entirely unconvincing" because "no evidence would ever make the American people believe that a man like Woodrow Wilson, cast so perfectly as the apothecary's clerk, could ever play Romeo!"

Wilson won the presidential election with 435 electoral votes, compared to 88 for Roosevelt and 8 for Taft. A few days after his inauguration, Wilson wrote to Mary in Bermuda that he had finally found the time "for which I have waited with such impatience, to write to my dear, dear friend." Her letters, he insisted, were a help to him in the midst of his troubles. When he did not hear back from her, he protested, "Do you really want to know what the present President of the United States lacks and *must* have, if he is to serve his country . . . He needs *pleasure* and the unaffected human touch!" He urged her to contribute to the "success of a national administration" by writing him.

When Wilson moved into the White House, the staff was a bit afraid of him "because the President looked so stern with his long, lean face," according to one. But they soon learned of Wilson's joy in playfulness. "The strangest thing about the President was that he was really a frustrated actor," wrote Lillian Parks, whose mother, Maggie Rogers, worked as a White House maid. "Mama would find him making faces, clowning and doing a jig with his daughters, or taking a very serious part in a play, and speaking with one arm raised dramatically."

As first lady, Ellen stepped outside the traditional role of hosting social events and took a particular interest in improving the slum housing—often with no running water—in Washington's numerous alleyways. A serious, joyless individual, she disliked wearing beautiful gowns, even complaining that she had to put on a clean blouse every day or her White House maid would quit. When Eleanor Roosevelt came to Washington in 1913 as the wife of the new assistant secretary of the navy, she described the first lady as "a nice, intelligent woman but not overburdened with charm."

The White House staff, however, loved her. According to Lillian Parks, her mother "always came home shaking her head in amazement because a woman of such importance and such high rank could be so gentle. It was as if Mrs. Wilson wanted to make the world around her a little better place to live in."

Ellen's despondency must have been increased by Mary Hulbert's visit to the White House beginning on May 9, 1913. The first lady absented herself, pleading other commitments. Wilson took Mary on drives in the Virginia countryside with his cousin Helen Bones, who served as Ellen's personal secretary, as chaperone. Helen remarked that the first lady had proved herself "a pretty good politician" by inviting Mary Hulbert to stay in the White House, giving the "friendship" the gloss of respectability.

And so things continued with President Wilson and his two women, until the summer of 1914 when everything changed. On June 28, Wilson received a telegram that Austro-Hungarian Archduke Franz Ferdinand and his wife had been assassinated in Sarajevo. As Europe prepared for war, Wilson kept the U.S. firmly on the sidelines, hoping to mediate. It was a hot summer, and Ellen became unwell and feverish, despite the newfangled White House "cold-air machine": swiftly revolving fans blowing over seven tons of ice in the White House basement. The first lady had a hard time keeping her food down and grew weaker by the day. Doctors diagnosed Bright's disease, an obsolete term that included various diseases of the kidneys. She had experienced her first kidney trouble twenty-five years earlier after her third pregnancy.

Now she was suffering the symptoms of kidney failure: swelling of the face, nausea, and backache. Her nights were "full of pain."

As the European powers lurched into a world war, Wilson spent every moment he could with Ellen, holding her hand with his left hand as he wrote urgent memos with his right. Now and then, he was forced to leave the room to deal with the looming bloodbath in Europe. When he was away, she called for him continually. In a moment of clarity, she took the hand of her physician, Dr. Cary Grayson, and said, "Doctor, if I go away, promise me that you will take good care of my husband." She also told Grayson that the "Peck affair," as she called it, was the "only unhappiness her husband had ever given her."

"Even in the last moment of her life, her thoughts were with others," wrote Lillian Parks. "The President was with her when she died on August 6, 1914, and he came out of the room saying that her last words had been for the slum-dwellers of Washington, asking that something be done for them." When Wilson realized she was gone, he wrenched himself away, staggered to the window, and wept bitterly. Dr. Grayson later said, "A sadder picture no one could imagine. A great man with his heart torn out."

Lillian Parks wrote, "Mama heard the President talking to his dead wife as he stood beside the body. She happened to be in the room at twilight when the President came in and stood looking at his wife's face. He picked at the lace on her dress, and Mama could hardly keep from crying at this wistful, hopeless scene. The President spoke aloud, brokenly, 'Never, never, never.' Then he walked out."

Americans—especially American women—mourned Ellen Wilson greatly. Lacking in charm though she might have been, she had in many ways transformed the role of first lady. As the first to undertake social welfare causes, Ellen was a tremendous inspiration to Eleanor Roosevelt when she became first lady nineteen years later. Ellen was also the first to campaign with her husband and watch him address Congress. And she left the American people a lasting legacy by creating the White House Rose Garden.

Within hours of Ellen's death, Wilson wrote Mary, "Of course you know what has happened to me; but I wanted you to know direct from me. God has stricken me beyond what I can bear . . . I never dreamed such loneliness and desolation of heart possible."

Mary had already fired off a letter as soon as she heard the news. "It seems incredible," she wrote, "that this terrible thing has come to you now, when you need that sweet love to help you in this terrible time."

Wilson told his chief adviser and longtime friend, "Colonel" Edward House, that he could "not think straight" and "had no heart in the things he was doing." He wanted and needed a woman. Washington socialites made bets on whether he would remarry before his first term expired. Mary, knowing him as well as she did, understood better than most that he could not live long without a female companion. She hoped, when the time came, it would be her, after all the love they had shared. Yes, she was older and not as attractive as she had been eight years earlier when the affair began. The stress of her divorce, a drunken adult son, and her financial difficulties had affected both her health and her appearance.

There was, of course, the added disadvantage that marrying a divorcée—and one whose name had been whispered with his while his lamented wife had been alive—might jeopardize his winning a second term. But why not marry after his reelection, more than a year after the mourning period was over? Ellen herself wouldn't have minded. She had told her friends, "I hope Woodrow would marry again. He cannot live alone."

Wilson found his new love quite unexpectedly, in March 1915, as he rounded a corner on the second floor of the White House and almost smacked into a striking woman with muddy shoes. She was forty-three-year-old Edith Bolling Galt, five foot nine, with Rubenesque curves, who had accompanied her friend Helen Bones—Wilson's cousin—to her White House apartment to have tea. The president was gobsmacked by the sight of her, muddy shoes notwithstanding. Edith had a wide, handsome face, thick, black hair, deep blue eyes, and strong, dark eyebrows. As they chatted, he found she was charming, confident, and amusing. He invited her for dinner and, after her departure, pumped Helen for information about her.

Edith had been born to a family of modest means in rural Virginia. In 1896, she had married Norman Galt, owner of Galt's Jewelers, known as "the Tiffany's of Washington," and helped her husband run the revered establishment where Thomas Jefferson had bought a silver service for the White House in 1802. Edith was not terribly attracted to Norman, but she was attracted to his lifestyle and the Washington social scene, and they lived happily enough. In 1908, Norman Galt died of a liver infection at the age of forty-five, leaving his childless thirty-five-year-old widow with some $6 million in today's money. In early 1915, she became acquainted with Helen Bones, and the two frequently walked in Rock Creek Park for fresh air and exercise. When Helen invited Edith to tea in her White House apartment that day, Edith demurred. She wouldn't want to run into the president of the United States wearing muddy shoes. Helen assured her there was no chance of that; the president was out playing golf.

Edith dined at the White House for the first time on March 23 and soon became a regular guest. "She's a looker," said Pat McKenna, the White House doorkeeper. "He's a goner," said Arthur

Brooks, Wilson's valet. "He couldn't," said some. "Wait and see," others predicted. "Suddenly the President was effervescent and full of jokes," wrote Lillian Parks.

Two months after their first meeting, Wilson proposed to Edith. But she said it was too soon. His wife had only been dead nine months. Wilson protested that it had already been "a life-time of loneliness and heartache" since Ellen's death. "I would be less than a gentleman if I continued to make opportunities to see you without telling you that I want you to be my wife," he said.

Wilson wrote her, "Here stands your friend, a longing man, in the midst of a world's affairs which he cannot face with his full strength unless you come into this heart and take possession. Will you come to him some time, without reserve and make his strength complete?"

Edith told him her first marriage had not been a passion-ate one and indicated she had never much liked sex. "If you can quicken that which has laid dead so long within me," she wrote, "I promise not to shut it out of my heart." He would gladly un-dertake the task, he rejoined. "There is a heart to be rescued from itself—a heart that never made complete surrender . . . that final divine act of self-surrender which is a woman's way to love. She must be taken by storm—and she shall be!"

Wilson was evidently successful in awakening Edith's inter-est in sex. They would drive out into the countryside, park, and close the curtains on the car windows. And there was certainly something going on between them in Wilson's private White House quarters (etiquette forbade the president from calling on a private citizen). "Seeing you as I saw you last night," he wrote, "my radiant, wonderful Darling, is like being present while life is created." Wilson was overwhelmed at being "the instrument of it." He wrote that she "turns to her lover and throws the gates wide—no, not quite wide yet, but wide enough to show him the sweet and holy places where her true spirit lives."

Having had a look at Edith's sweet and holy places between the gates, he would lie awake at night pretending she was in his arms. He complained that his lips "can speak nothing worthwhile all day long for lack of your kisses." He started signing his letters "Tiger."

She was his "*perfect playmate*," one who could "match and satisfy every part of me, grave or gay, of the mind or of the heart— the man of letters, the man of affairs, the boy, the poet, the lover." Indeed, Edith, with her vivacity, her unabashed self-confidence, and her hearty laugh, was far more suited to Wilson than Ellen had been.

What interested Edith even more than sex, however, was power: sharing *power* with the president of the United States. She enjoyed his romantic letters, she wrote, but "I enjoy even more the ones in which you tell me of what you are working on for then I feel I am sharing your work and being taken in partnership as it were . . . I feel so close to you when I know what you are doing."

Wilson, who was still writing to Mary, hadn't mentioned a word about Edith, nor had he told Edith about Mary. This caused him some awkwardness when, in May 1915, Mary, who had been staying in Hot Springs, Virginia, wanted to visit her lover at the White House on the way home to New York. Wilson tried to discourage her from coming, citing his busy schedule. She did not take the hint, however, and arrived at seven thirty on the morning of May 31. That afternoon, Mary accompanied Wilson, his daughter Margaret, and Helen Bones to Arlington Cemetery, where the president made a speech observing Memorial Day. They all made sure Mary was on the four o'clock train to New York. It was a stroke of great good fortune that Edith had been unable to attend the Arlington events as she had houseguests. Wilson must have mopped his face with his handkerchief in relief as Mary's train whisked her north.

In June, Wilson proposed again, and this time Edith accepted him, though they couldn't release the news until after the year of mourning was over. Now the president was in a real pickle. What should he do about Mary? He decided to send her some money. She had written him that her son wanted funds to start yet another business, this one in California, where she would be joining him. Wilson bought two mortgages she held for $7,500 ($190,000 today). Though Mary had never given him the slightest hint that she considered blackmailing him with his letters, he must have been worried what a scorned woman might do when she heard about his engagement to Edith.

Despite the world war raging in Europe, Wilson was "simply obsessed" with Edith. Some of his staff were concerned that the president of the United States was acting like a lovesick teenager while Europe was consumed by war and his wife's body was still cooling in her grave. In a bizarre, cruel manipulation, Wilson's son-in-law Treasury Secretary William Gibbs McAdoo lied to the president about having received an anonymous letter claiming that Mary Hulbert Peck was showing around the president's love letters. McAdoo hoped Wilson's fear of scandal might cool his relationship with Edith.

But the maneuver backfired spectacularly. Wilson reckoned that if he did not tell Edith about Mary before the papers broke the story, she might very well dump him. The same day, September 18, 1915, he sent Edith a scrawled note, asking to meet in her home—etiquette be damned—to discuss "something personal." Edith agreed at once, and that evening, Wilson confessed to his affair with Mary Hulbert Peck. Though we don't know exactly what was said, we do have the letters Wilson wrote Edith in the following days rehashing his story, which he called "a passage of folly and impertinence, long ago loathed and repented of."

He insisted his embarrassment was not because "the lady to whom [the letters] are addressed was not worthy of the most sincere admiration and affection, but because I did not have the moral right to offer her the ardent affection which they express." The revelation of his affair would, Wilson said, "make the contemptible error and madness of a few months seem a stain upon my whole life." He added, "I am deeply ashamed and repentant . . . But none of this lessens the blame or the deep humiliating grief and shame I suffer, that I should have so erred and forgotten the standards of honorable behavior by which I should have been bound."

As Edith listened, she must have felt that she was watching Wilson fall off his pedestal in horrifying slow motion. She could not bring herself to forgive him immediately and told him she would think about their relationship. But by the next morning, she was "ready to follow where love leads" and promised that "whether the wine be bitter or sweet, we will share it together." The wedding was still on. Wilson was further delighted to hear from Edward House that Mary had not, in fact, tried to sell his letters.

And so on that October day, Mary read of her lover's upcoming marriage in the newspaper. She must have been equally devastated that Wilson had not had the courtesy to write to her before the public announcement, that he had been so uncaring as to let her learn the news in this hurtful way. When she did receive his letter, she saw that it had been postmarked only two days before the announcement, not long enough for it to travel all the way to California. He had "not been at liberty to speak of it sooner," he

wrote. It seems likely that Edith, who had been micromanaging
the announcement, did not want to give Mary any special prefer-
ence.

It took Mary a few days to pull herself together enough to
respond on October 11:

Dearest Friend,

*I have kissed the cross. We are very glad you have found happiness
and that you had time to think of us in the midst of it. I need not tell
you again that you have been the greatest, most ennobling influence
in my life. You helped me to keep my soul alive and I am grateful. I
hope you will have the happiness that I have missed. I cannot wish
you greater. We are well, and both working at the business that your
friendly purchase of the mortgages made it possible for us to embark
upon . . . She [Edith] is very beautiful and sometime perhaps I
may meet her. I wish you had told me before, for your letter was
only mailed the 4th, and the newspapers had already published the
fact. The cold peace of utter renunciation is about me, and the shell
that is M.A.H. [Mary Allen Hulbert] still functions. It is rather
lonely, not even an acquaintanceship to make the air vibrate with
the coming warmth, perhaps of friendship. God alone knows—and
you—partly, the real woman Mary Hulbert, all her hopes and joys,
and fears, and mistakes. I shall not write you again this intimately
but must this once . . . Write me sometime, the brotherly letters
that will make my pathway a bit brighter. And believe me ever*

Your friend,
Mary Allen Hulbert.

*P.S. This is rather a whine but it is the best I can do—now.
God bless you!*

It was a stunningly gracious letter from a woman suffering such utter heartbreak. Wilson's engagement to Edith was a slap in the face of not only Mary, but also of Ellen. On the back of Wilson's letter to her, Mary scrawled, "How could he so soon?" She then swallowed hard and wrote Edith a letter wishing her happiness. Wilson, feeling more miserably guilty than ever, sent Mary another $7,500.

Woodrow Wilson and Edith Galt were married on Saturday, December 18, 1915, at her house, with only forty guests in attendance. A Secret Service agent reported that the day after the wedding, he saw Wilson dancing down a White House corridor singing a popular song, "Oh, you beautiful doll, you great, big, beautiful doll!" and clicking his heels.

Wilson's money didn't last Mary very long, probably because her son wasted it. By 1916, she was reduced to "tramping the streets of California towns," she later wrote, "selling books which nobody seemed to want; buying furniture at auctions and trying to sell it to affluent people, sitting in the casting offices of moving picture studios in Hollywood hoping to do 'atmosphere' parts for five or ten dollars a day, cooking for ranch hands." She sold her own furniture to make ends meet and was evicted from one apartment for not paying rent. She had fallen far from the unrivaled queen of the winter social season in Bermuda.

And so, when a Republican operative knocked on her door asking to buy her letters from President Wilson, he assumed she would eagerly accept the huge sum he offered. The 1916 presidential election was coming up, and the Republican Party wanted to prevent Woodrow Wilson's reelection at all costs. According to Mary's recounting of the event, her visitor looked around her modest room and remarked that a woman of her breeding should have a larger apartment. Surely an extra $250,000 ($6 million in today's money) would come in handy? She stared at him. Or $300,000 ($7.3 million)? Or more? The men he represented could raise just about any sum she wanted. She would, however, have to travel abroad for a time. The United States would no longer be a suitable place for her to reside.

Having heard him out, Mary told him that the letters were honorable ones that would only reflect well on President Wilson's character, adding "I am not that sort of a woman." Then she told him to get lost. Offers continued to roll in up to half a million dollars (nearly $12 million today). The answer was still a firm no. Woodrow Wilson had been—would always be—the love of her life. She would rather suffer all the indignities poverty could offer than betray him. Concerned that someone might break in and steal the letters, she put them in a safe-deposit box. It was a good thing, too. Because Wilson only narrowly defeated the Republican candidate, Supreme Court Justice Charles Evans Hughes, with 277 electoral votes to 254. If Mary's collection of the president's love letters to her while he was married to Ellen had been published, he likely would have lost the election.

It is uncertain, though, that they would have been published at all in a major newspaper. Back in the 1912 election, journalists were well aware of Wilson's relationship with Mary Peck—among themselves they called Wilson "Peck's bad boy"—but didn't print a word about it. At the Democratic National Convention that year, journalist David Lawrence heard rumors involving Wilson and Peck "whispered about the corridors." And in 1915, reporters knew the supposedly inconsolable widower was having an affair with the voluptuous Edith Galt. Considering the shrieking newspaper articles about Alexander Hamilton and Maria Reynolds, Thomas Jefferson and Sally Hemings, and Grover Cleveland and

Maria Halpin, why were journalists so painfully discreet about Woodrow Wilson and Mary Peck?

Wilson benefited from a sudden radical shift in American journalism. From the dawning of the American colonies until the early twentieth century, members of the press were considered socially inferior tradesmen like carpenters, wielding not saws but pens to produce sleazy articles. Then journalists organized themselves into an elite profession, founding the National Press Club in 1908 and adhering to a code of ethics. Journalism schools were established at universities. The 1914 Journalist's Creed stated, "I believe that no one should write as a journalist what he would not say as a gentleman." And gentlemen did not gossip about other gentlemen's love lives.

Moreover, early twentieth-century legislators passed laws to prevent muckraking journalists publishing articles on political sex scandals. In 1900, the California legislature prohibited the publication of any article "which tends to expose the individual so caricatured to public hatred, ridicule or contempt." Other states quickly followed suit. The sponsor of Pennsylvania's law stated that "the Commonwealth is interested that those who render her service should be treated with deference and respect, so that when they go forth in performance of her functions those to whom they are sent may feel that they are vested with authority." Political opponents could, however, have printed up their own pamphlets and distributed them, causing outrage and protests, which may have been covered by major news outlets.

As America's leaders confronted the great struggles of World War I, the press became even more determined to insulate presidents from sex scandals. Still, one journalist must have had the good old days of salacious news stories somewhere in his subconscious when, on October 9, 1915, the *Washington Post* printed the most embarrassing typo in its long history. In describing President Wilson's activities of the day before, a front-page exclusive stated that the president took his fiancée to the theater, and "rather than paying attention to the play the President spent the evening entering Mrs. Galt" instead of "entertaining Mrs. Galt."

On April 6, 1917, the U.S. finally declared war on Germany. Though the conflict lasted only nineteen months for America, the losses were staggering: 53,000 killed, 204,000 wounded, and another 63,000 dead of the influenza epidemic that swept the world beginning in 1918. Yet the other Allies had lost far more. They wanted revenge. And Wilson warned that harshly punishing Germany would create a backlash of anger that would only result in another world war. He worked tirelessly to create a League of Nations, a body where disputes would be peacefully resolved. The Covenant of the League of Nations required members to respect freedom of religion and treat racial minorities fairly. It was incorporated into the Treaty of Versailles, which officially ended the war.

The Wilsons spent six months in Europe cleaning up the post-cataclysm mess at the Paris Peace Conference, where Woodrow started behaving oddly. He irritated the other statesmen by insisting they reopen issues that had already been settled. On occasion, the entire conference had to be adjourned because he hadn't read his papers. He accused his French servants of spying on him, and when his hosts removed some furniture in his official residence, he saw it as part of a diabolical plot. He ate less than ever and suffered excruciating headaches. On the morning of April 28, 1919, while Wilson was signing letters, his handwriting suddenly deteriorated. He could barely write his name when he signed the peace treaty. Back home, when several senators wanted amendments to the treaty before the U.S. agreed to it, Wilson stubbornly refused.

He decided to take his case for an unamended treaty to the American people and, against the wishes of Dr. Grayson and Edith, undertook an arduous twenty-seven-day trip to the West Coast, with speaking engagements all along the way. He spoke of his fear that American children would have to fight another world war if the League were not in place to prevent it. But Wilson was like Cassandra, the Trojan prophetess cursed with seeing a horrifying future that no one believed.

In Los Angeles on September 21, the Wilsons met with Mary, whom Wilson had not seen in four years. Edith, just like Ellen before her, went reluctantly along with the visit to show her "disdain" for the "slander" about his relationship with Mary. Edith damned Mary with faint praise, describing her as "a faded, sweet-looking woman," while the ever-slender Mary later commented how shocked she was at Edith's weight; she was much fatter than she had appeared in newspaper photos. When Wilson expressed his regret about the gossip Mary had endured because of their friendship, Edith snapped, "Where there's so much smoke, there must be some fire." Mary, who had heard rumors that Edith had been sleeping with the German ambassador before the war, retorted, "Then maybe you were von Bernstorff's mistress!"

Perhaps the strain of the meeting, on top of his exhaustion and unceasing, years-long stress, tipped Wilson over the edge into a full-on stroke. Just three days later, his face suddenly changed. He said, "I am not in a condition to go on. I have never been in a condition like this, and I just feel as if I am going to pieces." Then he started to cry.

Canceling the remaining five stops on the trip, the presidential train raced to Washington, seventeen hundred miles away.

The president could barely walk from the train to his limo. He began drooling from the left side of his mouth. Back in the White House, at 8:00 a.m. on October 2, Edith found him awake but unable to move. A specialist arrived and discovered that Wilson's left leg and arm were completely paralyzed. He had no feeling on the left side of his body, the left half of his face was drooping, and he was completely blind in his left eye.

The Constitution had no provision for a president suffering a serious physical disability. Edith, unwilling to inform the American people of her husband's condition, decided she would run the country for him until he improved. She forced Dr. Grayson to lie about Wilson's health, claiming he was merely suffering from exhaustion. The vice president, Thomas R. Marshall of Indiana, was not allowed to see him. He kept up with the president's health by reading the newspapers every morning, filled with lies Edith had given them.

Edith took important papers into Wilson's bedroom and came out with his "instructions." It was unlikely the president was able to issue any instructions. Ike Hoover, who served as White House chief usher, recalled, "He appeared just as helpless as one could possibly be and live." In the middle of the night, Wilson would pick up a little flashlight and turn it toward a picture of his first wife, stare at it, turn off the flashlight, and do it again. And again. Grayson said that the president "could articulate but indistinctly and think but feebly."

Members of Congress were refused permission to see Wilson and guessed what was happening. They knew the country needed strong leadership to deal with unemployment, inflation, and striking workers. Instead, the acting president was a former jeweler's wife who had never completed high school. Senator Albert Fall, a Republican from New Mexico, spoke for many when he pounded his fist on the table of the Senate Foreign Relations Committee and shouted, "We have a petticoat government! Mrs. Wilson is President!"

Even though Wilson slowly improved, with the irascibility of a stroke victim, he refused to make the changes to the treaty that Congress wanted. It would be all or nothing. On March 19, 1920, the treaty was voted down. If Edith had allowed her husband to resign and the vice president to take over, the U.S. would likely have ratified the Treaty of Versailles and joined the League of Nations. Though more than forty countries from around the world joined the League, without the force of the U.S. behind it, it was a creature without a spine, powerless to alter the events leading up to World War II.

Perhaps Wilson's most bizarre plan of all was to run for a third term as president. There were no rules to limit a president to two terms until 1951, and Wilson hoped the delegates to the 1920 Democratic National Convention would nominate him. Fortunately, they did not. They chose James Cox, whose running mate was a handsome, up-and-coming young man named Franklin Delano Roosevelt.

Deeply depressed after Warren Harding's inauguration in 1921, Wilson moved to an elegant home not far from the White House where Edith took care of him, reading to him, tucking his napkin under his chin at meals, and holding his hand when he burst into tears. On February 3, 1924, as he lay dying, he told Dr. Grayson, "I am a broken piece of machinery. I am ready." He called out to Edith when she stepped away from his bedside. Her name was the last thing he ever uttered.

For the next thirty-seven years, Edith Wilson devoted herself to creating a fitting legacy for her husband. Her first step was to get those blasted letters back from Mary Hulbert. Edith had authorized Ray Baker, Wilson's press secretary at the Paris Peace Conference, to write Wilson's definitive biography; now she instructed him to visit Mary and persuade her to turn them over. Mary told him she needed the money the letters could bring, and she would be happy to sell them to a buyer friendly to Wilson's memory. A donor, Wilson's friend and adviser Bernard Baruch, stepped up and bought them for $31,500 (some $473,000 today).

Several months after she had sold them, Mary wrote Baker, "You understand that the loss of those documents leaves me bereaved. I hated selling them. I wanted to give them. I am satisfied however that they have found their safe and right honors . . . I am grateful for your beautiful and delicate handling of the friendship." Mary died in New York City in 1939 at the age of seventy-seven. We can imagine she cherished those eternally sunlit Bermuda days with Woodrow Wilson until her last breath.

Edith Wilson was successful in burnishing her husband's reputation. By the time she died, Wilson was considered one of the best U.S. presidents ever with an astonishing vision that foresaw World War II and the formation of the United Nations. Active socially and philanthropically on the Washington scene, she was on the inaugural platform on that bitter cold day in January 1961 when John F. Kennedy took the oath of office, discreetly sipping bourbon from a silver flask to keep herself warm. She died that year on December 28, Woodrow Wilson's birthday, at the age of eighty-nine, in the same bed, in the same room where he had died. Perhaps her greatest legacy to the American people is the Twenty-Fifth Amendment, enacted in 1967, which provides measures to ensure that the vice president becomes "acting president" if the president is "unable to discharge the powers of duties of his office."

6

WARREN G. HARDING'S EXCRUCIATING JOY

*W*arren Gamaliel Harding exuded a raw animal magnetism irresistible to many women. His security guards had to keep his female fans from following him around and making embarrassing scenes. Pundits of the day believed he won the 1920 election only because featherbrained women—newly given the vote—were smitten by his sex appeal rather than his policy goals.

Harding's sex life involved a rotating buffet of delectable young women. But the American public had no idea of the president's philandering until his former mistress, the mother of his illegitimate child, wrote a scandalous tell-all book, the first of its kind, that shook the nation.

★ ★ ★

On a hot summer's day in 1922, First Lady Florence Harding marched grimly to the Oval Office. This time she was determined to catch her husband, Warren, red-handed with a girl. Her trusted Secret Service agent Harry Barker had just informed her that Harding's trusted Secret Service agent Walter Ferguson had smuggled a blonde into the office five minutes earlier.

But as Florence approached the door opening onto the hallway, Ferguson blocked it, explaining that Secret Service regulations permitted no entry from that door, not even to the first lady. She would have to go through the office of Harding's secretary, George Christian. As Florence turned around and raced to Christian's office, Ferguson entered through the hallway door he had been guarding and told the president—who had taken the girl into a closet to muffle the noise—that his wife was on the way. As Harding pulled up his trousers, Ferguson grabbed the girl, took her out the hallway door, and told her to meet him at his car. Meanwhile, the first lady was delayed a few moments by George Christian, who knew what was up. When she barged into the Oval Office, she found her husband sitting innocently at his desk, quietly perusing papers. She flew back through Christian's office and into the hallway to find Ferguson idly guarding the door. Perhaps he was studying his fingernails. "She stood and glared at me like she couldn't believe it," he reported.

President Theodore Roosevelt's acid-tongued daughter, Alice Roosevelt Longworth, heard all about the episode from White House chief usher Ike Hoover. "It was really rather a close call," she said. "Stumbling in closets among galoshes, she pounding on the door, the girlie with panties over her head. That sort of thing. My God, we've got a President who doesn't know beds were invented, and he was elected on a slogan of Back to Normalcy!"

Florence was long used to her husband's infidelities. A good-natured fellow who didn't want to hurt anybody, Harding just couldn't help himself when it came to sex. Tall and well-built, with a face of bold, carved features like those of a Roman god, he exuded pheromones of such wild sexuality they turned women into howling cats in heat, even as he grew portly and gray. Debutantes, actresses, wives, widows, prostitutes, teenagers, and socialites stalked him, sent him love letters, and boldly offered their bodies. His staff had a name for women they needed to extricate him from: "lollapaloozas."

Ironically, thirty years earlier Florence had been a lollapalooza herself. The daughter of Amos Kling—the richest and meanest man in Marion, Ohio—at nineteen she became pregnant by a neighbor, twenty-year-old Henry DeWolfe. Amos threw her out of the house. Scholars debate whether Florence and Henry ever married, but all agree that DeWolfe, a hopeless alcoholic, abandoned Florence and their son in less than two years, and after an estrangement of four years she divorced him (which she could also have done for a common-law marriage). Her father agreed to raise her son, but Florence, defiantly independent, did not go home in shame. She supported herself by teaching piano to local children. When she was thirty, she went to the home of Dr. George Harding to teach his daughter. There she met the girl's older brother, Warren. Five years her junior, Harding owned a struggling newspaper, the *Marion Star.*

Smitten to the core, Florence avidly pursued him. She rudely interrupted his conversations with other women at social events. One day, hearing that he would be returning from visiting a girl-friend, Florence waited for him at the train station. Spotting her, he tried to escape out of the other side of the train. "You needn't try to run away, Warren Harding," Florence cried. "I can see your big feet!" He allowed her to drive him home in her buggy.

Harding liked beautiful, feminine young women, and bossy bespectacled Florence wasn't pretty, even in her youth. But she had an intelligent face, alert blue-gray eyes, and thick, dark hair.

She also had a keen sense for business and saw enormous opportunity in Harding's newspaper. He listened with interest as
she described ways to make the paper profitable. Harding knew
himself to be a bit too lackadaisical to achieve great success;
his favorite pastimes were sex, drinking, and playing poker. In
Florence, he saw a woman who could organize his life and perhaps help him realize his dream of becoming a politician. And it
wouldn't hurt if she one day managed to inherit some of old man
Kling's money. At their 1891 wedding, Florence announced that
she was now going to work to make her husband president of the
United States.

A *Star* writer said, "She had faith in his future. She believed
he had the making in him of a great man. She urged him on
and on." Florence immediately took the newspaper in hand. She
negotiated lower interest rates for loans, greatly increased circulation by drafting an army of schoolboys on bicycles to provide
home delivery, and raised advertising rates. A strong advocate of
women's rights, she hired Ohio's first female reporter, and she
even learned how to wield a wrench to fix the printing presses
herself. As Warren put his feet up on the editor's desk and smoked
a cigar, Florence made the paper a tremendous financial success.
"Florence Harding?" said one Marion lady. "Runs her house, runs
the paper, runs Warren; runs everything but the car, and could
run that if she wanted to."

But Warren didn't much like being run by the "Duchess," as
he called her, and escaped as frequently as he could. He traveled
to Republican meetings across the state where he drank, played
poker, and had sex with women. After eighteen months of marriage, he fell into a deep depression and eventually checked into
the renowned Battle Creek Sanitarium run by Dr. J. H. Kellogg,
who believed that the cereal he invented—cornflakes—would

cure depression and reduce the insatiable libidos of his male patients.

The cornflakes didn't work for Harding's libido, alas. Soon after returning from the sanitarium in 1894, Harding got Florence's best childhood friend, Susan Pearl McWilliams Hodder, pregnant. Susan left for Nebraska, where Harding sent child support for their daughter. Her pregnancy so upset Harding that he bounced back to Battle Creek.

But no matter how many cornflakes Warren Harding ate, he never did manage to give up women. The men in town understood. One of them said, "Anyone who lives with Florence Harding *deserves* extra-curricular activities." Another recounted the story of plumbers going into the home of a local widow to fix a sink. "And who comes out of the master bedroom but Harding in shirt sleeves. He had obviously just bedded down the woman of the house. He guffawed and then asked the plumbers to give him a ride downtown."

Florence knew, of course, about her husband's illegitimate daughter and the constant stream of women. She vacillated between blazing fury and resigned acceptance. As far as emotional pain was concerned, she wrote in her diary, she learned to "shut it away in my mind's secret cupboard and lock the door upon it." She also chose to enjoy her life no matter how badly the men in it were behaving. "No man, father, brother, lover or husband, can ruin my life," she wrote. "I claim the right to live the life the good Lord gave me, myself."

In 1899, Harding ran for state senate and, though a Republican, won in a heavily Democratic district. A charismatic speaker, he was extremely popular with other legislators for his ability to find a compromise. His constituents, too, loved him, particularly the women. Florence never let him out of her sight, even sitting in the statehouse gallery to watch the legislators at work. Harding became Ohio's lieutenant governor in 1904 and started to get national headlines as one of the most popular speakers on the Midwest summer lecture circuit. Gripping his arm tightly, Florence went along on the tour. "The way to keep a husband," she often said, "is never to let him travel alone."

But the biggest threat to Florence's marriage would not be a one-night stand with a stranger. It would be Florence's best friend. Carrie Phillips—tall, voluptuous, with wide blue eyes and strawberry-blond hair—was married to Jim Phillips, owner of a prosperous Marion hardware store. In 1905, when Florence was in the hospital with kidney disease and Jim Phillips in the Battle Creek Sanitarium eating cornflakes for depression, Warren and Carrie began a torrid affair. Even though Carrie lived nearby, Harding wrote her passionate letters—thirty, forty, fifty pages long. Hopelessly romantic, deliriously ardent, he blended the physicality of sex with rapturous poetry and apocalyptic religion. Indeed, reading the missives alone might suffice to tip some women into an earth-shattering orgasm.

My Darling:

There are no words, at my command, sufficient to say the full extent of my love for you—a mad, tender, devoted, ardent, eager, passion-wild, jealous, reverent, wistful, hungry, happy love— unspeakably encompassing, immeasurably absorbing, unendingly worshipping, unconsciously exalting, unwillingly exacting, involuntarily expounding, everlastingly compensating . . . It is the prayer and benediction of my heart; the surpassing passion of my body, the conviction and consecration of my mind, and the

*hope and heaven of my soul. I love you thus, and more. I love you
more than all the world and have no hope of reward on earth or
hereafter, so precious as that in your dear arms, in your thrilling
lips, in your matchless breasts, in your incomparable embrace. To
have and to hold you, in happiness to you, exclusively in satisfying
and satisfied love, would be the triumph of living and loving.*

In another, he told her, "I'd pet and coddle and kiss and fon-
dle and admire and adore, utterly impatient until I made you the
sweetest and purest and darlingest wanton . . . There is one en-
gulfing, enthralling rule of love, the song of your whole being
which is a bit sweeter—the 'Oh Warren! Oh Warren!' When
your body quivers with divine paroxysm and your soul hovers for
flight with mine . . ."

When Florence returned from the hospital, she was not
healthy enough to travel with him on the next summer's speaking circuit. Harding and Carrie met in hotel rooms across the
Midwest. Back in Marion, they met in each other's homes when
their spouses were out. One morning, the Harding cook spotted
Carrie wearing bright-colored shoes at the market. A few hours
later, when the cook started to enter the Harding kitchen through
the rear, she was stopped in her tracks by the sight of Warren,
his trousers about his ankles, standing with his back to the door,
and Mrs. Phillips spread out "on the kitchen table—still in those
shoes!"

Oddly, Florence's sharp, suspicious eye never fell on her best
friend. When the two couples cruised to Europe in 1909, Warren
and Carrie made love on the ship's deck after their spouses had
gone to bed. "I want to weld bodies, to unite souls," he wrote
soon after. "I want the divine embrace, the transcending union,

the blissful affinity, and with them all the excruciating joy and unspeakable sweetness that I never did know and can only know when fastened by you."

In 1911, encouraged by all those letters, Carrie suggested they both obtain divorces and marry. But Warren hemmed and hawed. True, Florence had aged greatly since their wedding twenty years earlier. Her hair was gray, her face rather puckered and sunken. Though she was still trim, her ankles had swollen. Harding no longer found her sexually attractive—if he ever had—and, it seems, they had stopped having sex some time ago. But Florence stalwartly supported him, his newspaper, and his political career with her wily acumen and forceful determination. Even if they were no longer lovers, they were partners and friends. His wife was bossy, to be sure, but she buoyed him up while nasty Carrie tore him down, deriding his dreams of high political office. There was more than self-interest in his reluctance, however. He knew of Florence's painful past—the father who beat her bloody with a switch, the pregnancy, the abandonment, the years of shame and grinding poverty. He could not hurt and betray her.

Furious, Carrie sent a love letter to his home hoping Florence would open it. She did. And realized that she had been doubly betrayed. Florence wrote in her diary, "Most of the pain in this world is located in the hearts of women . . . Passion is a very transient thing. To me, love seems to have been a thing of tragedy." Raging, Florence dragged her husband to a divorce lawyer.

But Warren didn't want a divorce. He wanted wild raucous sex with Carrie and a marriage partnership with Florence. Somehow Florence and Warren came to an agreement. They would stay married. After this crisis, she became bossier than ever, and he became more deferential to the Duchess.

"Love, to a man," she wrote bitterly in her diary, "is a sensation only. Never a complete giving of himself to one forever." She wrote that her relationship with him was "platonic affection, good fellowship."

In September 1911, Carrie Phillips took her fourteen-year-old daughter, Isabelle, to Germany, leaving behind her rather stupid husband—who remained blissfully unaware of his wife's infidelity with his best friend—to run the hardware store. But she secretly met Warren in Montreal for a New Year's Eve rendezvous. As both of them reached their climax, the bells of midnight pealed out their joy at the New Year in a kind of orgasm all their own. "The bells rang the chorus," Warren recalled in a letter, "while our hearts sang in rapture without words, and we greeted the New Year from the hallowed heights of heaven." He continued, "Fate timed that marvelous coincidence. It was impossible for us to have planned, and I count it to be one of the best remembered moments of my existence."

After another quick tryst in New York, on September 15, 1913, he wrote, "At New York, I had given you all—the very last passions, I thought, in a perfectly ecstatic loving, and I was prostrate from the excessive joy of it, dead from rapture . . . You set me aflame with the fullness of your beauty and the fire of your desire, and you loved me, gave me your unfailing kisses, and intoxicated me with your breasts, and then imprisoned me in your embrace and gave me transport—God! my breath quickens to recall it."

When an ocean came between them, Harding liked to put on his bathrobe—which she wore when they were together—and, wrapped in her scent, masturbate in front of a roaring fire in his study. One evening, he wrote Carrie, he dreamed of her "to alarming release. I called your name aloud thrice, begging you to come, and a voice upstairs responded, wanting to know what I wanted."

It was Florence, wondering what he was yelling about.

After war broke out in Europe in 1914, Carrie—who had become a rabid supporter of the kaiser and all things German—moved back to Marion with her daughter, much to Florence's chagrin. Warren was now running for the U.S. Senate, and he met Carrie in hotel rooms as he campaigned across the state. He won the Senate seat by more than 102,000 votes.

After the election, Carrie demanded Warren buy her a car. At first, he refused, but then, remembering all those letters, he caved and got her a Cadillac. Florence had no idea that the impressive new set of wheels her former friend and current enemy drove around town had been paid for by Warren. And poor, dim Jim Phillips didn't think there was anything odd about his best friend buying Carrie a Cadillac.

In 1915, the Hardings moved to Washington, D.C., and Warren took up his seat in the U.S. Senate. While he was popular with just about everyone, Florence hated her new city and felt the other politicians' wives were harshly judging her. She was right. One Washington society matron wrote of the Hardings, "That evening, I decided that the junior senator from Ohio was a stunning man with a powerfully masculine quality to charm a woman. That night his white-haired, kidney-troubled wife, whose chin was lifted haughtily each time she scented challenge, served all our drinks and did not play. Woman-like, I noticed her neck was withering and her ankles thickly swollen almost before I realized that she was rich in spirits, a determined and a jealous wife. By the calendar year she was five years older than her husband, but by all that matters in a marital partnership, she was far, far older than her easy-going, play-loving partner. Ill-health and a tendency to worry over what might happen, plus her nagging temperament had helped to wear her body . . . Hers was the ambition, what he had was charm, an ability to get along with assorted persons, friendliness and a love of jovial companions."

Millionaire Evalyn Walsh McLean, owner of the Hope Diamond, was much kinder. "She had been lovely in her youth," Evalyn wrote. "Anyone could tell that. Her eyes were blue, her profile finely chiseled, but her mouth was a revelation of her discontent. She was ambitious for herself and Warren."

When Florence fell ill with the old kidney complaint, Evalyn visited her. "You know, this town, Washington, is an awful place," Florence muttered, lying flat in bed, "the most awful town I have ever lived in."

"Why, Mrs. Harding, I love Washington. Why don't you like it?" Evalyn inquired.

"I'll tell you," she said, pushing herself up to a seated position. "Every woman in this town is after Warren . . . It's so. I'll keep him close to home, until I am up again."

Evalyn wrote, "At parties she was bound to grow alert each time he vanished from her sight. 'Where's Warren?' she would ask and then more shrilly pipe, 'Warren!'"

Though there was a twenty-six-year gap in their ages—when Florence moved to the capital she was fifty-five and Evalyn twenty-nine—they soon became best friends, and Florence settled into Washington life. Always an advocate for helpless, abused things as she herself had been, Florence joined the Animal Rescue League, the Humane Society, and the SPCA. When she saw a drunken man whipping his horse after it had fallen in front of the wagon, she ran into the street, tended to the horse, pulled the whip out of the man's hand, and gave it to his wife. "If you have to, use the whip, but not on the horse," she advised.

As pressure mounted on the U.S. to join the Allies in the European war, Carrie Phillips so defiantly defended the German cause back in Marion that the Secret Service investigated her as a possible German spy. Harding, made aware of the investigation, begged her to tone down her shrill defense of the kaiser. In response, Carrie wrote Warren that if he voted for war with Germany, she would reveal his love letters to her husband and the public. But when Congress—including Senator Harding—voted to declare war in April 1917, she kept his letters to herself. Revenge, of course, is sweet. But money is sweeter. She would hold on to them awhile.

Even after her threat to reveal his letters, Harding couldn't stop writing new ones. He concluded one such missive by asking her to destroy it. "Such a letter is a peril," he wrote. "I know and ought not send it. I endanger you, and no sane man ever pens such a missive. But no sane man ever loves as I do . . ."

In the midst of war, hot sex, and Carrie's threats of blackmail, Warren must have been intrigued to receive a letter from a twenty-year-old girl he had known in Marion. Nan Britton was the daughter of Sam Britton, a friend of Harding's. When Sam died in 1913, his widow, Mary, asked Harding for help, and he arranged a teaching position for her. "Maybe I can do something for Nan," he told Mary.

It had been a joke in Marion that Nan, at twelve years old, had developed a burning crush on Harding, who was thirty-one years her senior. She hid outside the *Star* office until he emerged and followed him home. She scribbled in her schoolbooks "Warren Harding—he's a darling" and wrote "I love Warren Harding" on her classroom blackboard. She covered her room with his campaign posters.

"Nan was a pretty girl, blonde and slender," recalled her best friend, Ellen Metzger. "In those days, we girls were movie crazy and we couldn't wait until school was out to go to a movie or to read movie magazines. But Nan wasn't interested in the movie stars; all she could talk about was Harding . . . I don't believe Mr. Harding encouraged her in any way. He didn't have to. Nan ran after him. He was so good looking, women chased him."

Nan recalled, "His pictures hung directly in front of my bed so that when I awoke in the morning, I looked into the handsome face of him whom I loved and saw his likeness the last thing before turning off my light." Everyone in Marion laughed at Nan's schoolgirl crush, everyone except Florence.

Now, in May 1917, Nan was finishing up secretarial school in New York. She wrote Harding in Washington and asked if he could use his influence to find her a good secretarial position. Eager to leave the hornet's nest of Washington to flirt with a sweet young thing, he raced up to New York and met her in the lobby of the Manhattan Hotel, where he had often rendezvoused with Carrie. "We became immediately reminiscent of my childhood," Nan later wrote, "and my adoration of him, and he seemed immensely pleased that I still retained such feelings. I could not help being perfectly frank."

When Harding suggested they go to his room, the bridal suite, "so that we might continue our conversation without interruptions or annoyances," she eagerly agreed. There they kissed passionately. "Oh, dearie, tell me it isn't hateful to you to have me kiss you!" he exclaimed. But Nan did not find it hateful at all. He tucked thirty dollars (some $600 in today's money) into her silk stockings and said, "I love you more than all the world, and I want you to belong to me. Could you believe me, dearie? I want you and I need you so."

Harding arranged for Nan to be hired as the secretary of the chairman of the U.S. Steel Corporation headquartered in New York. He continued to see her, dabbling in foreplay, even as he rendezvoused with Carrie. Finally, in July 1917, Harding and Nan met at New York's Imperial Hotel—a shady place used for such assignations where important men wouldn't run into anyone they knew except one another—where he registered as Mr. Harwick. They finally made love that afternoon. "I became Mr. Harding's bride—as he called me—on that day," Nan recalled.

As Nan and Warren were getting dressed, two house detectives broke into the room and caught the pair. They demanded to know Nan's name and age; she was, in fact, under twenty-one, the legal age of consent. Warren feared his entire career was ruined. He sat "disconsolately on the edge of the bed, pleading for them to allow me to go," Nan wrote. "'I'll answer for both, won't I? Let this poor little girl go!'" A detective told him they had already called the police and "You'll have to tell it to the judge!"

Then, one of the detectives picked up Harding's hat, saw his name on the band, and recognized him as a U.S. senator. They immediately apologized and even helped them sneak out of a side entrance before the paddy wagon arrived. Harding thankfully gave them a twenty-dollar bill. "I thought I wouldn't get out of that for under $1,000!" he said to Nan as they raced off in a taxi.

Harding and Nan frequently met in New York and Washington. Their rendezvous often lasted long, luxurious hours. "So potent was this spell which we had for each other," Nan wrote, "that for whole evenings we were its willing prisoners, living as in a dream, neither of us coming out from the intoxication of each other's presence until long after separation." Harding must have been a hot handful of man in the sack.

He sent her a photo of himself standing on the steps of the U.S. Capitol which she kissed so much it cracked and fell apart. "He confessed that it had been many years since his home situation had been satisfying," Nan wrote. "He spoke very freely to me about what he would do if Mrs. Harding were to pass on, he wanted to buy a place for us and live in the country. 'Wouldn't that be grand, Nan? You'd make such a darling wife!'"

In January 1919, Nan visited Harding in his Senate office and made love without a condom as, she wrote, "The Senate Offices do not provide preventive facilities for use in such emergencies." A month later, Nan knew she was pregnant.

In April, she returned to Washington and met Harding at the Willard Hotel, where she informed him of her condition. Calmly, Harding offered to procure her an abortion. Her sister Elizabeth, too, thought that was the only sensible route to go. But Nan, in awe that she was carrying the child of the man she idolized, refused. "I could not bring myself to destroy the precious treasure within me," she explained. Allowing Nan to make her own choice, Warren gave her a sapphire-and-diamond ring and the two performed a pretend marriage ceremony. "The ring was indeed a great comfort to me, helping to sustain me . . . It was a material evidence of a relationship which no wedding ceremony could have made more solemn or more sacred than that very own ceremony between ourselves, with God as our witness."

But Harding was still involved with Carrie, regularly adding more love letters to her mountain of blackmail material. And after he hired a tall, blond, beautiful new secretary, Grace Miller Cross, he started an affair with her, too, a sadomasochistic one, as sometimes she cut him and made him crawl in front of her naked, begging for forgiveness. Then there was a Washington woman named Augusta Cole, whom he also impregnated. He must have been relieved that Augusta, at least, agreed to have an abortion. A New York matron whose name has been lost to history committed suicide when Harding didn't divorce Florence and marry her. And amid all these histrionics and threats, there was little

Nan, sweet, undemanding, and grateful for whatever crumbs of attention he gave her. She was delighted when he gave her a winter coat.

Carrie Phillips, on the other hand, would not be silenced with a coat. In August 1919, she wanted him to buy her another new car and give her $10,000 ($150,000 today). By then her husband Jim was deeply in debt, and she saw her luxurious lifestyle slipping away. She once again threatened to release Harding's letters if he didn't cough up the money and the car. They came to an agreement.

When Nan's pregnancy began to show, she left her job at U.S. Steel and, with funds provided by Harding, rented rooms in a boardinghouse in the seaside resort of Asbury Park, New Jersey. She used an alias and pretended to be the wife of a soldier serving abroad. There, on October 22, 1919, she gave birth to a daughter whom she named Elizabeth Ann. Nan seems to have suffered from postpartum depression, exacerbated by being the single mother of a U.S. senator's child. She ate poorly, cried a lot, and said her nerves were "shattered." Finally, her sister took her to Chicago, leaving Elizabeth Ann in Asbury Park with a nurse. Harding had suggested they give the baby to his sister Charity to raise in California. But Nan could not give her up. Warren then promised that when Florence finally died of her kidney ailment, he would take the baby himself "and make her a real Harding!"

Florence, meanwhile, had no idea her husband had fathered a child with the obnoxious little girl from Marion who used to follow him around. Her mind was focused on politics. She watched hopefully as support in the Republican Party grew for choosing Warren as the 1920 presidential candidate. Jovial, glad-handing Harding had been an across-the-aisle bridge-builder in the Senate, finding the middle ground between progressivism and conservativism. He had been chosen to give the keynote address at the 1916 Republican National Convention, a nod to a man with a possibly presidential future.

In January 1920, Harding outlined his America First theme, which seems strangely familiar to us a century later, though in Harding's case, it was a reaction to the massacre of American men in the Great War. "Call it the selfishness of nationality if you will," he said, "I think it an inspiration to patriotic devotion. To safeguard America first. To stabilize America first. To prosper America first. To think of America first. To exalt America first. To live for and revere America first." Most Americans were disgusted at the cost America paid to extricate foreign nations from a bloodbath of their own making and heartily agreed with him. Additionally, Harding wanted to severely restrict the number of immigrants from southern and eastern Europe.

Florence, always interested in astrology and the occult, went with her friend Evalyn McLean to visit Washington's top fortune-teller, Madame Marcia. Wearing a dark veil so the seer wouldn't recognize her as the senator's wife, Florence gave her Warren's date of birth and asked what the future held for him.

Madame Marcia replied, "If this man runs for the presidency, no power on earth can defeat him. But you must know he will die a sudden death, perhaps of poison . . . This person will be the next president of the United States, but he will not live out his term. He will die in a sudden if not violent death. The end, when it comes, will be sudden, after an illness of short duration." Florence didn't know if she should be delighted that Warren would become president or horrified that he would die in office.

Carrie Phillips, too, was thinking about Warren's becoming president. Now that the stakes were higher, the orgasmic love letters were more valuable than ever. Carrie threatened to publish them if he didn't divorce Florence immediately and drop out of the presidential race. Warren politely offered to withdraw from the race, if that was her choice, to avoid disgrace. Or, if she waited until he became president, he would be in an excellent position to pay her substantial sums. He also assured her (despite the recent pregnancies, abortions, and suicides of his lovers) that he had never cheated on her. No fool, Carrie opted for the money.

Warren told Florence about Carrie's blackmail attempt and wondered if he should drop out of the race before the Republican National Convention, held in Chicago in June. Before the advent of the primary system in 1968, the Republican and Democratic national conventions were not the coronations they later became. They were cliff-hangers, where wheeling and dealing took place among a party's power brokers in smoke-filled rooms. And so, Florence traipsed back to Madame Marcia, having revealed her true identity. "He must stick," the psychic announced. "He will not be nominated until after noon on Saturday of the convention. But he will be nominated."

She was correct. At 6:00 p.m. on Saturday, June 12, Warren Harding was nominated as the Republican candidate for president. Three weeks after his nomination, Jim Phillips—informed by Carrie about the affair and not terribly upset about it—showed up at Harding's Senate office to ask about blackmail payments. Warren—prosperous but never rich—finally had to tell the Republican Party bosses about Carrie's extortion. They were horrified. The election of 1920 was the first time that American women would vote for president. Twenty million new female voters would not ignore a sex scandal the way most male voters had back in 1884 when Maria Halpin had accused Grover Cleveland of rape.

It is unlikely that any newspaper would have printed Carrie's steamy love letters. Harding benefited from the hands-off approach the press had with political sex scandals, just as Woodrow Wilson had. During the 1920 campaign, three newspaper reporters were invited to dine at the home of one of Harding's neighbors, an attractive widow. After dinner, the woman's eight-year-old child took them upstairs and proudly showed them Harding's toothbrush in the bathroom, explaining, "He always stays here when Mrs. Harding goes away." None of them investigated the matter further.

Harding even had the audacity to announce to journalists at the National Press Club, "It is a good thing I am not a woman. I would always be pregnant. I just can't say no"—perhaps the greatest headline never printed. Journalists also knew that during Prohibition, the Harding White House offered a full bar. Alice Roosevelt Longworth recalled, "No rumor could have exceeded the truth . . . trays with bottles containing every imaginable brand of whiskey stood about."

Perhaps Carrie was planning on publishing Harding's letters in pamphlet form and distributing them herself. Pamphlets could do great damage by causing protests and uproar that the press was obliged to cover. To solve the problem of Carrie Phillips, the Republican National Committee (RNC) solicited donations from Harding's richest friends and supporters to create an ample slush fund. An RNC representative called on Carrie in Marion. He would give her a lump sum of $25,000 ($321,000 today) and the promise of $2,000 ($26,000 today) a month, he said, as long as Harding remained in public office. In return, she would never discuss her relationship with Harding, never show the letters to anyone, and would betake herself and her husband on a very long cruise to Japan before the election. Carrie agreed.

With Carrie hushed up, the campaign moved forward at full speed. Florence came up with the idea of the front-porch campaign. Their Marion house—which she had helped design—had an enormous front porch with a circular area bulging out at one end and a white railing. The Hardings would not travel to meet voters but would invite the voters to come to them. In a rocking chair, Florence knitted and darned socks as Warren chatted amiably with supporters. It was a kind of before-the-war Disney World of traditional family values, a stage set where all that bloodshed on foreign soil had never happened, a dreamlike place of baseball games, apple pie, and church socials with fried chicken and watermelon, of good old American values like hard work and decency. It was a "Return to Normalcy," as his campaign slogan stated. Every storefront had red, white, and blue bunting except the hardware store owned by Jim Phillips.

Harding recognized Florence's campaigning savvy, which included novelties such as the extensive use of press photographers and newsreels, and the support of major Hollywood stars such as Charlie Chaplin. Warren "placed implicit confidence in his wife's judgment," said Florence's Marion neighbor Jane Dixon. He told his political advisers, "I'll consult Mrs. Harding about that and let you know." "Better ask the Duchess." "Talk with my wife. She will understand."

H. L. Mencken thought Harding's campaign pledges were tripe of the blandest, most bloviating kind, and we can only wonder what he would have thought of his love letters. "He writes the worst English that I have ever encountered," the writer remarked. "It reminds me of a string of wet sponges; it reminds me of tattered washing on the line; it reminds me of stale bean soup, of college yells, of dogs barking idiotically through endless nights. It is so bad that a sort of grandeur creeps into it. It drags itself out of the dark abysm of pish, and crawls insanely up the topmost pinnacle of posh. It is rumble and bumble. It is flap and doodle. It is balder and dash."

Still reeling from the horrors of bloody war, most Americans longed for the comforts of wet sponges and barking dogs. On November 2, 1920, Harding's birthday, he won in a landslide: 404 electoral votes compared to the Democratic candidate's 127 and thirty-seven out of forty-eight states in the most overwhelming presidential victory since 1820.

Nan Britton had been living with her sister Elizabeth and her husband in Chicago and working at the Harding campaign headquarters there. Upon hearing of her lover's victory, she took the midnight train for Marion. The next morning, Harding's Secret Service agent Tim Slade took her to a small house used by campaign clerical workers. There she sat on Warren's lap and cooed, "Isn't it wonderful that you are president?"

"This is the best thing that's happened to me lately, dearie," he replied. He asked about Elizabeth Ann, and Nan delightedly showed him pictures of the thirteen-month-old. Then he gave Nan $1,500 in the form of three $500 bills (about $20,000 today).

In January 1921, as Harding worked with his transition team, he arranged for Nan's sister Elizabeth to visit him in Washington. Hustled into his office, Elizabeth listened as the president-elect begged her and her husband to adopt Elizabeth Ann, who was still in New Jersey in the care of a nurse. Nan, he explained, with her bouts of severe depression and physical weakness, was in no position to take care of her. Moreover, he wanted the child to have a name and a traditional family. He volunteered to send Elizabeth $400 a month ($5,700) for the baby. Elizabeth saw the wisdom of his suggestion and pressed Nan to agree. The adoption took place in February, and the baby was brought to Chicago. Though Nan was delighted to be living with her child, the girl now had three parents, all arguing about how to raise her.

In the wee hours of the night before the inauguration, Warren snuck out of the presidential suite at the Willard Hotel to meet his former secretary, Grace Miller Cross, who had also taken a room there. But men from the Republican National Committee had heard about the planned rendezvous and, eager to avoid a new scandal, waited in the hall outside Harding's suite. When he emerged after midnight, they pushed Harding firmly back inside his room, then chased Grace out of the hotel with violent threats. Soon, however, they sent her, too, on a luxurious monthslong cruise abroad. Other young women kept popping up with Warren's love letters demanding money. There was a *Washington Post* employee named Miss Allicott, an Evalyn Ruby, and chorus girls Maize Haywood and Blossom Jones. The RNC slush fund would need constant replenishment throughout Harding's time in office.

Harding's 1921 inauguration was one of firsts: the first time the principals were driven in motorcars, the first time the wife of the new president had voted for her husband, and the first time the president took the oath of office with a loudspeaker so people could actually hear him.

As the band played "Hail to the Chief," Florence's joy was tempered by the memory of Madame Marcia's doom-filled prediction. She had been right about the nomination and the election, after all. Would her prediction of Warren dying in office also prove to be correct? She told Indiana senator Jim Watson, "I am filled with fear . . . It is the proudest day of my life, but we will not live through the four years."

Yet her ambition overcame her fear. As she stood on the North Portico waiting to enter the White House for the first time as first lady, she asked a senator, "Who was the most successful First Lady of the Land?"

"Mrs. Cleveland or Dolley Madison, I suppose," he replied.

"Watch me," Florence rejoined.

Then she turned to her husband and said, "Well, Warren Harding, I have got you the Presidency. What are you going to do with it?"

Feeling already the weighty responsibility of his position, he said, "May God help me, for I need it."

A week later, the debilitated President Woodrow Wilson and his wife, Edith, who had moved to a house nearby, drove past the White House. The place had been transformed. The Wilsons had shut off all public access for security reasons during the war and then due to the president's ill health. The White House, grim and darkened, where people talked in whispers, had been something like a funeral home. But Florence insisted that all the gates to the grounds be flung open, and hundreds of people were milling about the lawn. "The crowds of visitors were so interested in what was going on in the new administration," reported the *Los Angeles Times*, "that almost no one noticed the former President passing by."

Florence loved interacting with the public. At one reception she shook 6,756 hands. According to Lillian Parks, whose mother worked as a maid, "She would go running down the steps and greet the tourists, who came in to look around, with a big hello. They would be really startled!" The first lady was immensely popular with American women who saw her as a self-deprecating, folksy suffragette, a beloved auntie always ready with a witty quote.

Many commented that Florence enjoyed being first lady much more than Warren enjoyed being president. He hated having his every movement monitored and told Nan, "The White House is a veritable prison . . . I'm in jail, Nan! And I can't get out. I've got to stay." Wherever he went, he was trailed by Secret Service agents. And when he brought a girl into the White House, Florence's Secret Service agent Harry Barker would tell her. Which is what happened the day Florence almost found him in the closet having sex.

Perhaps because of that day, Florence finally learned that Nan Britton—the blonde in the closet with Warren—had become his mistress and had had his child. Gaston Means, an agent of the Bureau of Investigation who undertook special missions for the Hardings, reported in a 1930 book that Florence Harding asked him to follow Nan. Though Means was a crook and a swindler and later repudiated many of the shocking accusations in his book, his sex stories seem to have been accurate. Gaston wrote that Florence instructed him to get on Nan's train in Chicago bound for Washington. He noticed Nan immediately. "She was a most attractive young woman," he wrote, "blonde, fresh, vital. I took a seat in that car and watched her, and I also noticed that the other men in the car were watching her. She was decidedly the type to attract men.

"This attractive young woman," he continued, "with her bobbed blonde hair peeping from a closely fitting cloche, was really after all no more alluring than many other girls and women in whose presence I myself have seen President Harding all aflutter. But she was young, eager, panting, calling for sex-fulfillment, dazzled by his masculine beauty and his position, determined, flattered, seductive. And he loved girls . . . I had already seen enough of the President to know that he could no more resist a pretty girl or woman than he could resist food when hungry."

According to Means, Florence assigned him to investigate Nan's behavior with men from the age of twelve, when she had first started stalking Warren. Promiscuity with other men, she hoped, might indicate that her child was not Warren's. Means, interviewing schoolfriends and landladies, found that Nan had never shown any interest in the male sex—except for Warren Harding. Florence must have been deeply disappointed. She was even more so when Harding started sneaking out again, taking a few loyal Secret Service agents with him on his trysts.

The White House staff sensed Florence's nervousness. "The President was spending a lot of time away from the White House," wrote Lillian Parks. "Mama knew Mrs. Harding kept worrying about whom he was with . . . The more he stayed away, the more tense Mrs. Harding would get . . . She would try to keep him home, and once Mama was very shocked when Mrs. Harding shouted at him over the banister, 'You are not leaving this house tonight!'"

One night, when Warren was partying at the Love Nest, a rowdy bordello near the White House on K Street, a prostitute was hit on the head with a champagne bottle. As her friends tried to revive her, Harding, who was leaning against a mantel, drunk, was hustled out of the building by his Secret Service agents. The woman died.

If Nan had heard of Harding's extracurricular activities, she would have been devastated. Even believing as she did in his fidelity, she remained deeply depressed. "It is breaking my heart!" she wrote. "Our baby lost to me, and the world has my sweetheart!" When Harding gave her large amounts of cash—thousands of dollars in today's money—she would spend it immediately to induce a kind of quick high. "A new trinket might help to make me forget, at least while its newness lasted," she recalled. "Whenever I found myself eaten to distraction with too much thinking, I would go out to purchase a gaily colored gown or a hat or a pretty pin, eventually giving it away perhaps, but easing myself at least during the moment of buying. I used to drag my darling baby around with me on these mad hunts for happiness which, alas, never sparkled for the desolate even in caskets of diamonds and rubies . . . I surfeited Elizabeth Ann with toys. There was nothing she wanted that I did not immediately buy for her, often to my sister's disgust."

Harding's women troubles sowed the seeds of the corruption that would destroy his reputation. So many men had donated generously to his slush fund that he felt obliged to pay them back with high-level government positions. Harding trusted implicitly these good old boys who had gotten him elected, held the women at bay, and played poker with him.

He made his campaign manager, Harry Daugherty, the U.S. attorney general, a position Daugherty used to take hundreds of thousands of dollars in bribes to quash federal investigations. He also secretly sold liquor confiscated by agents enforcing Prohibition. Daugherty's assistant Jess Smith—who also accepted bribes for derailing investigations—committed suicide or was, quite possibly, murdered because he knew too much.

Harding's friend Charles Forbes became head of the new Veterans' Bureau, where, instead of looking after wounded veterans, he sold hospital medications to drug dealers, took kickbacks from purchasing agents, and gave himself commissions from selling army surplus material. His assistant, Charles Cramer, shot himself, leaving a suicide note addressed to Harding, which disappeared.

Another good friend, New Mexico senator Albert Fall, became secretary of the interior—where he caused the worst scandal of all, Teapot Dome, the name of a Wyoming oil field. Fall obtained control of the field from the navy, then leased oil production rights—with no competitive bidding—to Mammoth Oil. Suddenly, Fall was a wealthy man, with cattle ranches, several businesses, and a lavish lifestyle. It seemed clear that Mammoth Oil had rewarded him with huge bribes. Though the full scope of the scandal wouldn't come out for a couple of years, Fall had received $404,000 from the oil company (almost $6 million today).

"My God this is a hell of a job," Harding cried after hearing about the scandal. "I have no trouble with my enemies but my damned friends! My goddamned friends, they're the ones that keep me walking the floor at night." One night, White House chief usher Ike Hoover found the president sitting on the front lawn, sobbing that he hated his life. To friends he moaned, "And they called this the greatest position in the land—this nerve-wrecking, energy-sapping job—the Presidency of the United States!"

As Harding's popularity tanked, Florence pushed him to undertake an exhausting, fifteen-thousand-mile tour of the western states and become the first president to visit the American territory of Alaska. Harding wondered if it was a good idea. The stress of the office—exacerbated by the percolating corruption scandals—had taken its toll on his health. He had chest pains and, since he couldn't breathe lying down, he had to sleep propped up on pillows. Sometimes he had such shortness of breath he could hardly finish a sentence without gasping. His lips became puffy and blue, and his hands stiff and immobile. But Florence was determined to go. The trip would be good for him, she said, and would improve his popularity.

Harding's secretary George Christian begged him with tears in his eyes not to undertake the journey. "I can see nothing but a coffin in a funeral train coming back across the country," he said. But Warren—who had always wanted to see the beauties of

America's West and Alaska—decided to go. He made a new will shortly before his departure and sent Nan off on a cruise to Europe with some friends, hoping it would ease her depression.

As for the grueling "voyage of understanding," as the trip was called, Florence placed blind faith in her physician of many years, Dr. Charles Sawyer, called "Doc." Back in Marion, Doc had treated Florence for her numerous near-fatal, kidney-related illnesses. She credited him with keeping her alive, though that is debatable as Doc believed in the pseudoscience of homeopathy: giving patients minute doses of drugs that would produce symptoms in a healthy person similar to those of the disease. Doc was such an incompetent quack he couldn't tell that Warren was suffering from severe heart disease, even though other doctors who merely shook the president's hand could see it. And Doc wouldn't let his assistant physicians go near Harding if he wasn't around.

During the trip, Harding got sicker and sicker. Florence had to put ice on his swollen, blue lips. His eyes were so puffy he could hardly see, all signs that his heart could no longer pump sufficient oxygen through his body. At times, Florence had to give her husband's speeches for him. Coming back from Alaska on July 23, Harding and several others on the ship got food poisoning from shellfish. In Seattle on July 27, in the middle of a speech, he started gasping, dropped his remarks, and grasped the podium, probably suffering a mild heart attack. The rest of the trip was canceled.

Harding made it down to the Palace Hotel in San Francisco where he intended to recuperate. The incompetent Doc decided his attack had been caused by lingering food poisoning and Harding needed violent purgatives to get it out of his system. Quite possibly, Doc's medieval use of purgatives—which remove the body's potassium, a mineral required for healthy heart function— kicked Harding's already weakened heart into full-scale cardiac arrest. Sometime around 7:30 p.m. on August 2, Warren Harding died in his hotel bed. At the same time, 4:30 p.m. in Washington, D.C., the seer Madame Marcia told a gathering of her clients. "The President is dead."

Doc, in a panic, and Florence, protective of the man she believed had saved her life so many times, gave contradictory information about the president's exact time of death and who was in the room when it occurred. Florence refused to permit an autopsy, which would have revealed a heart attack as the cause of death and possibly resulted in a charge of negligent homicide against Doc. Doc wrote out a death certificate stating Harding had died of a cerebral hemorrhage. Given the conflicting stories about Harding's death, and the lack of an autopsy, many people believed Florence had killed her husband, either as punishment for his amours or to protect his legacy from all the corruption scandals about to break.

On August 3, 1923, Nan Britton was in Dijon, France, when she heard that President Harding had died the night before. "My heart pounded, and my cheeks felt strangely hot," she wrote in her autobiography. "Aloud I was saying to myself as I ran along, 'Oh, that could not be, that could not be! Of course, it is a mistake; oh, God, that just *could* not be!'" When she realized it was true, she wrote, "The world seemed without bottom. Things suddenly lost their meaning. I could not cry." And he had never once seen their daughter. She left on the next ship home.

Harding was placed in a coffin with a glass lid—his pallor covered by thick makeup, rouge, and lipstick, which only made him look ghastlier. The funeral train wended its way to Washington, exactly as his secretary had foreseen. People were disturbed to see that Florence never shed a tear. Indeed, she enjoyed looking at his dead body through the glass in his coffin. "Look at him," she told reporters as they gazed at the corpse, "more magnificent still in death!" For once in their marriage, Florence Harding knew exactly where her husband was and knew, too, he would never commit adultery again. Lillian Parks recalled, "Mama was shocked at how calm the First Lady was. 'She has turned to ice,' Mama said." Florence's odd behavior, too, added fuel to the murder rumors.

As soon as Harding was buried in Marion, Florence turned her attention to salvaging his reputation by dealing with his papers. Warren's secretary George Christian had a secret file marked "Heart-Throb Letters" which she proceeded to burn. There must have been many heartthrob letters because for five hot summer nights smoke billowed out of the Oval Office chimney. Realizing she didn't have enough time to read, sort, and burn all the compromising material before President Calvin Coolidge and his wife moved in, Florence instructed George Christian to stuff all the remaining presidential papers into ten-foot crates and cart them over to Evalyn McLean's suburban estate, Friendship. In the garden, she created a giant pyre of presidential papers, not all of them love letters. Many of Harding's official documents went up in that hecatomb. "We must be loyal to Warren," she said, "and preserve his memory."

During those days, Florence's face, hands, and arms were covered in soot as she fed papers to the flames: half of all Harding's presidential papers as well as many from his Ohio political career. She also destroyed much of her own correspondence and records of her early life. "Now that is all over," she told Evalyn as she shoveled the last embers, "I think it was all for the best." Curiously, her private diary escaped the conflagration, ending up in an Ohio barn auction, where it was discovered in 1997. Florence did not long outlive her husband. She finally died of her kidney ailment sixteen months after Warren on November 21, 1924.

Florence's bonfire of the vanities didn't help much to protect her husband's legacy. He was considered one of the least successful U.S. presidents, mostly because of the shocking corruption scandals associated with his administration that tumbled out in full public view soon after his death. Much anti-corruption legislation the Trump administration is coming up against was passed because of the Harding scandals: for instance, the 1924 change to the Internal Revenue Code allows the House Ways and Means Committee and the Senate Finance Committee to request the president's—or anyone else's—tax returns to conduct an investigation.

Carrie Phillips went to Germany in the 1930s, became the mistress of a prince, and lived in a castle on the Rhine. She returned to Marion, dumped Jim, who died in abject poverty in 1939, and raised German shepherds as a kind of paean to the dead kaiser. As senility settled in, she didn't bother to housebreak her dogs and lived in a house filled with their excrement. Sometimes she walked through downtown Marion—the scene of her former triumph as the town's wealthiest, most beautiful matron—naked except for a fur coat. She entered a nursing home, where she died in 1960. Soon after, her lawyer entered her house to see what valuables he might discover for her heirs. At the bottom of a closet, he found a shoebox crammed with poems and 250 love letters—some of them sixty pages long—from Warren Harding.

Desperate for money after Harding's death, Nan went to Warren's sister and told her about Elizabeth Ann. But unlike the shrewd Carrie Phillips, trusting little Nan had burned all of Harding's letters as he requested and had no proof that he had fathered her child. The family, already dealing with the corruption scandals ruining Warren's legacy, refused to give Nan anything. It would prove to be a massive mistake.

Nan wrote the first presidential kiss-and-tell book, *The President's Daughter*, published in 1927. As no publisher would take it, she decided to self-publish. When the government seized the printing plates from the printer, Britton successfully sued for their return. The book sold like hotcakes, making Nan a mint of money. On November 13, 1927, she held a press conference to introduce eight-year-old Elizabeth Ann to the world.

While the public reveled in Nan Britton's book about their affair, the press either ignored or disparaged it. One of the book reviewers explained the reluctance of journalists to cover any of Harding's indiscretions: "The majority feel . . . that it is not only beneath their dignity but a breach of their patriotic integrity to notice such terrible statements about a dead ex-President of the United States." Congressman John Tillman denounced Nan Britton's book on the floor of the House of Representatives, insisting that suppressing news of presidential adultery was "a matter of nation-wide interest and importance. It is a non-partisan question."

While many doubted over the years that Harding was Elizabeth Ann's father, proof came in 2015 when Elizabeth Ann's son, Jim Blaesing, was contacted by Peter Harding, Warren's grandnephew, suggesting a DNA test. It was a match.

"She loved him until the day she died," Jim Blaesing said. "When she used to talk about him, she would get the biggest smile. She just couldn't get enough of him. They were truly in love." Nan herself, who died in 1991 at the age of ninety-four, wrote that she looked back on the relationship "with absolutely no regrets. In the history of lovers, there was, I am sure, none to compare with Warren Gamaliel Harding. And to him I was, or so he has often said, the 'sweetheart incomparable.'"

7

FRANKLIN DELANO ROOSEVELT AND THE GOOD-LOOKING LADIES

*F*DR was one of the most beloved and successful U.S. presidents. His dynamic leadership hoisted the nation out of the Depression. He deftly guided U.S. diplomacy and the armed forces through World War II to victory. His wife, Eleanor, was a world figure on her own merits, endorsing the rights of workers and minorities. There was never a breath of scandal about the president and first lady during FDR's administration. And yet both had steaming-hot love affairs that came out decades later.

★ ★ ★

When Eleanor Roosevelt decided to unpack her husband's leather valise in September 1918, she had no idea it would irrevocably alter her marriage and the rest of her life. Franklin was in no condition to unpack it himself as he had just been carried off his ship on a stretcher, suffering from double pneumonia caused by the Spanish flu, a pandemic that would cull some fifty million people around the world. As assistant secretary of the U.S. Navy, he had spent ten weeks in Europe visiting battlefields and top military brass. But he had collapsed almost as soon as his ship left London. Eleanor had received a call to meet the ship in New York Harbor with a doctor and an ambulance.

Eleanor, raised to believe she was hopelessly ugly, compensated by being dutiful and helpful. She dutifully met her husband's ship with the doctor and ambulance and helpfully put her husband to bed in their Manhattan town house. And then, looking around nervously for new ways to be dutiful and helpful, she decided to unpack his valise, hang up his clothes, and see to his laundry.

But somewhere in between her husband's shaving kit and underpants she found something that caused her heart to skitter: a packet of faintly scented letters tied in a soft, blue ribbon, addressed to her husband in a hand she instantly recognized: that of her former social secretary, the beautiful Lucy Mercer. Almost against her will, her hands shaking, Eleanor opened one. Gasping, she read it and then ripped through all of them. They were love letters indicating a hot sexual affair that had gone on for years, letters sent via diplomatic pouch to all the cities Franklin had visited.

"The bottom dropped out of my particular world," Eleanor later said. Her husband's betrayal of her with a beautiful, charming woman brought back all the horrors of Eleanor's childhood. Though born to great wealth—she was the niece of Teddy Roosevelt, president from 1901 to 1909—her early life had been quite grim. Her mother, a New York society beauty, often told her, "Eleanor, I hardly know what's to happen to you. You're so plain that you really have nothing to do except be good." And "You have no looks, so see to it you have manners." Her aunt Edith said, "Poor little soul, she is very plain. Her mouth and teeth seem to have no future."

When Eleanor was eight, diphtheria killed her mother and younger brother. When she was ten, her father, an alcoholic, jumped out of an upstairs window while suffering withdrawal symptoms and died. As an orphan, she entered a surreal world of mixed Dickensian metaphors. She was sent to live at an estate something like Bleak House, presided over by her grandmother, a nasty old lady something like Miss Havisham, and a spinster daughter, the lamentably named Aunt Pussie. Living in seclusion with all the blinds pulled down, Eleanor wore hand-me-down clothes, was served inedible meals, and received harsh discipline, like Oliver Twist. Perhaps worst of all, her relatives constantly told her how ugly she was. Trying to shrink out of sight proved impossible when Eleanor grew to five foot eleven, grotesquely tall for a woman of the time. Yet she was not ugly. Her teeth protruded a bit in that age before orthodontia was common, and her chin was receding. But she had wide, soft blue eyes, thick honey-blond hair, and a flawless, milky complexion.

At fifteen, Eleanor was let out on probation to attend a school outside Paris, where she reveled in light and color and freedom, in friendships with other students, in discussions with brilliant female teachers. After three years, she was forced to return home to make her society debut, a hideously painful experience. Towering over most of the men, she stood, palms clammy, a wallflower, as few of the eligible bachelors asked her to dance. "I often felt that I'd like to have the floor open so that I could sink into it," she recalled.

Shockingly, the one young man who sought her out was the handsomest, most eligible bachelor in society, Eleanor's fifth cousin, Franklin Delano Roosevelt, often called FDR. Not only did he ask her to dance at balls, but he invited her for walks, games of tennis, and sailing. Franklin, two years Eleanor's senior, was the only child of James and Sara Delano Roosevelt. A child of privilege, he was his indomitable mother's obsession and her masterpiece. When his father died in 1900, his will stated that Sara controlled all of Franklin's inheritance until her death, which meant that she could, to a great extent, control him as well. Now, to Sara's alarm, her son was in love for the first time. Sara could hardly complain about the girl's family—it was the family she had married into, after all—but Franklin was still at Harvard. Though Sara tried repeatedly to break up the budding romance, her son refused to obey.

What did FDR see in this ungainly, timid girl? For one thing, Eleanor was different from all the pretty misses with perfect features and empty minds. She was smart, well-read, passionate about helping the less fortunate. It was a relationship something like that of Bill Clinton and Hillary Rodham seventy years later. A handsome, magnetic, popular man—who could marry almost anyone—chooses as his mate a brilliant but rather plain woman.

Franklin's proposal of marriage was like spring after a bitter winter, sunshine after an interminable rain. Eleanor—who thought no one would ever love her because no one ever had—suddenly saw a radiant future. "I am so happy. So very happy in your love dearest, that all the world has changed for me," she wrote him during their courtship. Resigned to the marriage, Sara insisted they wait until Franklin graduated Harvard. They married on March 17, 1905. The groom was twenty-three, the bride twenty-one.

But the first seeds of discord were sown during their three-month European honeymoon. For one thing, Eleanor did not enjoy sex. As she told her daughter, Anna, before her 1925 wedding, "Sex, my dear, is something a woman must learn to endure." Secondly, Franklin flirted with every pretty woman in sight, which just made Eleanor feel ugly and unloved all over again. The new-lyweds quarreled. Franklin, always cheerful, would joke about their disagreements soon afterward. Eleanor, serious as Death eating an onion, played the silent, wounded martyr. She had not found a loving soul mate, after all, just a husband she couldn't connect with and who jumped on her at night, and an interfering mother-in-law from hell.

When the young couple returned from their honeymoon, Eleanor found that Sara had bought two contiguous Manhattan brownstones—one for her, one for them—and knocked down doors between them on each floor so she could burst into Elea-nor's house and see if she was running Franklin's household prop-erly. Sara had also hired all of Eleanor's servants and furnished her house according to her own taste, without consulting Eleanor in anything. A few weeks after moving in, FDR found his wife sobbing uncontrollably that this was not her house, she had not chosen one thing in it. Franklin told Eleanor she was mad, shook his head, and left the room. Then there were public embarrass-ments. At one dinner party, in front of several society guests, Sara said sweetly to Eleanor, "If you just ran a comb through your hair, dear, you'd look so much nicer."

There was motherhood, of course, to distract her. But mother-hood didn't come easily to Eleanor. As one baby followed an-other, she realized she had no idea what she was doing. When her doctor told her that her first baby should be given regular airings, Eleanor dutifully hoisted the baby's bassinet outside her second-floor window on a rope until a neighbor, hearing the child's wails, threatened to call child welfare services. "This was a shock to me," Eleanor recalled, "as I thought I was a most modern mother."

Though FDR practiced law the first few years of his marriage, he intended to go into politics. In 1910, he was elected New York

State senator and developed a reputation for standing up to corruption and championing the poor against the powerful. In 1913, President Woodrow Wilson appointed him assistant secretary of the navy, which meant a move to Washington, D.C. Eleanor—who now had three children—was nervous at the social responsibilities expected of a top official's wife: calling on the wives of other administration officials, congressmen, Supreme Court justices, and ambassadors in strict order of precedence, and making charming small talk. Panic-stricken, she wrote her aunt, "I don't know a soul in Washington and am afraid of all kinds of stupid mistakes." She found herself making up to thirty calls a day, usually staying only six minutes as she had no idea what to say. Almost every night, there was a dinner.

One night, Eleanor burst into tears as dinner guests waited downstairs. "What's wrong, dear?" her husband asked. She sobbed, "I'm afraid I cannot face all those people, Franklin." Stunned, he said, "Do pull yourself together."

Insecure and overwhelmed, Eleanor had a hard time keeping track of her schedule and her correspondence—writing thank-you notes, accepting and declining invitations, and issuing her own. What she needed, her aunt said, was a social secretary to relieve her of the pressure, and she knew the perfect girl.

Twenty-two-year-old Lucy Mercer had an impeccable pedigree—she was a descendant of Charles Carroll of Carrollton, a signer of the Declaration of Independence—but her family had fallen on hard times. Her father was a drunk, her mother a spendthrift. Lucy had attended finishing school abroad and knew D.C. society like the back of her hand. Possessed of a regal grace, she remained unbowed by her family's recent misfortunes. She was five foot nine, with thick, dark-blond hair, a flawless complexion, and dreamy blue eyes. One of Lucy's friends later said of her, "I think she was the most beautiful woman I ever saw. It was a beauty the artist and photographer didn't catch. Her beauty was in her expression and in her graceful manner." As her cousin said, "Every man who ever knew her fell in love with her."

Eleanor interviewed Lucy and hired her immediately. Three mornings a week, Lucy competently arranged Eleanor's appointments and handled her correspondence. And when the Roosevelts found they needed a charming woman to liven up their dinner parties, it was Lucy they invited.

When Franklin moved to Washington, he was no longer the cute college boy who had courted the gangly debutante Eleanor. He was now a vital, virile man of thirty-one. A Washington journalist wrote of him, "The face was particularly interesting. Breeding showed there, cleanly cut features, a small, sensitive mouth, tiny lines running from nostrils to the outline of his lips, broad forehead, close cropped brown hair, frank blue eyes, but above all the straight, upstanding set of the head placed on the man." Nigel Law, a secretary at the British embassy, said that Franklin was "the most attractive man whom it was my good fortune to meet during my four years in America." The Roosevelts' son Elliott wrote, "Men and women alike were impressed by the sheer physical magnetism of Father. On meeting anyone, the first impression he gave was of abounding energy and virility. He would leap over a rail rather than open a gate, run rather than walk."

Elliott claimed that after his brother John was born in 1916, Eleanor, who had given birth to six children in ten years (one had died), had had enough of unwelcome sex and even less welcome pregnancies. She announced to Franklin that she had done her part and would do no more. In this case, it is understandable that a virile man like Franklin would look elsewhere for sex. And he did not have to look very far.

For Lucy—lovely, feminine Lucy in her fashionable, feminine clothes—was and would forever be FDR's ideal woman. Like Franklin, she had a playful sense of humor and loved to laugh. Poor Eleanor rarely thought anything was funny. Lucy spoke in low, dulcet tones; hers was a voice that soothed. Eleanor's voice was high-pitched, insistent, each word fraught with earnest significance. Eleanor hectored him, irritated him. Lucy calmed him, made him laugh and enjoy himself. And, as events would prove, Franklin needed the company of cheerful, alluring women to relieve his stress. "Nothing is more pleasing to the eye than a good-looking lady," he later told a friend, "nothing more refreshing to the spirit than the company of one."

We do not know exactly when Franklin and Lucy's affair began, but it was certainly going on by mid-1916. Many of the wealthier men in Washington, D.C., sent their wives and families to the country for the summer to escape the devastating heat, while the men enjoyed "summer wives" in the city. FDR sent his family to the Roosevelt retreat on Campobello Island, in the Canadian province of New Brunswick. To Eleanor's repeated invitations to visit them, he begged off, citing his workload as he enjoyed a romance with Lucy. By June 1917—two months after the U.S. had joined the war—Franklin was once again suggesting Eleanor should take the children and go far, far away for the summer. It seems that by this time Eleanor had heard rumors. She fired Lucy, which just made matters worse because she immediately got a job in the Department of the Navy working directly for Franklin.

When Eleanor and the children were back at Campobello

that summer, Franklin and Lucy grew reckless; they were seen driving and sailing together, and Lucy visited him at his home, servants be damned. Alice Roosevelt Longworth, Teddy Roosevelt's malicious daughter, allowed the two to use her mansion as a trysting place. When a family member reproached her for aiding and abetting adultery, Alice quipped, "Franklin deserved a good time. He was married to Eleanor."

Although Lucy had received a promotion and a perfect job performance evaluation at the Department of the Navy, she was abruptly fired in the fall of 1917, probably because FDR's boss, the puritanical U.S. Navy Secretary Josephus Daniels, had heard rumors of the love affair. Eleanor must have been relieved Lucy would no longer work with FDR. Perhaps she naively assumed they no longer had any contact.

But then, a year later, she discovered his letters. It would prove to be the most calamitous blow of her life. Her devastation indicates she had not been aware of a full-blown sexual affair; maybe she thought it had only been a flirtation heading in that direction, a flirtation that was over. The letters showed her just how wrong she had been. We will never know exactly what was written because Eleanor destroyed them, she later told a library curator. But we can imagine the impassioned avowals of love, the references to ecstatic sex, the times they sneaked away to the houses of friends.

Eleanor's heart broke. All the self-loathing of her childhood came racing back, threatening to engulf her—she was ugly, she would never amount to anything, no man would ever want her. Her mother, her grandmother, Aunt Pussie—they had all been right. Her own friends and relatives in Washington had abetted the affair. They must all think her a fool. Even her servants, knowing FDR had brought Lucy to his bedroom, must have thought her a fool.

At first, Eleanor did nothing other than see to Franklin's recuperation. And then, once he was better, she showed him the letters. Franklin admitted that he loved Lucy and wanted a divorce so he could marry her. And Eleanor, furious and betrayed, agreed to give him his freedom. It was Sara Roosevelt who was aghast. She had never wanted him to marry the unprepossessing Eleanor in the first place, but now she was adamant that they remain together. While many society couples had lovers, divorce was a social stigma. If Franklin wanted to throw away his family and political career for Lucy, Sara couldn't prevent it. But she could cut him off without a dime. And Franklin liked his country clubs and pleasure boats, his first-class cruises to Europe and expensive suits. He had always sent his bills to his mother to pay. Plus, to obtain his divorce he would have to admit betraying his faithful wife, the mother of his five children—poison to his burgeoning political career.

Sadly, Franklin accepted that he could not divorce Eleanor. But now Eleanor had her own conditions for staying in the marriage: that he would never see or contact Lucy Mercer again, and that he would never try to bed Eleanor again. He agreed. But he would keep only one of those promises.

Eleanor must have been relieved he was staying. The gossip and finger-pointing would have been horrible to bear, the comparison of her plain looks and Lucy's beauty, of her humorless personality and Lucy's charming one. And it would have been too painful to see Franklin walk into his future blissfully wedded to Lucy. Still, Eleanor never forgave him. Their son James later said that his parents' marriage was "an armed truce that endured until the day he died."

When Eleanor accepted that her marriage would never be a happy one, she began to feel something growing inside her for the first time ever—strength. She had survived the ruin of all her hopes. She began to take charge of her household affairs, firing all the white servants Sara had hired—Sara said African Americans couldn't be trusted—and replacing them with African Americans.

She wrote, "I think I learned then that practically no one in this world is entirely bad or entirely good . . . I gained a certain assurance as to my ability to run things and the knowledge that there is joy in accomplishing a good job. I knew more about the human heart, which had been somewhat veiled in mystery up to now."

In 1919, Lucy began working for Winthrop Rutherfurd, a wealthy widower in his late fifties known as the "handsomest bachelor in society." Rutherfurd owned a thousand-acre estate in New Jersey, as well as stately homes in Washington, New York, and Paris. Lucy had known Rutherfurd, a fixture in Washington society, for several years, when he was happily married. Now, however, with six motherless young children to raise, the youngest of which was only two, he hired Lucy to help look after them. Predictably, the two were soon engaged. Winthrop "worshipped the ground she walked on," her niece recalled. A friend of Lucy's said, "He was desperately in love with her. He kissed her every time he saw her." Shortly before Lucy's February 1920 wedding, Franklin and Eleanor were having tea with guests when someone mentioned that Eleanor's former social secretary was going to marry Winthrop Rutherfurd. Franklin "started like a horse in fear of a hornet."

Clearly, Rutherfurd's money and social position were attractive to Lucy, who had been mired in genteel poverty for years. She was not in love with him—her heart would always belong to FDR—but she strove to be the best wife, hostess, and stepmother she could possibly be. Lucy's stepson said, "She was never a stepmother. I never considered her anything but my mother. She was a fantastic woman, beautiful and very loving. We all got along very well." Late in 1920, Lucy had her only biological child, Barbara.

Luckily for Franklin, now that Lucy was a wealthy, respectable matron, whispers of their affair would evaporate. Eleanor, too, must have sighed with relief. In the 1920 presidential election, Franklin was the Democratic vice presidential candidate running on the ticket of Ohio governor James Cox. But Republican Warren Harding took nearly twice the popular vote. After the election, FDR accepted a job as vice president of the New York office of the Fidelity and Deposit Company.

It was Eleanor who suggested that FDR temporarily employ a personal secretary to help him deal with the mounds of correspondence he had neglected during the campaign. He hired twenty-four-year-old Marguerite LeHand, a striking young woman whose poise and regal bearing belied her blue-collar Boston background. Missy—as she came to be known by the Roosevelt children who could not pronounce her name—was not beautiful, which must have comforted Eleanor somewhat. Her face was too long, her jaw and nose too prominent, and her thick, dark hair would turn prematurely gray. But she had grace, confidence, and charm. Slender and five foot seven, she wore beautiful, feminine clothing, often in a shade of inky blue that exactly matched her eyes.

One acquaintance described Missy's "lovely throaty voice and quick upturn of the face . . . lips parted in that strange secret smile composed of cunning influence, forever baffling." Missy was discreet, hardworking, competent, and possessed of a delightful sense of humor. She was, in short, exactly the charming female company that soothed and relaxed FDR. After she completed her temporary contract, FDR asked her to stay on.

In August 1921, FDR was vacationing at Campobello when he became ill with a high fever, extreme fatigue, and chills. A couple of days later, he could not move his legs and slipped into delirium. The horrifying diagnosis was polio. Yet FDR remained defiantly optimistic that he would walk again. He developed his upper body strength to an extraordinary degree; his biceps, shoulders, and chest bulged with new muscles even as his withered legs shrank down to bones. Six months after his attack, FDR weighed 182 pounds, almost all of it muscle in his upper body.

He pulled himself out of bed on a bar dangling from the ceiling and lowered himself into his wheelchair. In a sitting position, he pushed himself upstairs backward until he was drenched in sweat, then turned and flashed his concerned family a radiant smile. Instead of using a bulky wheelchair, he had a kitchen chair outfitted with wheels so he could move easily through the brownstone's narrow doors and passageways. He learned to heave himself from the wheelchair to a regular chair and back so swiftly it was barely noticeable. FDR's main fear was burning to death immobilized. Wherever he slept, he planned an escape route in the event of fire.

In 1923, he decided to live on a houseboat in Florida for extended periods of time with a small crew and a cook. Appalled at the laziness of such a life, Eleanor didn't join him, but Missy did. Together they swam, fished, and lay in the sun. When Franklin's friends visited, Missy played the hostess and often sat on the lap of "FD," as she called him, in a bathing suit. His son James said that Missy "filled a need and made him feel a man again, which Mother did not do." Given the total paralysis in his legs, we might wonder if FDR was impotent. But a decade later, three top doctors examined him and reported that his private parts were fully functional.

How could Eleanor, who had been so heartbroken about Lucy, leave her husband with Missy on the houseboat? Eleanor had changed. She no longer defined herself as a wife but as someone who wanted to make a difference in the world helping others. In a magazine article, she wrote, "If anyone were to ask me what I want out of life, I would say the opportunity for doing something useful, for in no other way, I am convinced, can true happiness be attained."

Eleanor was actually relieved that Missy was looking after Franklin. "Missy alleviated Mother's guilt," son Elliott explained years later. "Knowing Missy was always there allowed Mother to come and go as she pleased without worrying about Father or feeling she was neglecting her wifely duties." FDR's wife and mistress were on very friendly terms, frequently shopping together and going for long walks.

Franklin had not given up his dreams of a political life and stayed involved, from a distance, in the Democratic Party, supporting candidates and writing newspaper columns. He wanted to run for public office himself, of course, but he knew no one would vote for a "cripple." But what if they didn't know the extent of it: What if he appeared to be only somewhat lame? FDR practiced for months to develop a kind of pretend walking. He locked his hips and legs into heavy metal braces under his suit pants, leaned on his eldest son, and rotated his wasted legs out from the hips, giving the illusion of slow, awkward walking, but walking nonetheless. FDR accepted the opportunity to speak at the 1924 Democratic convention in Chicago and knew that if he fell on his way to the podium, his political career would be over. Sweat dropped off his chin as he agonizingly made his way forward. Reaching the podium, he flashed his dazzling grin to a cheering crowd. And in that moment of victorious, exhausting sweat equity, his political career was saved.

That autumn, FDR bought a dilapidated resort hotel in Georgia, eighty miles southwest of Atlanta. He dubbed it Warm Springs for the warm thermal pools where handicapped people could swim as physical therapy and where, for the first time in three years, he could move his toes. He renovated the property and created the Georgia Warm Springs Foundation, which would cover the costs of polio victims to visit the resort for treatment. Eleanor hated the place—the abject poverty of local African Americans, along with strict segregation and cruel Jim Crow laws depressed her—so again, FDR stayed there with Missy, apparently living as man and wife. He designed a car he could operate with his hands and found a mechanic to make the changes. Soon he was driving Missy all over the area, a picnic lunch stashed in the back.

Meanwhile, Eleanor had become friends with a lesbian couple, Nancy Cook and Marion Dickerman, who helped her come out of her shell. The three of them went hiking, swimming, and riding. In 1927, they founded Val-Kill Industries, a furniture factory on the Roosevelt Hyde Park estate ninety miles north of New York City to generate income for local farming families. FDR built the three a little cottage near Hyde Park, where the linens were embroidered with the initials "EMN," as if they were some kind of marital trio. Naturally, there was some talk about this unusual relationship. FDR called Nancy and Marion "she-males." Alice Roosevelt Longworth acidly referred to them as "female impersonators." Eleanor didn't care. For the first time in her life, she was having fun.

When she was separated from Nancy and Marion, Eleanor felt their absence keenly. "I feel I'd like to go off with you and forget the rest of the world existed," she wrote. The three of them bought the Todhunter School in New York, a private girls' school, where Eleanor taught U.S. history and English and American literature.

FDR continued to deliver keynote addresses at state and national Democratic conventions, swinging his legs forward across the stage as he leaned on his son's arm. By 1927, he was bored with the houseboat and wanted to get back into politics in a serious way. He soon got his wish: in October 1928, he was chosen as the Democratic candidate for governor of New York.

The main question going into the campaign was whether a person known to be lame could have a political future. When the *New York Post* criticized his selection for this very reason, the outgoing governor and Democratic presidential candidate Al Smith replied, "We do not elect him for his ability to do a double back flip or handspring. The work of the governorship is brain work. Ninety-five percent of it is accomplished sitting at a desk."

On November 6, 1928, Franklin was elected governor of New York by a tiny margin. On New Year's Day, 1929, when the Roosevelts moved into the governor's mansion in Albany, Eleanor assigned Missy LeHand a bedroom off Franklin's room. Elliott Roosevelt wrote, "It was no great shock to discover that Missy shared a familial life in all its aspects with Father. What did surprise us was the later knowledge that Mother knew, too, and accepted the situation as a fact of life like the rest of us."

James Roosevelt, who disagreed with his brother's statement that the two were having an affair, wrote, "Elliott makes a lot of Missy being seen entering or leaving Father's room in her night-clothes, but was she supposed to dress to the teeth every time she was summoned at midnight? None of us thought anything of it." Though we can wonder why FDR summoned Missy at midnight.

Eleanor was not happy about being the first lady of New York State and was often absent, but she began to stay closer to home when she developed a crush on Franklin's handsome bodyguard, State Trooper Earl Miller. They went riding and swimming together and on camping trips with friends. They gave each other back massages at the pool and held hands. Was it a friendship? A flirtation? A sexual affair? Eleanor was a plain woman of forty-four, Earl a gorgeous, muscled thirty-two.

In his memoirs, James Roosevelt wrote, "I believe there may have been one real romance in Mother's life outside of marriage. Mother may have had an affair with Earl Miller . . . Victorian as Mother may have been, she was a woman, too, who suffered from her separation from Father." Franklin, who was no idiot, must have noticed how close Eleanor and Earl had become. But, James said, "He did not seem to mind." In the 1970s, the elderly Marion Dickerman told a historian that Eleanor had written her that she was going to leave Franklin and go off with Earl. Apparently, duty prevailed, or perhaps Earl objected. In 1932, he married a seventeen-year-old.

In two years as governor, Franklin built roads and hospitals and regulated public utilities to put money in the pockets of the public rather than in the pockets of rich industrialists. He gave frequent talks on the radio about the state of New York and what he was doing to improve it. Then, only ten months into office, the stock market crash of October 1929 presaged the Great Depression.

Soon, one American in three was jobless. FDR created a state program, the Temporary Emergency Relief Administration (TERA), to provide food, clothing, and shelter for the destitute, the first time that impoverished people could seek help from the government rather than charitable institutions. He asked the brightest minds at universities for advice in combatting the worsening economic situation. FDR radiated hope, confidence, energy, and new ideas. He was reelected in 1930 by a margin thirty times that of 1928. On July 2, 1932, he was chosen as the Democratic presidential candidate, running against President Herbert Hoover.

When it came to dealing with the Depression, Hoover was the one who was truly paralyzed, unwilling for the federal government to intervene in the nation's precipitous economic slide. By 1932, more than five thousand banks had failed. Bank foreclosures on homes were up to one thousand per day. Thirty-four out of forty-eight states had shut down their banks, meaning the public had no access to their funds. People couldn't buy gas and, when it ran out, just abandoned their cars in the middle of the road. Journalist Joseph Alsop recalled driving along Manhattan's East River and seeing people, "mostly respectable-looking older men and women, climbing precariously about on the enormous dumps in the hope of finding bits of edible garbage." FDR campaigned energetically, offering exciting new ideas to put people back to work. Hoover rejected those ideas, counseling starving, homeless people to be patient. He was heckled and bombarded with eggs and rotten fruit.

Neither FDR's wife nor his mistress wanted him to become president. Missy resigned herself to it. Eleanor, however, was almost hysterical at the thought of becoming "a prisoner in the White House, forced onto a treadmill of formal receptions, openings, dedications, teas, official dinners." Nancy Dickerman was convinced "she won't do it. She'll run away with Earl Miller . . . She'll file for divorce."

Back in 1887, when Franklin was five, his father took him to visit Grover Cleveland in the White House. The president came out of his office, clearly exhausted, patted Franklin on the head and said, "My little man, I am making a strange wish for you. It is that you may never be President of the United States." Grover Cleveland's wish did not come true. FDR won the election with the biggest electoral lead up to that time. He received seven million votes more than Hoover, won 42 of the 48 states, and took 472 electoral college votes while Hoover received only fifty-nine.

That night, as twenty-four-year-old James Roosevelt helped his father into bed, FDR said, "All my life I have only been afraid of one thing—fire. Tonight I am afraid of something else. I'm afraid I may not have the strength to do this job."

But Franklin—bursting with plans to stop the run on banks and the foreclosures of homes and farms—had to cool his heels a frustrating four months between the election and the inauguration. The Founding Fathers had chosen November as the month for presidential elections as the harvest was in and the roads had not yet become icy, which presented a danger for horses and buggies. Starting with George Washington's second inaugural in 1793, inauguration day was always March 4. There were two reasons for this four-month delay between the election and inauguration; the first involved the time it took to hand count the votes and then send messengers with the tabulations riding around the country. By that time, winter was setting in, and everyone wanted to wait for the March thaw to travel to the inauguration. Even with the advent of improved vote tallying and transportation by the early twentieth century, the March 4 date remained because it had become a historic tradition. But in the winter of 1932, Americans literally starved to death on the streets of Washington as Herbert Hoover glided by in his big black limousine, unmoved.

In 1937, FDR would successfully push for the Twentieth Amendment to the Constitution, changing the inaugural date to January 20.

On March 4, 1933, a black limousine picked up Lucy Mercer Rutherfurd from her sister's house on Q Street, NW, in Washington, D.C., and drove her to the inauguration. Sitting next to her husband, Eleanor had no idea that Lucy was in the huge audience, watching the man she still loved become president of the United States.

As soon as he took office, FDR instructed White House switchboard operators to accept calls from a Mrs. Paul Johnson, a code name for Lucy. The two went for long drives when the first lady was out of town. Eleanor was unaware that her husband was breaking his 1918 promise never to contact Lucy again. She was embarking on a love affair of her own. Lorena Hickok—known as Hick—was the nation's top female journalist and covered the presidential campaign in the fall of 1932 for the Associated Press. Foreseeing that Eleanor would be a first lady unlike any other, she worked hard to win her trust. Eleanor's usual reserve melted when she realized that she and Hick had some things in common. Hick, too, had had a Dickensian childhood, though hers had been the truly impoverished version. Abused by her violent father and kicked out of the house by her wicked stepmother at fourteen, Hick scrubbed floors to support herself. She managed to graduate high school with top grades and attend college for two years before joining the *Battle Creek Journal* as a nineteen-year-old cub reporter in 1912.

Most women journalists of the time wrote about society parties and fashion. Those wanting to cover news and politics had to be fiercely competitive and tough as nails. Hick worked her way up to become the AP New York City bureau chief by the time she was thirty-five, writing articles on politics and crime. At five foot eight, Hick weighed two hundred pounds. She had a wide, friendly face, a beautiful complexion, and wore the requisite skirt, makeup, and earrings when on the job. Off the job, however, she wore men's clothes, smoked cigars, played poker, swore like a sailor, and drank the men under the table with bootleg bourbon. Immensely popular, Hick was kindhearted, outspoken, and emotional.

During the campaign, Eleanor would frequently dismiss the other reporters and socialize alone with Hick. They ate dinner together, went to the theater, and spoke on the phone often. The afternoon after the inauguration, White House servants were confused when Eleanor, who had been giving Hick an interview in the sitting room, took her into the bathroom to conclude it. One maid who witnessed it wrote, "It was hardly the kind of thing one would do with an ordinary reporter. Or even with an adult friend." Later, Eleanor explained that they had retired to the bathroom because they kept getting interrupted.

The true nature of Eleanor and Hick's relationship did not come to light until 1979 when former *New York Times* reporter Doris Faber was researching Eleanor Roosevelt's letters at the Roosevelt Library in Hyde Park. There she found some two thousand letters between the women that had just been made available to the public, and apparently Faber was the first researcher to read them. Late in life, Eleanor had returned Hick's letters to her, entrusting her with both sides of the correspondence. Hick apparently destroyed the most sexually explicit letters but gave the rest to the library on the condition they not be released for ten years after her death.

Soon after the inauguration, Hick returned to her job in New York. The same day, Eleanor wrote, "Hick my dearest, I cannot go to bed without a word to you. I felt a little as though part of me was leaving tonight, you have grown so much to be a part of my life . . . Oh! I want to put my arms around you, I ache to hold you close . . . My pictures are nearly all up & I have you in my sitting room where I can look at you most of my waking hours! I can't kiss you so I kiss your picture good night & good morning . . . I miss you so much and I love you so much & please never apologize . . . Oh! I wanted to put my arms around you in reality instead of spirit. I went & kissed your photograph instead & tears were in my eyes."

Hick wrote Eleanor, "I remember your eyes, with a kind of teasing smile in them and the feeling of that soft spot just north-east of the corner of your mouth against my lips. I wonder what we'll do when we meet—what we'll say."

Eleanor wrote, "Dearest, it was a lovely weekend . . . Each time we have together <u>that</u> way—brings us closer, doesn't it."

Separation was painful. Moreover, Hick realized she no longer had journalistic impartiality when covering Eleanor. She resigned from the AP in the summer of 1933 and took a three-week road trip with Eleanor—and no Secret Service—to Quebec in a Plymouth roadster convertible. After the trip, Hick moved into the White House. Eleanor gave her a small bedroom in the second-floor family quarters and arranged a job for her at the Women's Division of the Democratic National Committee. Lillian Parks, now a seamstress in the White House, recalled many occasions when "Hicky, as we all called her behind her back, slept in the First Lady's bedroom suite, on the daybed in her sitting room. Supposedly, the reason was that there were so many guests."

Hick became a source of friction between FDR and Eleanor. Lillian said, "When the Roosevelts first arrived in 1933, there was a short honeymoon stage around the White House when Hick was an open guest, welcomed by the President, joining the family for dinner. But eventually, so the *sub rosa* story went, he got the drift and feared the situation could give the White House a bad reputation. The President was heard raising his voice to Eleanor, telling her, 'I want that woman kept out of this house.' That woman meant too much to Eleanor, and instead of keeping her out of the house, she simply kept her out of FDR's sight."

Franklin, who loved feminine women in pastel chiffon swishing around him in a cloud of delicate perfume, couldn't stand the sight of Hick stomping around in men's clothes chewing on a cigar. He put up with her as much as he did because he knew it made Eleanor happy.

Missy LeHand also lived in the White House, in a room on the third floor. As in the governor's mansion in Albany, servants became accustomed to seeing her in and out of the president's suite at all hours clad only in a nightgown and robe. Initially, White House staff were confused by this four-way living arrangement. "What goes?" one servant asked. "FDR was spending his evenings with Missy LeHand, while Eleanor Roosevelt was spending evenings with Lorena Hickok."

Lillian Parks wrote, "After you accepted the situation, there was no shock in seeing Missy come to FDR's suite at night in her nightgown and robe or sitting on his lap in the Oval study." She added, "A man has no secrets from his valet. The valets knew there was nothing incomplete about FDR's love life." His only concern during sex, she said, was that "he just didn't want anything heavy pushing on his legs."

Odd though the servants found the living arrangements, they soon grew to love Missy LeHand, who was "sunshine and laughter," Lillian Parks recalled. Realizing her significance in the president's life, "When Missy gave an order we responded as if it had come from the First Lady . . . We really had two mistresses in the White House." The servants concluded "that Missy was the substitute wife, and we honored her for it . . . As we saw it at the White House, Missy gave him the companionship, the rapt attention, the ego building boost that men sometimes find in their wives. Mrs. Roosevelt was not the kind of woman who would give blind praise or blanket approval. For that kind of warm support and recognition, no matter what he did, the President turned to Missy."

Eleanor—in a position now to do something truly useful— crusaded for racial justice, decent wages and housing, women's equality, and a host of other social issues. Hick persuaded her to hold regular press conferences—often open only to female reporters to encourage papers to employ more women—and write articles that became a nationally syndicated column, *My Day*. A blur of action, Eleanor would race out of the White House clutching her flower-bedecked hat, tumble into a waiting limo, and ask, "Where am I going?" Often, she burst into her husband's presence with a list of important tasks he must do—immediately— just when he was hoping to relax.

The Roosevelts' daughter, Anna—called Sis by the family— recalled an evening when Missy was mixing cocktails for Franklin and a few friends when Eleanor arrived in high-hectoring mode. "She came in and sat down across the desk from Father. And she had a sheaf of papers this high and she said, 'Now Franklin, I want to talk to you about this.' I just remember, like lightning, that I thought, 'Oh God, he's going to blow.' And sure enough, he blew his top. He took every single speck of that whole pile of papers, threw them across the desk at me and said, 'Sis, you handle these tomorrow morning.' She just got up. She was the most controlled person in the world. And she just stood there half a second and said, 'I'm sorry . . .' Intuitively I understood that here was a man plagued with God knows how many problems and right now he had twenty minutes to have two cocktails . . . He wanted to tell stories and relax and enjoy himself—period. I don't think Mother had the slightest realization. She could pester the hell out of him."

Though he lost his temper with Eleanor's pushiness, Franklin appreciated her efforts to help the less fortunate and often ended up doing exactly what she wanted. Sometimes, when he tried to give her a big old hug, "She would recoil and back away," according to Lillian Parks. White House usher J. B. West said he "never saw Eleanor and Franklin Roosevelt in the same room alone together. They had the most separate relationship I have ever seen between man and wife." James Roosevelt said that there were "several occasions I was to observe in which he in one way or another held out his arms to Mother, and she refused flatly to enter his embrace."

While White House servants were surprised at the Roosevelts' domestic arrangements, they were delighted with their warmth and generosity. The day the Roosevelts moved in, the servants were shocked to see Eleanor carrying chairs and stacks of books, pitching in to help the moving men. That day at lunch, she helped the butlers serve the guests. Lillian recalled, "All the changes Mrs. Roosevelt made were for the comfort of other people—for example, she assigned a nice dining room for the help, and a room to lie down in if you were ill."

Former first lady Lou Hoover had actually used hand signals to instruct servants when to move or not move, when to speak and not speak, as if they were dogs. Strangely, the Hoovers also demanded that servants remain unseen. When the president or first lady was coming, a bell would ring and all the servants would jump into broom closets—maids with mops and buckets, butlers holding trays over their heads—all of them squeezed in together so the Hoovers would not see them. Outside, when the bell rang, gardeners wielding hedge clippers dived into bushes. FDR and Eleanor were mystified to hear bells ring and see servants throwing themselves into closets and bushes. They put a stop to the practice immediately.

Eleanor brought homeless men she found in nearby parks to the White House for dinner. The staff cleaned them up as best they could before they sat down with the president and first lady, and sometimes they stole the silver, but the Roosevelts didn't care. FDR had other worries. Knowing that the White House was a firetrap, he had the Secret Service install special chutes to get him out of his bedroom window and down to the ground in record time. His agents held regular drills.

At first, Eleanor was miserable in her new role. She wrote to Hick, "I know I've got to stick. I know I'll never make an open break & I never tell FDR how I feel. Darling I do take happiness in many ways & I'm never likely to fight with F. I always shut up." In another letter, Eleanor wrote Hick, "I realize FDR is a great man, & he was nice to me but as a person, I'm a stranger and don't want to be anything else."

Franklin and Eleanor were fortunate that the press continued to maintain a patriotic silence about their private lives. In 1933, journalist Raymond Clapper wrote in his diary that gossip about FDR's continuing affair with Lucy Mercer Rutherfurd "buzzed around Washington," yet nary a word was printed. Journalists also heard of just how private a private secretary Missy LeHand was. They reported the almost telepathic closeness of FDR and Missy and stopped there. Additionally, FDR's paralysis was seen as a state secret. Knowing he could control the press, he often said, as cameras rolled when he was being lifted out of his wheel-

In 1797, the relationship of U.S. treasury secretary Alexander Hamilton with a blackmailing prostitute resulted in the first U.S. political sex scandal. *John Trumball (painter)*

In 1786, Thomas Jefferson served as U.S. ambassador to France where he began a thirty-year relationship with his enslaved woman, Sally Hemings. *Mather Brown (painter)*

Though the American public learned that Grover Cleveland had impregnated a woman in 1873, that didn't stop him from winning the 1884 presidential election. Voters cared more about his honesty in public office. *Library of Congress Prints and Photographs Division*

In 1886, forty-nine-year-old Cleveland married his ward, twenty-one-year-old Frances Folsom. Cleveland was the only U.S. president to marry in the White House, and Frances was the youngest first lady ever. *George "Geo" Prince (photographer), Library of Congress Prints and Photographs Division*

Cleveland's illegitimate child became fodder for political cartoonists, and "Ma, Ma, I want my Pa!" became a rallying cry for his opponents.

Frank Beard (artist), Library of Congress Prints and Photographs Division

Despite his prim appearance, Woodrow Wilson was quite the lady's man, writing steamy letters to his mistresses. *Harris & Ewing, Inc. (photographers), Library of Congress Prints and Photographs Division*

After his wife's death in 1914, Wilson ditched his long-term mistress to marry a wealthy, statuesque widow, Edith Bolling Galt. *Harris & Ewing, Inc. (photographers), Library of Congress Prints and Photographs Division*

The Ɠ

Warren Harding had thousands of lovers, several long-term mistresses, and more than one illegitimate child. *Harris & Ewing, Inc. (photographers), Library of Congress Prints and Photographs Division*

Florence Harding often publicly berated her husband for his love affairs. When he died unexpectedly in 1923, many believed she had poisoned him. *Library of Congress Prints and Photographs Division*

Nan Britton was unable to support her daughter with President Harding after his death. In 1927, she wrote the first presidential sex tell-all and earned a fortune. *Alamy Stock Photo*

esident's Daugh

Franklin Delano Roosevelt in 1916, the year he began having an affair with his wife Eleanor's social secretary. Lucy Mercer would be the love of his life. *Alamy Stock Photo*

Though she married a multi-millionaire, Lucy Mercer always remained close to FDR and was with him when he had his fatal stroke in 1945. *Alamy Stock Photo*

Journalist Lorena Hickok was, almost certainly, the lover of Eleanor Roosevelt, who never got over her husband's betrayal of her with Lucy. *Courtesy of the FDR Library*

FDR's secretary of twenty years, the coolly efficient Missy LeHand, lived with him on a houseboat at times. Servants frequently saw her in the President's bedroom. *Harris & Ewing, Inc. (photographers), Library of Congress Prints and Photographs Division*

Kay Summersby was the driver and right-hand assistant of General Dwight D. Eisenhower during World War II. Their love was doomed to remain unconsummated, despite their best efforts. *Alamy Stock Photo*

Lyndon Baines Johnson in 1934, the year he married Texas heiress Lady Bird Taylor. The rising congressional aide always said he would marry for money. *Courtesy of the LBJ Library*

Lady Bird Johnson learned to accept her husband's many mistresses with such equanimity that she even tidied up their undergarments in her husband's hotel rooms. *Courtesy of the LBJ Library*

Alice Glass, six feet tall with golden red hair, had a steamy affair with young congressman Lyndon B. Johnson. *Courtesy of the LBJ Library*

Good-time girl Judith Campbell had an affair with both President John F. Kennedy and Chicago mob boss Sam Giancana at the same time. *Alamy Stock Photo*

chair and deposited in his car, "No movies of me getting out of the machine, boys."

Those who were clueless enough to take such pictures often found their cameras knocked from their hands, lying broken on the pavement with a roll of exposed film. No newspaper would print such a photograph. A story about the president's love affairs or his paralysis might have derailed his efforts to heave the country out of the Depression. By the time the U.S. joined World War II, it would have been seen as nothing less than treason. When, after his death, the American people learned the extent of FDR's paralysis, they were shocked.

As soon as Franklin was inaugurated, he began issuing legislation that Congress readily passed. The first step was to restore confidence in the banks. His initial bill would reopen the banks under Treasury Department licenses that guaranteed them. If a bank had insufficient cash, the Federal Reserve Board would lend the bank the money it needed. In his first fireside chat on March 12, he said, "I want to talk for a few minutes . . . about banking. When the people find out that they can get their money—that they can get it when they want it—the phantom of fear will soon be laid . . . I can assure you that it is safer to keep your money in a reopened bank than under the mattress." The following morning, the long lines in front of banks had vanished. In fact, people soon formed lines to put their money back into the banks.

He also addressed the crisis of farm mortgages, thousands of which had been foreclosed on, telling Congress, "At the same time that you and I are joining in emergency action to bring order to our banks, I deem it of equal importance to take other and simultaneous steps . . . One of these seeks to increase the purchasing power of our farmers and at the same time greatly relieve the pressure of farm mortgages . . ." Franklin allocated $2 billion for the plan, which utilized federal credit agencies to refinance farm mortgages at 4.5 percent—far lower than what farmers had been paying—with far more time to pay.

Another of FDR's first efforts to lessen the grip of the Depression was to end Prohibition. Only eighteen days after taking office, on March 22, 1933, he signed an act allowing the manufacture of beer and wine. The Eighteenth Amendment enacting Prohibition was repealed entirely in December, allowing the manufacture of hard liquor. In the depths of the Depression, the government needed the revenue from the sale of alcohol, which before Prohibition had been 14 percent of all federal, state, and local revenue. Just as important, repeal stimulated employment and the economy. Breweries, wineries, and bars opened back up. Across the country, restaurants did a booming business again. And, with some booze in them, Americans just generally felt more optimistic.

FDR created many new federal agencies to buoy the American economy: the Federal Deposit Insurance Corporation, the Federal Housing Administration, the Tennessee Valley Authority, the Social Security Administration, the Public Works Administration, and the Securities and Exchange Commission. Public money went to hire the unemployed and build much-needed infrastructure such as schools, hospitals, sewers, roads, parks, and government buildings. In 1933, four thousand banks failed, most before he took office. In 1934, only nine banks failed. Over the course of FDR's first term, the number of unemployed dropped by a third. American businesses, which had lost $2 billion in 1932, made $5 billion in profits in 1936. In the 1936 presidential election, FDR won 46 out of 48 states and swept the electoral college by 523 votes to 8.

Before the reelection, the relationship of Eleanor and Hick had begun to cool as Eleanor became a national figure with less and less time for her personal life. Deeply hurt, Hick became jealous and demanding, which just drove Eleanor further away. "You have a feeling for me that I may not return in kind," Eleanor warned. Hick moved out of the White House and on to other relationships with women. She would move back into her old room from 1941 to 1945 as she wasn't earning much money and had nowhere else to go. Eleanor, though no longer in love with Hick, would always look out for her.

FDR dreamed of buying a Florida Key and opening up a fishing resort after his second term. Yet, when the time came, he felt his work wasn't done, particularly with war raging in Europe. He ran and won an unprecedented third term, defeating the Republican candidate by five million votes. With Eleanor off saving the world, he spent more time with Lucy who, at fifty, was still beautiful. White House staff recalled that FDR would return from their long drives "relaxed and happy." Missy LeHand, who knew what FDR was doing every minute of the day, must have been devastated.

She had devoted her entire life to Franklin Roosevelt. Attractive, personable, and certainly well connected, Missy had received a great deal of male attention over the years and dated a few men. But when a friend asked her if she wanted to marry, Missy replied, "Absolutely not. How could anyone measure up to FD?"

Lucy wasn't Missy's only rival for FDR's love. When the glamorous thirty-seven-year-old Princess Märtha of Norway fled Hitler's takeover of her country in 1940, Franklin offered her and her three young children sanctuary at the White House. The princess joined FDR for cocktails, accompanied him on long drives in the countryside, laughed and flirted with him. When she moved to an estate nearby, FDR visited her there. Then there was Margaret Suckley, known as Daisy, FDR's sixth cousin, who saw him frequently. Nine years his junior, she became a close confidante, possibly more. FDR instructed Daisy to burn his letters, and we can only wonder why.

By 1941, Missy, aged forty-three, had devoted twenty years of her life to Franklin. Now she found herself just one of many women in his life, and not even the favorite. "I don't think she ever felt that she was his great heart's desire," Elliott Roosevelt said. "She was too honest with herself for that."

In 1941, Missy—who had always been so cool, calm, and efficient—uncharacteristically began throwing shocking temper tantrums. On June 10, 1941, at a White House dinner for staff, after FDR rolled himself up to bed Missy fell to the floor with a minor stroke. Seventeen days later she had a major one, paralyzing her entire right side and robbing her of the power of speech forever. Franklin changed his will so Missy would receive half his estate, should he die before her, to pay for her medical care. As it turned out, Missy died on July 31, 1944, aged forty-seven. FDR's grandson Curtis Roosevelt, who grew up in the White House, concluded, "I think it's not entirely speculative to tie Missy's eventual breakdowns to her frustration with the fact that she was in love with somebody who was probably not in love with her."

With Missy out of the picture, FDR saw more of Lucy than ever, in the White House and out, sometimes for two or three hours at a time. His divorced daughter, Anna, moved into the White House to take over Missy's social tasks—mixing drinks and entertaining visitors—and one day walked into the Oval Office to find a strange woman on her knees massaging the president's wasted legs. Franklin grinned at Anna and introduced "my old friend, Mrs. Winthrop Rutherfurd." He made her promise not to tell her mother. She didn't.

On March 19, 1944, Winthrop Rutherfurd died, aged eighty-two, after several years of illness. Lucy told James Roosevelt's first wife that "although she loved Winthrop Rutherfurd and owed him much, FDR had nonetheless been the love of her life."

After the U.S. had entered World War II in 1941, Roosevelt calmed and inspired the country with his frequent radio addresses. But the stress of running a nation in a world war clearly affected his health. By 1943, he was gray-faced and seemed shrunken in oversized clothing. Sometimes his breathing was labored, and he started a sentence only to forget what he was going to say. His doctor discovered he was suffering from severe hypertension; his blood pressure was 210 over 120, his arteries were hardening, and the left ventricle of his heart failing. He was, in short, dying. As with Woodrow Wilson's hypertension forty years earlier, physicians could diagnose high blood pressure, but had no means of treating it other than advising rest and relaxation. And FDR couldn't jaunt off to Bermuda; he was planning the D-Day invasion.

Realizing how ill her father was and the tremendous stress he was under, Anna decided to assist his romance, even if it meant betraying her mother. She facilitated Lucy's visits and often joined her father and his mistress for cocktails and dinner. Anna said that Lucy's visits "were occasions which I welcomed for my father because they were light-hearted and gay, affording a few hours of much needed relaxation for a loved father and world leader in a time of crisis."

By the fall of 1944, FDR knew he was a dying man. He also knew he had to see the war to its end, and then, possibly, he could resign. Announcing his decision to seek a fourth term of office, he said, "All that is within me cries out to go back to my home on the Hudson River, but the future existence of the nation and the future existence of our chosen form of government are at stake."

In early April 1945, FDR arrived in Warm Springs for some rest and relaxation. His cousin Daisy Suckley was there, along with another cousin, Laura Delano. On April 9, Lucy arrived with a portrait painter named Madame Elizabeth Shoumatoff, who was to paint the president, and a photographer, Nicholas Robbins, who would photograph him for Shoumatoff. On the morning of April 12, FDR sat at a card table he used as a desk in his living room, reading documents as the artist painted him. He said, "We have got just about fifteen minutes more to work."

Suddenly, FDR's head slumped forward, and his hands shook violently. He put his left hand to the back of his head and said, "I have a terrific pain in the back of my head." He had just had a massive stroke. Lucy knew she needed to get out of there immediately, before the press arrived. As doctors attended him, she threw her clothes in a bag and, sobbing, raced out of the resort with the artist and photographer. She later learned he was pronounced dead at 3:35 p.m. He was sixty-two.

After his death, Eleanor discovered he had been seeing Lucy all along. In time, she forgave her daughter, Anna, for arranging the meetings, and she came to forgive her husband, as well. "The act of being physically unfaithful seems much less important to the average man," she said, and a man finds it "hard to understand why the woman he loves looks upon it as all important. He might have been happier with a wife who was completely uncritical. That, I was never able to be, and he had to find it in other people." Of Lucy she said, "She deserves forgiveness as much as anyone." Looking back, Eleanor described herself as "pig-headed" and said, "If only I had found the courage to talk to Franklin. I should have said, 'Let's bury this whole matter and begin over again together.'" Recalling how she had badgered him, she said, "I felt akin to a hair shirt."

Daisy Suckley best summed up the Roosevelt marriage. "Poor Eleanor Roosevelt, I believe she loved him more deeply than she knows herself, and his feeling for her was deep & lasting," she said. "That fact that they could not relax together, or play together, is the tragedy of their joint lives, for I believe, from everything that I have seen of them, that they had everything else in common. It was probably a matter of personalities, of a certain lack of humor on her part—I cannot blame either of them."

Eleanor continued to travel, write, and lecture for social justice. She became a delegate for the United Nations General Assembly in December 1945 and chairperson for the UN Commission on Human Rights the following April. She made sure that Hick, who had diabetes and was going blind, had enough money to live on and moved her to a cottage on the Roosevelts' Hyde Park estate to be close to her. In 1947, at sixty-three, Eleanor fell in love one last time with an attractive, forty-five-year-old doctor, Dave Gurewitsch, whom she engaged as her personal physician. He accompanied Eleanor on thirteen international trips she made for the United Nations. Eleanor wrote or called him almost every single day. "I'm glad you love me," she gushed in one missive. "I love you dearly and send you my most devoted thoughts," and "I love you as I have never loved anyone else." She kept his photo on her bedside table, and she insisted that he was "the love of her life." She knew he would eventually marry a young, pretty woman, and he did. The three of them moved into a Manhattan town house where they lived in separate apartments but saw one another often. Eleanor Roosevelt died November 7, 1962, aged seventy-eight. Hick survived her by six years and died at seventy-five.

Lucy Mercer Rutherfurd lost FDR, her mother, and her sister, who committed suicide, in the space of three years. Perhaps it was too much for her to bear. In the spring of 1948, she was diagnosed with leukemia, which quickly advanced. Living her last weeks on morphine, she died in July, at fifty-seven.

"As far as emotions were concerned," Anna Roosevelt said, "Lucy was Father's emotion for life."

8

DWIGHT EISENHOWER OUT
OF PRACTICE IN LOVE

A World War II hero who successfully invaded France and Germany, and a two-term president, Eisenhower was known for exuding the quintessential American spirit: optimism, integrity, duty, and determination. The American public had no idea until after his death that during the war, Eisenhower fell deeply in love with his driver and aide.

★ ★ ★

Things are never the way you think they'll be. At least, that was what Kay Summersby discovered when she finally found herself in the arms of General Dwight D. Eisenhower in his London town house in January 1944. Their intimacy had grown slowly but surely since the fall of 1942 when she first became his driver. Working twelve- and fourteen-hour days together, seven days a week, to save the Free World had resulted first in mutual respect, then fondness and, finally, love. Ike had confessed his feelings for her eight months earlier, and she had enthusiastically responded, but theirs had remained a chaste relationship, a squeeze of the hand, a stolen kiss.

Now, their passion knew no bounds. "Our ties came off," Kay wrote in her 1975 autobiography. "Our jackets came off. Buttons were unbuttoned. It was as if we were frantic. And we were."

They kissed and groped and moaned, enjoying—finally— the tantalizing sensation of skin against skin. She waited to feel him inside her. And waited. But General Eisenhower—supreme commander of the Allied Forces—couldn't command his penis to rise to the occasion. Perhaps it was age-related erectile dysfunction. After all, he was a chain-smoking, whiskey-belting, fifty-three-year-old bundle of stress upon whose shoulders rested the salvation of mankind. Or perhaps it was his old-fashioned values of honor and integrity. When it came right down to it, he just couldn't betray his wife.

Whatever the case, there they were naked. With nothing to do.

"This was not what I had expected," Kay wrote, and we can imagine that was an understatement. "Wearily, we slowly calmed down. He snuggled his face into the hollow between my neck and shoulder and said, 'Oh, God, Kay, I'm sorry. I'm not going to be any good for you.'

"You're good enough for me," she insisted. "What you need is some sleep."

Perhaps, as Kay looked under the couch for her bra, she reflected on the long, strange path that led her to that moment of unbearable embarrassment. It had all been Hitler's fault. On September 2, 1939, the day after Great Britain declared war on Germany, the thirty-one-year-old decided to forge a new path in life. Daughter of a wealthy Irish landowner, in 1936 she had married a handsome young publisher in London's social set and found a life of constant partying soul-numbing. They soon separated.

Kay became a model for the Worth fashion house and found that equally stultifying. With war in the offing, her family begged her to return to the safety of County Cork, but Kay could not see spending the war "sitting on a horse properly and pouring tea correctly," as she wrote. She wanted to make a difference, to offer something of substance to people in need. An excellent driver in a time when most women didn't have driver's licenses, she decided to become a London ambulance driver. Within months, the Blitz began. And she got more than she bargained for.

She described it as "living, driving, and working in a bomb-made hell where blood and death were as commonplace as a cigarette . . . Driving ambulances loaded with bodies, the stench of burnt flesh, being turned away by morgue after morgue with 'Sorry, we're full' . . . A cinema with the lights on but the front row stalls filled with bodies, all headless . . ." She kept a flask of whiskey with her to mask the taste of dead flesh in her mouth.

Kay was skilled at driving in blackouts and the thick yellow fog which periodically crouched over the city. What's more, all the street signs in Britain had been removed to confuse any German troops who might invade. Ambulance drivers needed a photographic memory of every street in London.

When the United States joined the Allies after Pearl Harbor in December 1941, a host of American military bigwigs arrived in London, and their drivers got hopelessly lost even in the cold, clear light of day. The solution was to provide them with British ambulance drivers. Kay was assigned to drive General Dwight Eisenhower—known as Ike—when he arrived in London in May 1942. She recalled their first meeting when their eyes locked. "Brilliant blue eyes. Sandy hair—but not very much of it. A fair, ruddy complexion. A nice face—not conventionally handsome, but strong, and, I thought, very American. Certainly very appealing. And I succumbed immediately to that grin that was to become so famous."

What did Ike see when he first met his new driver? A trim, shapely brunette five foot eight inches tall, with a wide forehead, high cheekbones, and a strong jaw. Though pretty, to be sure, her most attractive feature was the light in her face, an expression of alert intelligence, competence, and good humor ready to bubble up into laughter.

And laugh she did at the shocking informality of the Americans. When she drove Eisenhower and one of his senior commanders, Major General Mark Clark, they would eat boiled cabbages for lunch, start farting in the car, and roll down the windows as they howled with laughter. Ike often invited her to join him for lunch, something a British senior officer would never do. He even invited her mother. As she waited in his office all day for him to order the car around, she pitched in answering the phone and making his appointments. Soon she became an invaluable aide.

Focused on winning the war, Eisenhower hated wasting time attending social events. As a down-to-earth American, he ridiculed "all that la-di-da" of London's upper crust. After one reception, he slid into the car and told Kay, "I don't think my blood pressure can take it if one more silly woman calls me 'My deeaaah general.' I'm nobody's goddamned 'deeaaah general,' and I'm not fighting this war over teacups."

He hated his hotel suite, too, in the lavish Claridge's. He thought the black-and-gold sitting room "looks like a goddamned fancy funeral parlor," and the bedroom was decorated in "whorehouse pink. Makes me feel as if I'm living in sin." He hated the noise and crowds of London, and whenever he walked outside, people stopped and stared at him. Or asked him about the war. Or saluted. "I'm a captive," he complained. "I can't even go for a walk without starting a parade."

As Eisenhower, stressed and harried, planned the first Allied invasion against Hitler's armies, he needed a homelike atmosphere where he could truly relax. He moved out of the hotel and into Telegraph Cottage, a Victorian five-bedroom, mock-Tudor home in a ten-acre park. Only a forty-minute drive from London and minutes from Bushy Park, the U.S. Army Air Forces headquarters, Telegraph Cottage offered privacy away from the crowds and noise of London. The general and his male aides stayed there three or four nights a week, while Kay had a room with a nearby family. Together, Eisenhower's "family" cooked, drank, played bridge, and practiced their golf swings in the garden.

Kay wrote, "In the middle of a vast world war, the commanding general had managed to establish a happy home in that precarious calm of the eye of the storm."

Kay felt that one thing only was missing to make Telegraph Cottage the perfect home. One day, as she was driving the general, she remarked, "I miss having a dog. We always had dogs around the house." She talked about her favorite, a Scottie named MacTavish.

"Kay, would you like a dog?" Ike asked. "Another Scottie?"

She braked the car suddenly. "Would I like a dog? Oh, General, having a dog would be heaven!"

"Well," he said with a grin, "if you want one, we'll get one. I think I can manage that. I'd like to do something for you for working all these crazy hours and everything." Eisenhower knew tongues would wag if it got out that he had given his attractive female driver a dog, so he pretended it was for him. He named the black Scottie puppy Telek, a combination of Telegraph Cottage and Kay, "two parts of my life that make me very happy," he said.

Telek was presented to Ike at his birthday dinner, wearing a big red bow, as the general's wartime family toasted his health. After dinner, Kay and Ike found themselves alone in front of the fire having a drink, as they so often did, the puppy asleep in Ike's lap. "Thank you, Kay," he said, "for bringing so much gaiety into my life. I don't know what I'd do without you." From that time on, Telek accompanied them almost everywhere.

Kay met numerous celebrities during the war. She dined periodically with Prime Minister Winston Churchill in the basement of 10 Downing Street—the upstairs had been bombed. Churchill was "a menace at the table," Kay recalled. "His manners were atrocious. He would slurp his soup, spill things, pick up food with his fingers. He would pick his nose while listening to the rare person who managed to get a word in edgewise and would quite uninhibitedly unzip his siren suit to scratch his crotch. Make sweeping gestures while telling a story and knock glasses and pitchers to the floor. Pay no attention whatsoever to what he had done and keep talking as servants raced to clean up the mess. All these possibly purposeful gaucheries seemed trivial when he started talking. He had the most fabulous command of the English language. I could have listened to him forever."

One day, Kay gave U.S. general George Patton a tour of London. As she pointed out bombed ruins of a school, an apartment building, or a shop, he would say, "The bastards! The dirty mother-fucking bastards!" and apologize immediately. "Excuse me, Miss Summersby. I beg your pardon. My tongue ran away with me." Seconds later he would erupt in expletives again. "The sonsabitches! The bloody sonsabitches!" And apologize again.

Kay drove King George VI of Great Britain, who usually didn't talk, and later, FDR, who insisted on holding Telek in his lap. When he found a good place for a picnic, the U.S. president asked, "Won't you come back here, child, and have lunch with a dull old man?" She wrote, "FDR was enjoying himself immensely, laughing and telling stories. He had the gift of putting a person completely at ease, and I soon got over my awe of him and was chatting away as if I had known him all my life."

Kay also met entertainers who came to perform for the troops. Vivien Leigh, whom she found more beautiful in person than she had been in *Gone with the Wind.* Bob Hope. Noël Coward. Her hobnobbing with celebrities disturbed her fiancé, U.S. Army Lieutenant Colonel Dick Arnold, who rarely saw her.

"My God," he said one day, "you know all those top generals, the ones the rest of us only hear about. And Winston Churchill calls you Kay."

"It's only because it's my job," she said. "It has nothing to do with me."

Dick shook his head and said, "You know, when the war is over and we are living in the States, you won't be associating with prime ministers and three-star generals."

Kay knew this to be true, but she also found it impossible to envision life after the war. Though she and Dick were wrapping up their divorces and expected to marry the following summer, she "simply could not imagine leading any other life. I was completely caught up in the moment. I loved Dick. I really did. But at the moment, I felt closer to Ike. It was not a time for love, I felt. We all had a mission that was far more important than our personal lives and desires."

Thirty years later, as Kay lay dying of cancer, she looked back on the war and saw things with the twenty-twenty clarity of hindsight. Those fighting the war, she wrote, existed "in their own special dimension. Their preoccupation is so great, their commitment so complete, their energies so all-absorbed that it is as if their days were being lived out in a tunnel . . . They are people apart . . . This knowledge was something that the General and I shared. His own family was far away. He rarely mentioned them. This was not through lack of caring. It was simply that we were in another world. And one could not share it with outsiders. The war was an irresistible catalyst. It overwhelmed everything, forced relationships like a hothouse so that in a matter of days one would achieve a closeness with someone that would have taken months to develop in peacetime."

Soon after Pearl Harbor, President Roosevelt and Prime Minister Churchill had agreed that Americans must carry out a major invasion into Nazi-occupied territory within the year. At first, both believed the invasion should be in northern Europe, envisioning an operation much like D-Day would turn out to be. But FDR quickly realized that the U.S. was not prepared for the conquest of Europe. Civilians were being drafted and trained, tanks and ships built. They would not be up to their full force for some time. The first U.S. operation needed to be smaller, more focused. FDR decided to invade northwest Africa, held by the Vichy government of France, which was cooperating with Hitler. Such a move would surprise the Germans, who were expecting a European attack. The invasion was called Operation Torch.

As Eisenhower prepared to leave for North Africa in early November 1942, Kay believed her months of excitement and glamour were over. She would be transferred back to routine driving duties for whichever military official needed her in London. But Eisenhower asked her to follow him to North Africa once the battle was over and things had settled down. "From that time on, I felt as if there were clouds under my feet instead of pavements or a gas pedal," she recalled.

When Eisenhower's wife, Mamie, heard that Kay would be

joining him in North Africa, she evidently wrote him a scathing letter. For months, she had seethed with outrage whenever she saw the attractive brunette standing next to him in photos and newsreels, even on the cover of *Life* magazine.

"She is terribly in love with a young American colonel," Eisenhower replied, "and is to be married to him come June, assuming both are alive. I doubt that *Life* told you that."

The Eisenhower marriage had gone through many ups and downs. When Ike and Mamie married in 1916—she was twenty, he twenty-six—the young officer told her, "The country will always come first. You will come second." Several months later, the U.S. was in World War I. Ike stayed stateside, much to his frustration. A son born in 1917 died in 1921 from scarlet fever, and suddenly the marriage was different, tarnished, something irrevocably lost, though a second son born in 1922 helped improve the relationship. Mostly, Ike focused on his work, Mamie on being the perfect officer's wife. Though Mamie would move a total of twenty-eight times over the course of her husband's long career, she particularly hated Ike's posting to Panama in the early twenties and the Philippines in the mid-thirties. She spent as much time as possible in the U.S.—often away from Ike—and was now living in Washington, D.C.

At the outbreak of war in 1941, Mamie Eisenhower was a slender forty-five-year-old with merry blue eyes, youthful apple cheeks, and dark hair with inexplicably short curled bangs that would be her signature look until her dying day. Her life in Washington was proving difficult. Unwilling to be seen partying while so many men fought and died, she had poured herself into volunteering for the Red Cross and other organizations to help the war effort. But that, too, would be curtailed due to a lack of balance that had her walking into walls and unable to navigate stairs.

Though she would later be diagnosed with Meniere's disease—an inner ear disorder—word got out that the supreme commander's wife was a raging alcoholic. Often too dizzy to leave her apartment, worried about her husband serving in Europe and her only child, John, who would graduate West Point on D-Day, she grew sleepless and irritable. On top of everything else, she frequently heard about the young, beautiful Kay Summersby always hovering at her husband's side.

Operation Torch began November 8, 1942. More than a hundred ships disgorged a hundred thousand American soldiers onto the coasts of Morocco and Algeria, supported by British warships and aircraft in the largest amphibious landing in U.S. history. Losses were minimal, and the invasion was over by November 11, after which Eisenhower established an Allied headquarters in Algiers.

Five weeks later in her London flat, Kay joyously packed a suitcase with satin nightgowns. Her fiancé, Dick Arnold, was stationed in Algiers, and his divorce had been finalized. Her own divorce papers would arrive soon, and the two would marry. But between Spain and Algiers, Kay's huge troop transport ship, the *Strathallan*, struck a German mine. She made it to a lifeboat—but her nightgowns did not—and she arrived in Algiers the following morning wet and bedraggled.

Though Operation Torch had been a success, Eisenhower still found himself fighting in North Africa as German troops in Tunisia attacked U.S. troops from the east. His stress levels were through the roof. The American Army had not been prepared for the torrential rains; tanks and jeeps sank in the mud. Eisenhower's commanding officer, U.S. Chief of Staff George Catlett Marshall Jr., took one look at the stressed, sleepless, chain-smoking general and ordered him to balance his work with some time off.

Ike decided he needed another Telegraph Cottage, a place where he and his war family could relax. He chose a white stucco farmhouse called Sailor's Delight, only ten miles from his headquarters in Algiers. The property had tennis courts, stables, and a sea view. He and Kay often went riding.

"We would leave the office in the middle of the afternoon several days a week," Kay recalled, "drive out to Sailor's Delight, ride for a couple of hours, shower, have a drink and supper and then drive back to Algiers. Once in a while we would spend Saturday night and all day Sunday, doing all the things we had done at Telegraph Cottage. We played bridge, sat outdoors when it was warm enough, knocked a few golf balls around the grass and practiced target shooting."

In Algiers, one of Eisenhower's closest aides, Colonel Ernest Lee of Texas, called Tex, took Kay aside and said, "I think you ought to know, Kay, that there's a lot of gossip about you and the Boss. People are saying that you—uh-oh . . ." He was too embarrassed to continue. "That we what?" she asked innocently. "That you, uh—well, that you sleep together when you go on trips."

Indeed, many powerful men assumed the two were sleeping together. As soon as Franklin Roosevelt returned to the White House, he roared with laughter about it as he drank cocktails with his staff. Winston Churchill assumed it. Ike's deputy chief of staff, General Everett Hughes, said, "Leave Ike and Kay alone, she's helping Ike win the war." Another aide said the general and his driver were "as close as two coats of paint."

Kay was amused at the gossip. "Don't worry, Tex," she said. "If anyone says anything more, just tell them that I'm engaged to be married and that the General and I are certainly not interested in each other that way. It's ridiculous." Yes, she and Ike had a special relationship. But it wasn't romantic. Theirs was a mutual respect, a kind of telepathy. "He would often look over at me in the course of a conversation and say, 'Kay knows what I'm talking about.' And I did. I did indeed."

The Axis forces in North Africa surrendered on May 8, 1943. Churchill proclaimed, "This is not the end. It is not even the beginning of the end. But it is, perhaps, the end of the beginning." Soon after the victory, Kay's divorce papers arrived. She and Dick could finally get married. But now Dick's regiment was ready to leave Algiers for a few weeks of mine clearing. The wedding would have to wait until he returned sometime in June. And then news came in early June that Dick had been blown up in a minefield.

It was Ike who broke the news to her, after handing her a stiff drink at Sailor's Delight. Then he put his arms around her and guided her to the sofa. "Go ahead," he said. "Go ahead and cry. It's the only way. Just let it out." And she did, crying like a baby as he patted her shoulder and said, "There, there." He handed her a handkerchief to blow her nose. He fixed her a cup of tea and spooned it into her mouth.

Kay soon realized she had known very little about Dick, whom she had seen so rarely. "Each time we met it had been as exciting as a first date," she wrote, "and probably for that very reason our knowledge of each other had not progressed much beyond the first-date stage. Ike knew more about me and had seen more of my family than Dick ever had. I knew very little of Dick's family. It was as if we had met and loved in a vacuum. Now when I tried to mourn him, I discovered that I did not really know the man I was grieving for . . . The realization that I had never really known him was as shocking as the knowledge that now I never would."

Work helped ease her grief; Eisenhower was now planning the invasion of Sicily. Horseback rides on the beach with Ike helped, and listening to music with him after dinner. Dick had served as a kind of wall between them. With him gone, there was nothing to stop their true feelings from rising to the surface. One day, Ike told her he had a surprise—new uniforms, a luxury at the time. "You do so many nice things for me," she said with a smile. "How can I ever thank you?"

"You can't possibly know how much I would like to do for you," he replied, his voice strangled. Then Ike removed his reading glasses and touched her hand. "Kay, you are someone very special to me," he said. Kay wrote:

> We just sat there and looked at each other. I felt overpoweringly shy. We were both silent, serious, eyes searching eyes. It was a communion, a pledging, an avowal of love. And it was an absolutely shocking surprise.
>
> So this is love, I thought. I had been in love before, but it had never been like this—so completely logical, so right. For over a year, Ike and I had spent more time with each other than with anyone else. We had worked, worried and played together. Love had grown so naturally that it was a part of our lives, something precious that I had taken for granted without ever putting a name to it. Yes, I loved this middle-aged man with his thinning hair, his eyeglasses, his drawn, tired face. I wanted to hold him in my arms, to cuddle him, delight him. I wanted to lie on some grassy lawn and see those broad shoulders above me, feel the intensity of those eyes on mine, feel that hard body against mine. I loved this man.

Then one of his aides burst in with some papers for the general. The moment was lost. But the joy was not. Kay recalled,

"That morning, life took on a sweetness that was almost unbearable. I floated on a cloud of happiness, delighting in my secret, exploring the feelings I had hidden from myself for months. I felt peaceful and fulfilled." And later that day, Eisenhower told Kay he loved her. He realized he would probably be transferred to Washington, D.C., to work at the Pentagon once the war was over, and if that happened, he would find a way to take her with him. "I'm never going to let you go," he vowed.

But their physical intimacy was limited to a quick kiss or holding hands a few seconds. While many officers had mistresses during the war, Eisenhower had to maintain a sterling reputation for the sake of morale. He was known as a man of the strictest integrity and the deepest sense of honor. His life had to be seen as above reproach.

He confessed to Kay the agony he felt the night he learned her ship had gone down. "If there was ever any question in my mind as to how deeply I felt about you, that night answered it. I had never let myself realize quite how dear you were to me before. But for God's sake, I never thought that I would be talking to you like this. Never. I was never going to tell you how I felt. And sweet Jesus Christ, I don't know how I ever had the guts to. I'm very out of practice in love, Kay." She didn't understand what he meant. That he didn't love his wife anymore?

General Marshall ordered Ike back to the States for twelve days over Christmas 1943 to spend time with Mamie, whom he hadn't seen in a year and a half. Stewing in Algiers, Kay was fretting with jealousy during the visit, but she needn't have bothered. Ike and Mamie didn't have a happy reunion because he kept calling her Kay.

In early January, Kay returned to London and a few days later picked up Eisenhower at the airport. She took him to his new London town house—she doubted she could find Telegraph Cottage in the thick fog that night—and they drank whiskey by the fire as they always did. Then they found themselves in each other's arms, and their clothes came off. And nothing happened.

One morning soon after, in that same living room of shame, Ike spoke to Kay of his relationship with Mamie. After the death of their three-year-old son, he said, nothing could recapture the love and happiness they had shared. Both had hurt each other over the years.

"Kay," he said, "I guess I'm telling you that I'm not the lover you should have. It killed something in me. Not all at once, but little by little. For years I never thought of making love. And then when I did . . . when it had been on my mind for weeks, I failed. I failed with you, my dearest. Didn't I?"

Kay sat on the arm of his chair, her head against his shoulder. "It's all right," she said. "I love you. It's all right." They couldn't afford to focus on their love affair. Ike was planning D-Day, chain-smoking, nervous, and exhausted. He had headaches and diarrhea. The night of the invasion, he and Kay stood on the roof of the 101st Airborne Division headquarters building in Newbury to watch the bombers take off for Utah Beach in Normandy.

Kay wrote, "The planes were taking off, roaring down the runways and climbing, climbing. Soon there were hundreds circling above us. It was a full moon, so brilliant that it cast shadows. The planes, wheeling like some immense flock of birds, blotted it out from time to time. It was such a gigantic moment! My heart was pounding, and I was practically crying. I knew I had never seen anything like it before and never would see anything like it again. We stayed on the roof a long time watching the planes. Ike stood there with his hands in his pockets, his face tipped toward the sky. The planes kept circling and then they began tailing off and headed toward Normandy."

Ike said, "It's very hard to look a soldier in the eye when you fear that you are sending him to his death."

As they walked to the car, he said, "Well, it's on. No one can stop it now." That night, he could have waited with Winston Churchill or Charles de Gaulle, leader of the French Resistance, or any of his top officers. But he only wanted to wait with Kay. At 6:00 a.m., they received word that despite heavy initial losses, the Germans had been caught by surprise and the invasion was going well. It was the beginning of the end of the war.

Later in June, Ike's son, John, visited his father in England, and Ike sent Kay back to the States with him for a much-needed vacation. Awkwardly, Mamie was waiting at the airport for her son. She greeted Kay pleasantly and invited her to a cocktail party that evening. "It was not much fun," Kay wrote. "I felt very stiff and foreign and military among these women in their fluttery light dresses. No other woman was in uniform. And certainly no other woman was being scrutinized as sharply as I was." Though Kay had heard the rumors of her affair with Eisenhower from friends serving with her in England, in Washington she experienced the outright hostility of other soldiers' wives circling the wagons to defend one of their own. "It was in Washington," Kay added, "that I became aware of the gossip about Ike and me. Of its virulence. No wonder the women at that little cocktail party had been eying me so closely. Wherever I went, I began to feel as if I were on display. I became increasingly sensitive to the whispers. Ike must have been protecting me from a lot of this. Friends told me that there had been several gossip-column mentions of the General's glamorous driver and nastily pointed insinuations about our relationship."

At first, Kay delighted in the luxuries no one in England had seen in years. Soft, feminine dresses. Steaks and chocolate. But after just a few days, she had had enough. She wanted to be back at the center of action, wearing her old uniform, eating canned fish. "I was glad when the holiday was over," she wrote. "I had enjoyed most of it tremendously, and I had fallen in love with the United States, but now I longed to be back where I belonged. I had stepped out of that special dimension in which Ike and I had been living, and I did not like the world I found outside, a world where war was only incidental. Not a crusade against evil things, not a way of life that demanded the best one had to give."

After a thirty-three-hour flight, Kay found herself in London again and was thrilled to learn that Eisenhower—with FDR's support—was getting her a commission in the U.S. Women's Army Corps (WAC) as a second lieutenant. "I'm trying to plan ahead," he said. "We're winning this war, although I'm not always sure of it, and I'm not going to be in Europe forever. I told you once that I was never going to let you go. If you're a WAC, I can keep you on my staff later on." One night, in front of the fire, they spoke about having a child together. When buzz bombs chased them to the shelter in the backyard, they fell asleep on cots, holding hands in the dark.

There were few opportunities for private moments after Ike moved his headquarters to Normandy in early August 1944. Kay told him, "If I ever write you a love letter, you'll have to tear it up and swallow it."

"You don't have to write me, Kay," he replied. "Every time you look at me, I see a love letter in your eyes."

When Kay received her commission as a WAC in October 1944, she could no longer drive the general but sat next to him in the backseat. Ike soon promoted her to first lieutenant and his official aide—the first woman aide to a five-star general in U.S. history. Winston Churchill awarded her the British Empire Medal. On the battlefield, victory followed victory. Things were happening so fast they barely had time to mourn FDR's death on April 12, 1945. Less than a month later, on May 7 at 2:41 a.m., German officers marched into Ike's office in the French city of Reims to sign the surrender. Kay, at her desk with Telek at her feet, watched them stride past and into Ike's office, where they clicked their heels and saluted.

A dozen of Ike's staff went to his quarters in an old castle and popped champagne. But it was a solemn celebration. No one even smiled. "We had won," Kay wrote, "but victory was not anything like what I had thought it would be. There was a dull bitterness about it. So many deaths. So much destruction. And everyone was very, very tired."

Having lived in the micro-bubble of war for so many years, Kay wondered what life would be like now. "For all tunnels come to an end," she mused. "Wars are won. Orgasm achieved; a vision captured. A child is born. The gates of death open—and close. Then one must emerge. Into what?" Ike had been working with FDR to cut through miles of red tape and get American citizenship for Kay; now he was communicating with President Harry Truman; it was urgent because he knew he would be assigned to the Pentagon by the end of the year. He kept mentioning the baby he wanted to have with her. She didn't ask him, but it sounded as if he might ask Mamie for a divorce.

After the surrender, Eisenhower and his staff moved to Frankfurt, Germany, where he took up his position as military governor of the American occupation zone. When his men reported to him the atrocities they discovered at Nazi concentration camps, he instructed them to photograph and film what they found for use in the Nuremberg Trials and to refute future Holocaust deniers.

On the afternoon of October 15, 1945, sitting on the sofa of his living room, Kay and Ike found themselves kissing passionately. "The fire was warm," Kay recalled. "The sofa was soft. We held each other close, closer. Excitedly, I remember thinking, the way one thinks odd thoughts at significant moments, 'Wouldn't it be wonderful if this were the day we conceived the baby—our very first time.' Ike was tender, careful, loving. But it didn't work."

Kay said, "Wait, you're too excited. It will be all right."

"No. It won't," he said bitterly. "It's too late. I can't."

They dressed slowly, sadly. It had happened again, on this second attempt at sex. Or rather, it had not happened again.

Ike ordered supper and the two sat there in companionable silence. "It's not important," Kay said. "It's not the least bit important. It just takes time. That's all. And I'm very stubborn. You've said so yourself."

"I know you are, but I'm not sure that you're right," he said.

Two weeks later, he told her he was going to Washington the following day to work at the Pentagon for a few weeks. Then he would return to Frankfurt, finish up some things, and bring his entire staff back to Washington by the first of the year.

Kay waited and, after a few weeks, learned that Eisenhower would not be returning due to a bad cold. His staff, however, received instructions to join him in Washington in ten days. Shortly thereafter, a telex arrived that Lieutenant Summersby was not to head to Washington. Mystified, Kay wondered if she was supposed to come before the group, or if he had an assignment for her and she would travel later. But there were no more orders.

"I was stunned," she recalled. "It took nearly an hour for the truth to sink in. I was not going to Washington with the others. The General did not want me to come earlier or later. I was here and he was there. I felt like throwing up."

Kay went to her room in the WAC house, threw herself on the bed, and cried for hours, going over their every moment together. Was there a clue, somewhere? What had happened? It was over. That was what had happened. Ike must have realized he would be sacrificing his military career if he divorced Mamie, and the political career he dreamed of might never get off the ground. His decision must have been confirmed by his impotence. A young, vital woman like Kay needed a man who could get it up. Kay finally received a typed letter from Ike.

Dear Kay,

I am terribly distressed, first because it has become impossible [any] longer to keep you as a member of my personal official family, and secondly because I cannot come back and give you a detailed account of my reasons . . . I am sure you will understand that I am personally much distressed that an association that has been so valuable to me has to be terminated in this particular fashion . . .

At the bottom he had written, "Take care and retain your optimism."

It was a cold, cowardly brush-off. The man who had faced down Hitler's armies couldn't face the woman he had loved for three years. Kay accepted a posting at an army guesthouse in Berlin, and then one doing public relations in California. Visiting old friends in Washington, she called on Ike at the Pentagon, Telek on a leash.

She was afraid she would cry if she touched him, even shaking hands, so she bent down and fiddled with Telek's leash to avoid it. "It was a strange experience," she wrote. "The General stood up to greet me as I came into the office. I stopped and let Telek off his leash, and he ran straight to Ike after all those months and rolled over on his back, paws in the air, to have his stomach scratched. I could tell that Ike was very much affected. He got all red . . . We chatted for a few minutes about my future plans." He told her to drop in again; busy as he was, he could always find a few minutes for her. She went back twice for equally brief, awkward visits.

In 1947, Kay applied for her discharge from the U.S. Army. For her, the war was truly over now. "What do you do," she asked, "when you have been caught up in the whirlwind of history and, after several years, the whirlwind sets you gently down back where you were? For the first time since I had been a very young woman in London, I spent my days sleeping late, having my hair done, lunching with friends, going to dinner parties and dancing all night. Weekends I would visit friends in the country and play bridge and golf . . . I was happy." She also wrote a book called *Eisenhower Was My Boss*, which left out all hints at romance, of course. It became a bestseller, earning her a fortune.

In 1948, she read in the paper that Eisenhower had become president of Columbia University in New York. Kay, who had been dating several charming men, became obsessed with seeing him again. She started walking around the campus several times a week, hoping to run into him. Finally, she did spot him coming in one of the gates. He was shocked to see her there. She feigned surprise, explaining that she was there to look up an old friend. He didn't believe her. Frowning, he said, "Kay, it's impossible. There's nothing I can do."

Kay knew Ike was being discussed as a U.S. presidential

candidate for the 1952 election. While the wartime gossip about them had faded, he could not afford to be seen with Kay Summersby again. Kay wrote, "I looked at him. There were tears in my eyes. But I tried to smile. 'I understand,' I told him. And I did. We had had a fabulous relationship, but it was over. Completely over."

In 1952, Kay married a stockbroker, whom she divorced six years later. Over the years, she eagerly followed Ike's career in the papers: he became the first head of NATO in 1950 and won the U.S. presidential election as a Republican in 1952. Popular until the end of his second term, he ended the Korean War in 1953, established the Interstate Highway System in 1956, authorized the establishment of NASA, and signed the Civil Rights Act of 1957, sending troops to enforce school desegregation in Little Rock, Arkansas.

Mamie was a popular first lady. Eleanor Roosevelt had been the perfect first lady during the war—rushing about to save the world in sensible lace-up shoes. But after the horrors of the war, the American public wanted a gracious hostess, a traditional wife, mother, and grandmother who never got involved in politics, someone who reminded them of that innocent time before all the death and destruction, and Mamie Eisenhower was all of that. She set foot in the Oval Office just three times in eight years, and only at her husband's invitation. Her love of all things pink popularized a shade known as "Mamie pink" in clothing, bathrooms, and kitchens, and she usually wore large crinoline dresses while holding ladies' tea parties. Though known for her charm, Mamie had a frosty dislike of Ike's personal secretary. Ann Whitman, forty-four when Ike became president, was trim, blond, and happily married. But perhaps she brought with her the sour whiff of Kay Summersby.

Memories of Kay must have haunted Ike, too. According to the White House dog keeper, Traphes Bryant, whenever Eisenhower was watching a movie with "too many women or a romance, he would get up and leave. He would say, 'Let the Secret Service and the rest of the fellows watch it. It's not for me.'" His relationship with Kay may have affected not just his choice of movies, but also his appointment of 175 women to high-level federal posts, including as ambassador to Switzerland and Italy, and delegate to the United Nations. Eisenhower knew firsthand just how efficient women could be.

Over his eight years as president, Eisenhower held more than two hundred press conferences, communicating directly with the American people, which Kay watched avidly. Even when he wasn't in the news, Ike would come suddenly into Kay's thoughts. The haunting melody of a song they used to play on the old Victrola at Telegraph Cottage would instantly take her back to those days, plucking at her heartstrings for the loss of so many beloved things. The saddest day, however, was when Telek died. Her constant companion for seventeen years, one morning the ailing dog could not get up. Tearfully, she took him to the vet.

"I picked Telek up, put him in my lap, and talked to him," she recalled. "I told him how much he had always meant to me, how much I had loved him. I told him that he was an important part of my life, that when I was sitting at home and he was curled up at my feet I never felt alone. I talked to him about Ike, I told that poor tired Scottie how much Ike had liked him. I reminded him of how he used to ride in the car with us, of how he had visited Buckingham Palace, of how President Roosevelt had held him, of all the adorable scampering puppies he had sired. I let my voice and my memories surround him. Then I put him on my bed, buckled his little tartan coat around him and carried him out to a taxi and to the veterinarian."

"Please put him to sleep," she said, sobbing.

"Such a gallant little dog," she wrote. "Such a faithful, loving friend. It hit me very hard. It was not just Telek's death I was mourning. He had been my last link to Ike, the man I had loved more than anyone else in my life. And I was grieving for my own loss. From now on there would always be something missing in my life, the spirit, the gaiety, the devotion of a small dog named Telek."

With great concern, Kay followed Ike's waning health over the years. He finally died of heart failure in 1969 at the age of seventy-eight; Mamie died ten years later at eighty-three. In the 1960s, Kay became a fashion consultant for the CBS network, and her last job was choosing costumes for the Hollywood cult classic film *The Stepford Wives*, released in 1975. A few months before the film's release, in the hospital with liver cancer, she read a newspaper story she could hardly believe.

A few years earlier, biographer Merle Miller had spent hundreds of hours interviewing former President Truman, who died in 1972. Miller reported, "Right after the war was over, he [Eisenhower] wrote a letter to General Marshall saying that he wanted to come back to the United States and divorce Mrs. Eisenhower so that he could marry this English woman."

Truman said, "Marshall wrote him back a letter the like of which I never did see. He said that if Eisenhower even came close to doing such a thing, he'd not only bust him out of the Army, he'd see to it that never for the rest of his life would he be able to draw a peaceful breath . . . and that if he ever again mentioned a thing like that, he'd see to it that the rest of his life was a living hell." Truman added, "One of the last things I did as President,

I got those letters from his file in the Pentagon and I destroyed them." Truman, apparently, did not wish them to leak out, ruining Eisenhower's reputation as a wartime hero.

Reading the article, Kay suddenly understood why Ike had dropped her like a hot potato all those years ago. With Eisenhower, Kay wrote, "Duty would always come first. He told me once that if there are two paths a man can take, both of them honorable, then all things being equal, he should take the path along which he will do the most good and inflict the least hurt. And that, I believe, is what he did."

Most of Eisenhower's family and friends were aghast at Kay's book, which came out soon after she died in January 1975 at the age of sixty-six. Kay's ghostwriter had made up the love affair after Kay's death to sell books, they said, though certainly a nice hard erection would have sold more books than a sad limp pizzle. President Truman's memory was faulty, they said, or maybe Merle Miller lied to sell more of *his* books. And Kay's story had to be a lie because Ike's letters to Mamie during the war were frequent and loving. Moreover, in one of them Eisenhower requested permission for Mamie to join him in Europe after the German surrender. "The strain of the past three years," he wrote General Marshall, "has also been very considerable so far as my wife is concerned and because of the fact that she has had trouble with her general nervous system for many years. I would feel far more comfortable about her if she could be with me." His request was denied.

But many men compartmentalize their relationships with their wives and mistresses, leading each one on. Perhaps, too, Ike was increasingly recognizing the hopelessness of his affair with Kay. We don't know the date of Ike's purported letter "right after the war" to Marshall asking for a divorce. Was his June letter asking permission for Mamie to join him in Frankfurt a response to Marshall's harrowing reply? Far away from Mamie, with Kay constantly at his side, was he uncertain which path to take until his second failed attempt at making love to Kay four months later?

Nor could the family deny the closeness indicated in a note Ike sent Kay during the war which appeared at auction after her death. "How about lunch, tea & dinner today?" he asked. "If yes: Who else do you want, if any? At which time? How are you?"

Eisenhower's son, John, who spent time with Ike and Kay at military headquarters, was less startled at the allegations than his mother, Mamie. In an interview with PBS, John described Kay as "the Mary Tyler Moore of headquarters. She was perky and she was cute. Whether she had any designs on the Old Man and the extent to which he succumbed, I just don't know."

Looking back, Kay wrote, "We were two people caught up in a cataclysm. Two people who shared one of the most tremendous experiences of our time. Two people who gave each other comfort, laughter, love. Now that I am very close to the end of my life, I have a strong sense of being close to Ike again. I can almost hear him say, 'Goddamnit, don't cry.'"

9

JOHN F. KENNEDY'S
TERRIBLE HEADACHES

O n November 29, 1963—a week after the assassination of President John F. Kennedy in Dallas—his widow, Jacqueline Bouvier Kennedy, sat down with Theodore White, a writer for *Life* magazine, and invented the myth of Camelot. Her late husband had loved the popular Broadway musical, she said (though many who knew him swore he had not), and loved to sing, "Don't let it be forgot, that once there was a spot, for one brief shining moment, that was known as Camelot."

Jackie was correct that the all-too-brief presidency was full of beautiful people. And, as in an early monarchy, there were many ladies-in-waiting, though none of them in the Kennedy White House had to wait very long. The comparison of Camelot was correct, too, in that adultery infected King Arthur's court like a plague, and his reign ended in bloodshed.

★ ★ ★

When Jackie Kennedy slid between her sheets one evening, her hand touched something odd beneath her pillow. She pulled out a pair of women's panties. While most wives would be perturbed to find such an item wadded up in their bed, the first lady merely dangled them from a finger and asked her husband, "Would you please shop around and see who this belongs to? It's not my size."

By the time she moved to the White House, Jackie was used to her husband's philandering. Given her background, she must have expected a certain amount of infidelity from anyone she married. She was the daughter of a serial adulterer—John "Black Jack" Bouvier—and a member of a privileged society where few saw the need to deny themselves anything. But Jackie had had no idea of Jack Kennedy's pathological need for sex with prostitutes, society matrons, schoolgirls, babysitters, debutantes, employees, actresses, strippers, and strangers picked up in bars, often with two women at once, or with two women and another man with the men swapping partners, some of those men his own brothers. The sex took place in closets, cars, brothels, hotel rooms, the homes of his friends, bathtubs, showers, swimming pools, yachts, and in Jackie's own bed. In 1962, during a summit in the Bahamas, Kennedy told British prime minister Harold Macmillan, "You know, I get a migraine headache if I don't get a strange piece of ass every day."

JFK's best friend from high school, Lem Billings, a frequent participant in those orgies, warned Jackie before the wedding that her fiancé could never settle down with one woman. Not for a moment did she consider canceling. Looking back, she said, "I saw it as a challenge."

Her friend, journalist Charles Bartlett, said that Jackie was not "prepared for the humiliation she would suffer when she found herself stranded at parties while Jack would suddenly disappear with some pretty young girl. Before the marriage, I think she found Jack's appeal to other women tantalizing—I suspect it reminded her of the magic appeal her handsome, rakish father had had with women, but once she was married and once it was happening to her, it was much harder to accept."

Three days before the inauguration, Jackie told a writer for *Life* magazine that she and Jack were "rather like an iceberg, one part fully exposed to public view and most of it quietly submerged."

And what the American people saw of the iceberg above the water was dazzlingly beautiful. For Jack and Jackie were, from the moment of their engagement, the most glamorous, photogenic couple in America. At six feet tall and 165 pounds, Jack was lean muscle, with gray-blue eyes, a thick mane of chestnut hair, and a million-dollar grin. At five foot seven and 120 pounds, Jackie was slender and athletic with a lithe grace. She had a square face with wide hazel eyes and dark hair teased into a kind of helmet. She had gone to the best private schools, spent her junior year of college in Paris, and graduated from George Washington University with a bachelor's in French literature. In 1951 she became an Inquiring Camera Girl for the *Washington Times-Herald*, photographing people on the street and asking them their opinions.

Jack was the scion of Joe Kennedy Sr., a bootlegging, womanizing, filthy rich tycoon who placed pornographic magazines on his son's bed when he was fourteen. Jack graduated from Harvard in 1940 with a bachelor's in government, his education derailed on numerous occasions due to ill health. His first major love affair began in 1941, when he was twenty-four, and the object of his desire was Inga Arvad, four years his senior, a reporter for the *Washington Times-Herald*. The statuesque former beauty queen was a native of Denmark who had written glowing articles about

Adolf Hitler's "kind heart." "The perfect Nordic beauty," according to the führer, Inga had been invited to Hermann Göring's 1935 wedding and was Hitler's personal guest at the Summer Olympics the following year. Suspecting that Inga was a Nazi spy, FBI director J. Edgar Hoover bugged her apartment, tapped her phone, and had her followed, discovering, to his horror, that she was sleeping with Kennedy, who was working in the U.S. Office of Naval Intelligence.

Hoover believed Inga might be wheedling naval secrets out of Kennedy and passing them on to the Germans. JFK and Inga knew they were being followed and recorded and continued to see each other, pure recklessness on Kennedy's part given his military position. Kennedy's superiors wanted to eject him from the navy for consorting with a woman they considered to be a Mata Hari. But because JFK's father was the rich and powerful Joseph Kennedy, who had been U.S. ambassador to Great Britain a year earlier, they merely transferred him to a desk job in South Carolina. Even then, the reckless pair didn't break it off. Inga drove down to Charleston or they met in hotel rooms in D.C. where Hoover presumably would not be listening in.

Soon, Kennedy saw action in the South Pacific. In 1943, he was commander of a PT boat when a Japanese destroyer collided with it, cutting it in half. Kennedy's actions to save his surviving crew—including towing a badly burned man to an island with his life preserver strap between his teeth—made him a war hero. Joe Kennedy was delighted as heroic actions could help propel a man into public office.

Irish Catholic Joe, son of a barkeep, was never really accepted into elite, Protestant Boston society no matter how many millions he made. He insisted on a son of his becoming president just to show them all. Jack's older brother, Joe Jr., had died in the war, so now the weighty mantle of paternal expectations fell on Jack, the second son. His campaign bankrolled by his father, in 1947, at the age of twenty-nine, Jack became a Massachusetts congressman. Handsome, dashing, and politically important, he found himself surrounded by beautiful women, including major Hollywood movie stars like Gene Tierney.

Many young bachelors enjoy sexual liaisons, but Kennedy seemed to have no control over his impulses and dropped his pants whenever the spirit overtook him, which was often. He didn't even bother to learn the names of many of his sex partners, calling them "kiddo" or "sweetie" for the ten or fifteen minutes he used them before they vanished from his life. "No one was off limits to Jack," said Florida senator George Smathers, one of his regular partners in carousing. "Not your wife, your mother or your sister." In 1952, Kennedy caused a ruckus when he locked himself and a woman in a closet at a white-tie benefit in Newport, Rhode Island. Guests had to wait until he was done to get their coats back.

By the beginning of 1953, now a newly minted senator, Kennedy was thirty-five and knew he needed to marry and start a family to remain popular with voters. Friends introduced him to Jacqueline Bouvier at a dinner, and he quickly saw that here was everything he could have asked for: Jackie was Catholic, beautiful, and intelligent. Her style and charm would help him politically. Oleg Cassini, Jackie's friend and dress designer, explained the attraction. "Jack wanted more than looks," he said. "He wanted courage, accomplishment. He wanted a champion, a star."

If Jackie suspected her husband might have an affair after a few years of marriage, she got a rude shock on her Mexican honeymoon. At a cocktail reception, Jack collected phone numbers on slips of paper from a crowd of women hovering around him.

Then, according to Michael Diaz, a lawyer from Mexico City, "At one point he brazenly walked off with one of the better-looking women and headed for a bedroom. They emerged twenty minutes later, looking flushed and spent. You had to feel sorry for Mrs. Kennedy."

In the first years of her marriage, Jackie saw her husband infrequently as he traveled both domestically and internationally without her. In the summer of 1955, Jack spent a week with a gorgeous twenty-three-year-old Swedish aristocrat, Gunilla von Post, at a resort in Sweden. He had met her in the south of France in August 1953, and they had, by her account, fallen in love during an evening of dinner and dancing. She was shattered to hear he would be getting married in a month. "If I had met you one week before," he said, "I would have canceled the whole thing." It was doubtful, given the prize Jackie was, that he would have jilted her, but the story did work in seducing Gunilla after two years of letters, phone calls, and complaints about his "cold" wife. They spent much of their week together in bed. Before leaving, Jack promised Gunilla he would talk to his father about getting a divorce so he could marry her. This comment shocked her, as she couldn't imagine a thirty-eight-year-old United States senator having to ask his father permission for anything.

We will never know if Kennedy actually spoke with his father about a divorce. But he told Gunilla that Joe Sr. said, "You're out of your mind. You're going to be president someday. This would ruin everything. Divorce is impossible . . . Can't you get it into your head that it's not important what you really are? The only important thing is what people think you are!" Jack offered Gunilla a job and financial support if she agreed to move to the U.S. She wisely turned him down and within the year married a wealthy Swedish landowner.

At the same time Jack was begging Gunilla to relocate, he was having a red-hot affair in Washington with a stripper named Tempest Storm. The following year, in a Malibu restaurant, he met twenty-four-year-old Joan Lundberg and began a three-year relationship, arranging for her to meet him in hotels all over the country. When she got pregnant—he refused to wear a condom, perhaps for religious reasons—he sent her money for an abortion.

In the summer of 1956, Jackie was seven months pregnant, having suffered a miscarriage the year before, when Jack went on a European cruise with his brother Teddy and Florida senator George Smathers. Soon after Jackie learned there were also three Scandinavian women on board, she began to hemorrhage and gave birth to a stillborn girl born a month early. When he heard the news, Jack was reluctant to return home, wondering aloud what he could do there. He called his younger brother Bobby, who said, "If you ever want to run for president, you had better haul ass back to your wife." He did, but Jackie nearly divorced him. Something had been irretrievably broken in their marriage.

Later that year, Jackie disconsolately sat for a taped television interview. "You're pretty much in love with him, aren't you?" asked the interviewer. "Oh no," she said, her eyes downcast. Almost surprised at herself, she raised her eyes and asked, "I said no, didn't I?" The director cut and they started over again. When asked if she was in love with her husband, she said carelessly, "I suppose so. I've ruined it, haven't I?"

In January 1957, Jackie and a gay friend, artist Bill Walton, took a trip to Hollywood. There they had dinner with one of the film industry's most popular stars, thirty-nine-year-old William Holden, and his wife. Walton said that Jackie quickly fell into bed with the actor and the affair was "primarily driven by Jackie's desire to seek revenge on Jack." Her desire for revenge increased the following year, according to White House dog keeper Traphes Bryant, when she discovered Jack had impregnated the fifteen-year-old babysitter of their infant daughter, Caroline. The babysitter, according to gossip, got an abortion, while Jackie once more threatened divorce. Rumor had it that her father-in-law bribed her to stay in the marriage.

It must have been an awful lot of money. Because the following year, Jackie, "always cheerful and obliging," according to campaign adviser Kenneth O'Donnell, campaigned hard for Jack's Senate reelection. "The size of the crowd was twice as big" when Jackie accompanied her husband, O'Donnell reported. She was, perhaps, his greatest asset on the campaign trail.

Despite Kennedy's popular wife, some of his friends were worried his women stories would get out when he threw his hat into the ring for the 1960 presidential campaign. Joe Kennedy Sr. ridiculed their fears, growling, "The American people don't care how many times he gets laid." Fred Dutton, a Democratic Party power broker, agreed. "There are more votes in virility than fidelity," he pointed out. Kennedy, he said, "was like a God, fucking anybody he wants to anytime he feels like it." The candidate was someone who, if the stories got out, most American men would envy.

Langdon Marvin, a Kennedy campaign worker, recalled that Kennedy would "dispatch me to a given town or city as a kind of advance man. I'd set things up for him. When he arrived, I'd pick him up at the airport. He'd clamber off the *Caroline*, the campaign plane his father had purchased for him, and he'd say to me, 'Where are the broads?'" Marvin would have several prostitutes lined up that Kennedy picked from. He usually chose two. A speechwriter for the 1960 election recalled, "It was just the way Jack felt—you weren't a man if you let a really incredible piece of ass get away."

On November 8, 1960, Kennedy won the presidential election by some 113,000 votes out of nearly 69 million total votes cast—49.7 percent versus 49.6 percent for Richard Nixon—the smallest victory margin in a century. It was a generational shift in America's power structure. At seventy, Eisenhower, the outgoing president, was the oldest person ever to serve in the office to that point; his wife, Mamie, was sixty-four. The president-elect was the youngest ever, forty-three. Jackie was thirty-one and almost nine months pregnant with their son John F. Kennedy Jr.

Giddy as many Americans were with their handsome young president, they did not know two essential pieces of information about him. One was the alarming state of his health. Sickly as a child, at the age of thirty Kennedy was diagnosed with Addison's disease, a rare endocrine disorder that caused severe lower back pain (which was greatly exacerbated by his war injuries), discoloration of the skin (resulting in his eternal orangey tan), abdominal pain, weight loss, diarrhea, headaches, impaired judgment, and high fevers. Severe stress could trigger an Addisonian crisis, with convulsions and dangerously low blood pressure, resulting in death. Kennedy was given last rites four times before he became president.

He wore a stiff, laced-up corset to stabilize his weak spine, slept on a special firm mattress, and often had his aides bring his rocking chair to private dinners. From time to time, his back was so bad he walked on crutches or with a cane, which, like FDR, he was careful to hide from the public. In the White House movie theater, he lay in a bed propped up on pillows. Kennedy strongly denied rumors that he had Addison's disease, claiming his back pain was solely the result of his heroic acts during the war.

His treatments—by three doctors working separately—involved hormones, steroids, vitamins, enzymes, and amphetamines,

with the potential side effects of hyperactivity, impaired judgment, nervousness, and mood swings. Kennedy was treated with
cortisone, in the form of pills, injections, and pellets inserted into
the skin. His father had the medicine placed in safe-deposit boxes
around the world in case Jack suffered a crisis in a foreign country. One of his physicians, Max Jacobson—who would lose his
medical license after killing a patient in 1969 with intravenous
amphetamine poisoning—was known as Dr. Feelgood. "I don't
care if it's horse piss," Kennedy snapped when his brother Bobby
warned him about the doctor's mysterious injections. "It works."

The other tidbit Americans didn't know was his reckless, obsessive philandering, much of it done in the White House when
Jackie wasn't there, which was often. Traphes Bryant explained,
"Usually when he wanted to be alone with his female company,
JFK passed the word that the private family quarters on the second floor were off-limits." One night, Bryant pressed the wrong
elevator button. "Just as the elevator door opened, a naked blond
office girl ran through the hall between the second-floor kitchen
and the door leading to the West Hall. Her breasts were swinging
as she ran by. There was nothing to do but to get out fast and push
the basement buttons."

After JFK had a tryst with a woman in the White House private quarters, either in his bed or—and here we shudder—his
wife's, housekeepers and Secret Service agents rushed in to clean
up the incriminating evidence before Jackie returned, according
to Bryant. This was especially true after the president had bedded
a blond, which he usually preferred. In that era, women's bouffant
hairstyles were nothing less than extraordinary feats of engineer-
ing sustained by relentless teasing, hair spray, and bobby pins.
Jackie may not have been suspicious if she found a long, dark hair
or dark bobby pin on her pillow. "Why can't he make it easier for

us?" the staff asked, cursing under their breath as they sifted the covers and floors on their hands and knees. "Why do we always have to be searching for blond hair and blond bobby pins? Why can't he get himself a steady brunette?"

Perhaps the most troubling aspect of this story is that the staff picked hairs off the sheets instead of changing them. Which leads us to ponder how many sets of sheets the White House possessed. Perhaps not enough to keep up with JFK's constant soiling of them? Fresh sheets would have offered the added advantage of whisking away all those pesky leftover panties, like the ones the first lady found wadded up beneath her pillow.

One evening, Bryant recalled, JFK, Bobby, and several women were swimming nude in the White House pool and knocking back daiquiris soon after Jackie left with the children for her country house in Virginia. Word came she had forgotten something and was at that moment entering the White House. "Suddenly the ushers were sounding the alarm," Bryant said, "and first thing I knew naked bodies were scurrying every which way. It was easy to get rid of bodies, but gathering up the drinks was another matter, and the help had a time clearing away the evidence—like highball glasses. Only the President remained in the pool. As I remember it, Jackie seemed not to notice anything amiss. Soon word came that she was getting back into her car, and then that it had driven off. But just in case, the President swam alone in the pool for a while."

Kennedy's unrestrained sexual appetite infuriated some of the men who were assigned to protect him. Secret Service agent Larry Newman remembered the "morale problems" that the president's indiscretions caused. "You were on the most elite assignment in the Secret Service," he said, "and you were there watching an elevator or a door because the president was inside with two hookers.

It just didn't compute. Your neighbors and everybody thought you were risking your life, and you were actually out there to see that he's not disturbed while he's having an interlude in the shower with two gals from Twelfth Avenue."

Then there was the issue of the president's personal safety. Agent Newman remembered joking with his colleagues about which one of them would testify on Capitol Hill if and when "the president received harm or was killed in the room by these two women." When Jackie was away, young women would show up at the White House unheralded, claiming the president had invited them over. The Secret Service agents had no time to vet the visitors, and Kennedy was in no mood to wait. Any one of these women could have killed the president when they were alone together in the second-floor residence. After sex, he often offered his lovers food his staff had left in his private kitchen, which had plenty of knives lying about. If a woman had attacked Kennedy, help would have been slow in coming as he had exiled all staff, including his Secret Service personnel, to other floors.

JFK's reckless philandering even threatened national security. Sometimes he ditched his Secret Service agents to meet a woman outside the White House, leaving behind the army officer with the nuclear security codes in a black briefcase handcuffed to his wrist. If the Soviets had launched an all-out attack with the president missing in action, America would have been unable to respond.

Though Kennedy probably had sex with hundreds of women while he was president, we only know the stories of a dozen. Two were purported spies. Kennedy's mistress Judith Campbell was a gorgeous good-time girl whose louche life, according to her autobiography, was a never-ending round of parties, dressing up, drinking, dining, swimming, and attending the midnight shows of Dean Martin or Frank Sinatra, after which she would disappear with a rich and famous man. A stunning, shapely brunette with ice-blue eyes, she claimed she was never paid for sex. And yet, reading her book, one wonders where she got all the money for the travel and designer clothing she described, as she had no visible means of support.

On February 7, 1960, one of her regular lovers, Frank Sinatra, introduced her to JFK in the lounge of the Sands Hotel in Las Vegas. There was immediate chemistry between the two. A month later, Kennedy arranged a tryst with her at the Plaza Hotel in New York, the day before the New Hampshire primary. He spent time with her in his Georgetown house, in a friend's home in Palm Beach, and at the Los Angeles Hilton during the Democratic National Convention. She is recorded as having visited the White House on twenty occasions. Judith confessed she was "caught up a little with the intrigue of it. The sneaking around, a mild form of cloak-and-dagger, the anticipation, the 'Boy, we didn't get caught!'"

But they would get caught in a scandal that threatened to derail Kennedy's entire presidency. Because Judith Campbell was also the mistress of the Chicago Mafia boss Sam Giancana, Al Capone's successor, who ran a criminal empire of some fifty thousand bookies, counterfeiters, murderers-for-hire, and assorted wise guys with an annual off-the-books revenue of $2 billion. In March 1962, FBI director J. Edgar Hoover, who eventually learned everything about everybody, informed Kennedy that the affair made him particularly vulnerable to blackmail by the Mafia. The president, who had been trying to reduce Hoover's unlimited power, clearly would not be able to do so now. Even worse, Attorney General Bobby Kennedy, who had been working to crack down on the mob, found his efforts hobbled. While some sources state that Kennedy ceased all contact with Judith after his discussion with Hoover, in a 1997 *Vanity Fair* interview, she claimed they last had sex in December 1962, some nine months after the president knew he was setting himself up for blackmail.

Ellen Rometsch was a gorgeous twenty-seven-year-old with a black beehive hairstyle, an hourglass figure, and a fetching little mole on the side of her pouting red lips. An East German, she had worked briefly as a secretary for Walter Ulbricht, head of the Communist East German government, before she and her family fled to West Germany in 1955. Soon after, she married a West German air force sergeant who was stationed at the embassy in Washington in 1961. She allegedly worked as a high-class prostitute at a hotel next to the Senate office building, servicing politicians. After his first date with Ellen, Kennedy called a friend and said, "That was the best blow job I ever had in my life." The two met for dinner privately several times at the White House.

Naturally, J. Edgar Hoover learned of it. He had his agents interview Rometsch and concluded she was probably a Soviet spy. One of her lovers, in fact, worked at the Soviet embassy in D.C. When Hoover informed Kennedy, for the first time ever he was worried about a sex scandal bringing him down. In June 1963, the British secretary of state for war John Profumo resigned in full-on tabloid disgrace after it came out that he had slept with a call girl—who was sleeping with the Soviet naval attaché—and then lied about it. Rometsch was sent packing back to West Germany. For once in Jack Kennedy's life, reason overcame recklessness.

His other lovers were far less dangerous. Twenty-year-old college junior Diana de Vegh met Kennedy during his 1959 Senate campaign at a political dinner in Boston. He arranged for her to work on Capitol Hill and then, after the inauguration, on the

National Security Council. When Jackie was out of town, he invited Diana to his private quarters in the White House for dinner. Afterward, they would go to the Lincoln Bedroom—Jackie's personal haven where she felt "the kind of peace . . . you feel when going into a church," with a high carved bed "like a cathedral"— and desecrate it. After a year, Diana had had enough of an affair with a married man. She quit her job, moved to Paris, became an actress in the soap opera *All My Children*, earned a master's degree in social work at Columbia, and became a psychotherapist.

Mary Meyer was the sister-in-law of *Newsweek*'s Washington bureau chief, Ben Bradlee, a close friend of JFK who in 1965 would become the editor of the *Washington Post*. Blond, spunky, and in search of a good time, Mary was the divorced mother of two and a painter of minimalist art. Though Mary had known the Kennedys ever since they moved in next door to her Georgetown house in 1954, her affair with Jack didn't start until October 3, 1961, when she arrived at the White House for an intimate dinner. According to White House logbooks, she would have at least thirteen such dinners over the next two years, though some sources say she had more than thirty, entering as the "plus one" of Kennedy's loyal special assistant Dave Powers. At a March 8, 1963, dinner dance, she disappeared for half an hour. Her date later reported, "Finally I went looking for her. She had been upstairs with Jack."

Mary's story had a very dark ending. She told friends she kept a detailed diary of her affair with JFK, including their experiments with LSD, marijuana, and cocaine. On October 12, 1964, while taking her usual walk along the C&O Canal towpath near her Georgetown house, she was fatally shot, and later that day Ben Bradlee found James Angleton, chief of CIA Counterintelligence, breaking into her art studio in Bradlee's backyard, looking for her diary. Bradlee agreed to give it to him, and Angleton burned it. The African American man police tried to pin the crime on was found not guilty, and the murder remains unsolved to this day.

When Helen Chavchavadze's affair with JFK began in 1960, she was a twenty-seven-year-old divorcée with two young children, studying for her master's degree in Russian at Georgetown University. The pretty brunette had met the Kennedys through Jackie's sister, Lee Radziwill, with whom she had gone to school. After the inauguration, when Jackie was traveling, Kennedy invited Helen for private dinners followed by sex.

Helen's affair came back to haunt her when, in the fall of 1962, she couldn't get a security clearance for a job she had been offered at the Foreign Service Institute. She realized that the denial was due to her affair with the president and that she was under surveillance. Falling into a deep depression, she had a nervous breakdown, was committed into a psychiatric hospital, and lost her house and custody of her children. Released from the hospital after a few months, Helen started teaching at American University, reclaimed her home and children, and met the man she would soon marry. She was standing by her ironing board when she heard the news of JFK's death and burst into tears. Yet, "When he was killed a tiny part of me felt freed," she told author Sally Bedell Smith.

Though Helen had suspected Kennedy may have had other lovers, she wasn't sure until it all came out years after his death. Looking back, she said of his rampant adultery, "It was a compulsion, a quirk in his personality. He was out of control. It may have looked like beautiful convertibles and women and sophistication, but it was the shadow destroying the self. For Mary [Meyer] and me it was our shadow too."

Curiously, Jackie invited Diana, Helen, and Mary to White

House luncheons and dinner dances, often sitting one of them next to her husband. An admirer of French ancien régime history, she seemed to have modeled herself on Louis XV's official mistress Madame de Pompadour, who selected young women for the king's enjoyment as a means of maintaining control. "Jackie was in charge choosing his playmates," Helen said. "It was very French."

Jackie even agreed to her husband's suggestion to hire his lover as her press secretary. Pamela Turnure, a fetching brunette, had been having an affair with Kennedy ever since she started working as his secretary in the Senate in 1958. Though Turnure had absolutely no experience handling the press, Jackie hired the twenty-three-year-old as her most visible staff member.

The president had other compliant young females close at hand whenever the urge struck him: two women dubbed Fiddle and Faddle. Fiddle, whose real name was Priscilla Wear, worked for Kennedy's private secretary Evelyn Lincoln; and Fiddle's close friend Faddle—Jill Cowan—was an assistant in the White House press office. They started working on Kennedy's presidential campaign when they were twenty and dropped out of college when he offered them White House jobs.

At lunchtime, both women enjoyed swimming with the president in the White House pool, returning to their offices with wet hair. They didn't do any work on the presidential trips Kennedy included them in. One day, National Security Advisor McGeorge Bundy and White House aide Myer Feldman walked into the Oval Office and saw the young women massaging gel into the president's scalp. Shocked, Bundy said he didn't think this kind of behavior was sufficiently dignified for the Oval Office. The president, looking at the balding heads of his visitors, said, "Well, I'm not sure you two plan your hair very well."

Jackie knew all about her husband's relationships with the girls. Once, while taking a reporter from *Paris Match* on a White House tour, she walked into Evelyn Lincoln's office and saw Fiddle sitting at her desk. Jackie turned to the reporter and said in French, "This is the girl who supposedly is sleeping with my husband."

Kennedy's most famous girlfriend was the immortal goddess of the silver screen, Marilyn Monroe. They met in the late fifties and had begun their affair by the 1960 presidential campaign. When JFK campaigned in Los Angeles, he and Marilyn made love in a bathtub, according to his brother-in-law and pimp, Rat Pack actor Peter Lawford. On the night of Kennedy's acceptance speech for the Democratic nomination, both Marilyn and Kennedy attended a nude swimming party at Lawford's Santa Monica beach house. Other times, the actress met the president on Air Force One, in the Beverly Hills Hilton, and in his two-story apartment in New York's Carlyle Hotel. Marilyn, perhaps the most recognizable woman in the nation, was smuggled in from a nearby apartment building through underground tunnels by Secret Service agents with flashlights. On the weekend of March 24, 1962, while Jackie was enjoying a camel ride in India, her husband had a rendezvous with Marilyn at Bing Crosby's Palm Springs home.

Marilyn had fallen hard for the president and dreamed he would divorce Jackie and marry her. When she called his private number in the White House residence, sometimes Jackie picked up and, hearing who it was, mutely handed the phone to her husband. Jackie wisely stayed away from the May 19, 1962, televised celebration of the president's forty-fifth birthday at Madison Square Garden. Marilyn sang a throaty "Happy Birthday, Mr. President" wearing a skintight, pink silk dress with sequins. One diplomat in attendance described the gown as "skin and beads only I didn't see the beads." The sexual electricity between the president and the actress was clear to the fifteen thousand spectators. Columnist Dorothy Kilgallen called it nothing less than "making love to the President in the direct view of forty million Americans."

After the event, Marilyn and the president spent the night together at the Carlyle Hotel. But five days later when she tried calling Kennedy, White House switchboard operators refused to put her calls through. Kennedy could no longer afford to continue the affair. He had learned from J. Edgar Hoover that the Mafia had bugged their meeting places and had recordings of them in bed. The president asked his brother Bobby to console her, which he did admirably. But after a scorching affair of two months, Bobby stopped taking her calls for the same reason. Hoover informed him that the Mafia would release tapes of him in bed with Marilyn if he continued coming down hard on organized crime. Furious at being dumped by both brothers in two months, Marilyn started speaking with the press. The president asked friends to talk some sense into her.

Her last call was on August 4 to Peter Lawford, who told police she instructed him to say goodbye to Jack and hung up. Lawford may or may not have been telling the truth. There are also reports that Bobby Kennedy was with Lawford that night. A few hours after that call, Marilyn Monroe was found dead of an overdose of barbiturates, a scrap of paper with a White House phone number in her hand. The scrap of paper disappeared, as well as all of her phone records from the offices of General Telephone.

Kennedy began his affair with the voluptuous, platinum blond actress Jayne Mansfield during his presidential campaign, and it lasted until his death. Mansfield had created a lucrative career by imitating Marilyn Monroe. Kennedy told Lawford, "She's so anxious to ape Marilyn, be Marilyn, we'll add to her credentials by giving her a roll in the hay."

"Why, think," Jayne told a friend, "I'll go down in history like that—what was her name—Madame O'Barry." Her friend had to tell her the famous eighteenth-century royal mistress was named Madame du Barry, and she was French, not Irish.

In 1962, Hollywood icon Marlene Dietrich received an invitation from the president to the White House for a drink the evening she was to receive an award for aiding Jewish war refugees. He immediately made it clear he wanted sex, according to film critic Kenneth Tynan, who heard the tale from Dietrich and immediately recorded this priceless pearl in his diary. "I hope you aren't in a hurry," Kennedy said. The sixty-year-old actress explained that two thousand people were waiting to give her an award in half an hour.

Undeterred, Kennedy grabbed her glass and led her to his bedroom. She recalled, "I remembered about his bad back, that wartime injury. I looked at him and he was already undressing. He was unwinding rolls of bandage from around his middle—he looked like Laocoon and that snake, you know? Now I'm an old lady, and I said to myself: I'd like to sleep with the president, sure, but I'll be goddamned if I'm going to be on top!"

After only six minutes, the president climaxed and fell sound asleep. "I looked at my watch and it was 6:50," Dietrich said. "I got dressed and shook him—because I didn't know my way around the place, and I couldn't just call for a cab. I said, 'Jack—wake up! Two thousand Jews are waiting! For Christ's sake get me out of here!' So he grabbed a towel and wrapped it around his waist and took me along this corridor to an elevator. He told the elevator man to get me a car to the Statler Hotel immediately—standing right there in his towel, without any embarrassment, as if it was an everyday event—which in his life it probably was."

There is one story that stands out from the kaleidoscope of sex tales involving movie stars, sophisticated socialites, and lonely divorcées. It is the tale of nineteen-year-old Mimi Beardsley, a fresh-faced college girl from New Jersey, who, on her fourth day as an intern in the White House Press Office in the summer of 1962, found herself thrown onto Jackie Kennedy's bed by the president of the United States and penetrated. On her way home afterward, she asked herself how it had happened and lamented that she would no longer be a virgin on her wedding night.

Mimi had first met Kennedy a little more than a year earlier, when she'd visited the White House for her high school newspaper. He had shaken her hand and asked her about herself. And then, months later, came an unexpected offer for a highly coveted internship. Mimi was a pretty girl who wore no makeup at all, her only adornments a wide white smile and a string of pearls. She had never been popular with boys. She blamed this on her height that, at five foot nine, was unfashionably tall for the time, and her build, thin and athletic rather than the rocket-boobs-hourglass figure women were supposed to have.

On her fourth day working in the Press Office, Kennedy's aide Dave Powers asked her to join him for a swim in the White House pool. Shocked, Mimi assumed this was some kind of White House custom and agreed. She soon found herself swimming with Fiddle, Faddle, and Kennedy and returned to the Press Office reeking of chlorine, her hair wet. And then, a few hours later, Powers suggested she join the president and a few of the staff for drinks up in the residence. Wide-eyed, Mimi guzzled daiquiris with Fiddle, Faddle, Dave Powers, and the president. When she learned that the first lady had taken the children to the

Virginia countryside, Mimi sensed there was something wrong; she shouldn't be there.

Then the president offered to give her a tour of the quarters. In the first lady's bedroom, she wrote in her 2012 autobiography, "He pulled down his pants and then he was above me. He paused briefly when he felt some physical resistance." He was gentler when she told him she was a virgin. Back home soon after, she wondered what she could have done to resist him. "When we were in the bedroom," she wrote, "he had maneuvered me so swiftly and unexpectedly, and with such authority and strength, that short of screaming I doubt if I could have done anything to thwart his intentions."

Mimi's shock and horror soon morphed into "the thrill of being desired. And the fact that I was being desired by the most famous and powerful man in America only amplified my feelings to the point where resistance was out of the question. That's why I didn't say no to the president. It's the best answer I can give. I wouldn't describe what happened that night as making love. But I wouldn't call it nonconsensual, either." It was the beginning of an affair that would last over a year. The president chose Mimi to accompany him on most of his trips, even though she did no work.

Mimi experienced some particularly cruel moments at the hands of the president. When Kennedy instructed her to perform oral sex on Powers, who was sitting on the edge of the pool, she swam up to him and complied. While visiting Bing Crosby's California ranch, Kennedy held out an orange capsule—which Mimi later believed to be poppers, or amyl nitrate—promised it would enhance sex, and asked Mimi to try it. When she refused, he snapped it open under her nose, sending her heart racing and bringing on a raging panic attack. Powers helped calm her as Kennedy had disappeared.

When Mimi returned to college, Kennedy arranged for her to spend some weekends at the White House and got her another internship in the summer of 1963. But by August, she was engaged to a young army reserve officer and stopped sleeping with the president. On the day of Kennedy's assassination, a grieving Mimi told her fiancé about the affair. Hurt, betrayed, but still in love with her, he married her but made her pay every day for betraying him with Kennedy while they were dating. There was no trust in the marriage, just bitterness and pain, and they eventually divorced.

What was in it for the president's women? Jack Kennedy was no Louis XIV, distributing castles, estates, and eye-popping jewels to his mistresses. While his aides paid prostitutes the going rate, women like Diana, Helen, and Mary received no payment. Mimi, a virgin who had practically been raped, came back for more.

Kennedy's women testified to his irresistible charisma, and the glamour and excitement of bedding the most important man in the world. Gunilla von Post wrote, "He cast a spell on people that I've never quite seen before or since . . . He embraced his life with ferocious energy. Jack burned like a brilliant comet in the sky. His grin was incandescent. His eyes were intensely blue, sparkling with joy, a smile that lit up his entire face. He was such a powerful, magnetic man, it was hard to deny my growing attraction to him."

Judith Campbell noticed that he had a knack for seducing people of all ages, male and female. "When he listened, it was as if every nerve and muscle in his whole body was poised at attention . . . When you talked to Jack there was total concentration and absorption. He really wanted to hear what you had to say. He had a habit when he listened of tilting his head slightly toward you, as if to facilitate the process, guarding against the possibility that a word might mischievously try to slip by him."

Mimi Beardsley explained, "He had that politician's gift of making you feel that when you were in his company, you were the most important and interesting person in the world . . . Being with the President and having his undivided attention was like taking this incredibly potent self-esteem drug. And that's a hard habit to kick. Despite the humiliation and uncertainty, I remained enthralled by his charisma and the glamour of traveling with his entourage. My college life of dorms, cafeteria dining, fraternity parties, homework, and moviegoing paled by comparison with Air Force One, Caribbean resorts, the Secret Service, and limos . . . The fact that I was desired by the most famous and powerful man in America merely amplified the thrill. I simply couldn't say no to the President."

While countless women were eager to jump into Kennedy's bed, those who landed there were almost always disappointed. Jackie confessed to her good friend, Dr. Frank Finnerty, that sex with her husband was unsatisfying because "he just goes too fast and falls asleep" and she wondered if she had somehow failed him. She portrayed herself as being "left out" of the sexual experience.

Marilyn Monroe, though hopelessly in love with Jack, lamented to a friend that his sexual performance was horrible. "A minute on and a minute off. Brutal and perfunctory in bed."

"He was in for quantity rather than quality," said his friend George Smathers, with whom Kennedy often engaged in partner swapping. "I don't know how the women ever tolerated it."

Actress Angie Dickinson reportedly said that sex with Kennedy was "the best sixty seconds of my life." Jayne Mansfield told Peter Lawford—who told author Lawrence Quirk—that Jack left something to be desired as a lover, preferring sex while on his back and pressing her to perform oral sex on him. "And once he's done, he's done, it's like you don't exist anymore!"

Judith Campbell, wrote, "When people make love, they should make love to each other. I mention this because, as I was to learn in my relationship with Jack, his attitude was that he was there to be serviced. Partly this was due to his back problem, and partly I think he had been spoiled by women. There is a world of difference between a man who expects to be made love to and two people making love to each other."

Like Roosevelt, Harding, and Wilson before him, Kennedy benefited from the unwritten journalistic rule that no stories of a president's sex life would make the news. This tradition was compounded by the fact that Kennedy served at the height of the Cold War, with emergencies like the Bay of Pigs, the Cuban Missile Crisis, and the building of the Berlin Wall. Diminishing the president's stature would diminish the strength of the entire nation. Journalists frequently saw Kennedy with women not his wife and never reported a word.

The press had protected Kennedy even before he became president. When he ran against Lyndon Johnson for the Democratic nomination in 1960, a Georgetown couple, Leonard and Florence Kater, mailed details of Kennedy's love affair with their former tenant Pamela Turnure to the newspapers. Devout Catholics, they had been disgusted to learn that Kennedy, a married man, had been sneaking into the building. They rigged up a tape recorder to capture sounds of their lovemaking and took pictures of him entering and leaving the apartment. When Kennedy moved into the White House, they protested out front with placards stating that an adulterer lived there. No paper covered the story.

Shortly before his 1961 inauguration, for three days Kennedy reportedly vanished into a Palm Springs vacation cottage with the blond, twenty-nine-year-old actress Angie Dickinson. A *Newsweek* reporter entered the room, saw her stretched out on a bed, and quickly closed the door.

In April 1961, Otto Fuerbringer, the managing editor of *Time* magazine, finished an interview with Kennedy in the White House private quarters and, a few minutes later, returned to retrieve a hat he had left on a chair. He recalled, "There sitting on the sofa was a striking blonde, about thirty-five years old, wearing a short black dress and pearls. Jack handed me my hat, and I left."

In early 1963, a cub reporter for a major newspaper was assigned to patrol the lobby of New York's Carlyle Hotel where President Kennedy was staying. When he saw a top Hollywood star—probably Marilyn Monroe—being hustled up to the president's floor—he told his editor. "No story there" was the reply. Photographs showing a goggle-eyed Kennedy staring at Marilyn's rear end at the "Happy Birthday, Mr. President" event at Madison Square Garden mysteriously disappeared from wire services.

Journalists hoped that staying on good terms with Kennedy would ensure them important scoops and invitations to fabulous White House parties. Not only did they remain silent on his adultery, they went out of their way to portray the Kennedy marriage as idyllic. Reporters and authors often submitted material to him and Bobby for corrections and comments before publication. In some ways, the press were greater prostitutes than the women Kennedy paid for sexual services.

Kennedy was well aware of his invulnerability with the press. "They can't touch me while I'm alive," he boasted to a friend, "and after I'm dead who cares?"

The press protection even extended to Jackie. No photos of her smoking—she had a three-pack-a-day habit—made the newspapers. If her skirt seemed too short in a photo, an artist would make it longer before a paper published it.

Thirty years after the assassination, in an interview with *Washingtonian* magazine, Kennedy's press secretary Pierre Salinger recalled a journalist's question about Kennedy and a woman. "I gave him a 1960s answer, not a 1990s answer. 'Look, he's the president of the United States. He's got to work 14 to 16 hours a day. He's got to run foreign and domestic policy. If he's got time for mistresses after all that, what the hell difference does it make?' The reporter laughed and walked out. That was the end of the story."

Jack's pathological infidelity deeply scarred his marriage. Jackie was trapped; no first lady had ever divorced her husband. To keep scandal from tarnishing the nation, she had to stay. She suffered depression and headaches that were treated by Max Jacobson, Dr. Feelgood, with injections of amphetamines.

While Jackie usually pasted on a smiling face with her husband's women friends, on at least one occasion, she became publicly enraged. Standing in a reception line, her eyes fell on a "blond bimbo" inching her way toward her. Jackie "wheeled around in fury" and scolded one of her husband's aides, "Isn't it bad enough that you solicit this woman for my husband, but then you insult me by asking me to shake her hand!" She managed to quickly compose herself and shake the blond bimbo's hand.

For all her fury and depression about her husband's philandering, Jackie Kennedy had two healthy and rewarding focuses as first lady. The first and foremost was motherhood. Jackie was a devoted mother, keeping her children firmly out of the press and creating a loving, learning environment. She played with them, read to them, insisted they have good manners, and built them their own little zoo on the White House grounds. She created a school on the third floor of the White House where Caroline and John-John were joined by children of White House employees. She told one reporter, "If you bungle raising your children, I don't think whatever else you do matters very much."

Her other focus was redecorating the White House. When the Kennedys moved in, the furnishings were a dumpy mishmash of more than a century of bad taste. Jackie raised funds, hired experts, and tracked down original White House pieces that previous presidents had blithely carted off with them when they left office. She founded the White House Historical Association and the Committee for the Preservation of the White House. Her February 1962 television show giving the viewers a tour of the refurbished White House was watched by 56 million Americans.

Jackie also found solace in punishing her husband in myriad manifestations of passive aggression, taking refuge in wild spending sprees—spending hundreds of thousands of dollars on designer clothing and budget-busting antiques in a year—that sent him into foaming-at-the-mouth rages. He always gave in to her, though. Under the circumstances, he had to.

In addition, she flirted outrageously with male friends in an effort to make her husband jealous. Traphes Bryant wrote, "I remember one particular White House party, Mrs. K. was loaded on champagne and flung her shoes off while dancing under the chandelier in the main lobby . . . Jacqueline seemed to flirt with every guy she danced with—making eyes, throwing her head back love-dovey. All the men danced with her."

One time she commanded Faddle to play tennis with her. When Faddle explained she had no tennis shoes, Jackie made her play on the hot court in bare feet. She knew the value of her style and beauty to her husband's popularity and tortured him with a thousand little cuts by simply not showing up for official events, sometimes at the last minute, embarrassing him deeply. She maintained that she would not be going to Dallas in November 1963 until Texas governor John Connally threw a raging tantrum, insisting he needed her there.

Jackie escaped from the White House at every opportunity, spending many weekends at Glen Ora, an estate an hour west of Washington, where she went riding and fox hunting. In the summer of 1962, she spent three weeks on the Amalfi coast of Italy with her children and her sister, and reportedly had an affair with the wealthy forty-one-year-old Italian industrialist Gianni Agnelli. Newspapers ran photos of the handsome pair joyfully walking through piazzas. Kennedy, alarmed, sent his wife a tersely worded telegram indicating she should be photographed more often with their daughter: "More Caroline, less Agnelli."

During Jack's final sixty-three days of life, he and his wife were apart for forty-two of them. On August 9, 1963, Jackie lost her premature son, Patrick, who survived only thirty-nine hours. Still deeply depressed several weeks later, she accepted an invitation from Greek shipping magnate Aristotle Onassis for an Aegean cruise on his luxurious yacht. Kennedy was aghast; a few years earlier, Onassis had been found guilty of U.S. tax evasion and fined $7 million. How would it look for the grieving first lady to kick up her heels with the playboy tax evader? But Jackie gleefully defied him, arriving in Greece October 3. Her sister Lee, who was having an affair with Onassis, joined her.

But events took a surprising turn when the shipping tycoon started courting the wife of the U.S. president. They flirted and laughed as Lee stewed. Onassis thought Jackie's jewelry was cheap, called Van Cleef & Arpels in Paris, and told them to fly a magnificent piece to the yacht. A few days later, Onassis gave Jackie a diamond-and-ruby necklace that cost $80,000 ($671,000 today). As for Lee, she complained that Onassis had only given her "three dinky little bracelets that Caroline wouldn't wear to her own birthday party." Onassis's friend Constantine Gratsos worried that what had happened on board that yacht would cost a lot more than $80,000. "I kept thinking: this could be the most expensive fuck in the history of the world."

Newspapers around the globe reported on Jackie's disgraceful behavior. Republican National Chairman William E. Miller denounced her "lack of decorum and dignity" carousing at "late night parties in foreign lands." Republican Congressman Oliver Bolton of Ohio condemned the first lady twice on the floor of the House for showing "poor judgment and perhaps impropriety in accepting the lavish hospitality of a man who has defrauded the American public. Why doesn't the first lady see more of her own country instead of gallivanting all over Europe?" Women picketed in front of the White House with signs demanding she return to the U.S. and do her job.

Instead of coming back, however, Jackie added another leg to her journey, visiting Morocco. She finally returned to Washington on October 17. To counter the rumors of problems with their marriage, Jack showed up with their two children to welcome Jackie as she glided off the airplane wearing her new $80,000 necklace.

Jackie would tell her sister Lee when she was upset about her husband's extracurricular activities, and Lee would talk to Jack. He had absolutely no guilt about it. "I love her deeply and have done everything for her," he would say. "I've no feeling of letting her down because I've put her foremost in everything."

According to her friend Dr. Frank Finnerty, Jackie wasn't certain her husband remembered most of his fleeting sex partners. "She was also sure that Jack felt no love or any kind of affection" for these women, he said. Jackie believed "he was just getting rid of some hormonal surge." Jackie said she was helpless to stop her husband's philandering, which was "an intrinsic part of his life," a "vicious trait" that he had "undoubtedly inherited" from his father.

"All Kennedy men are like that," she once told Ted Kennedy's wife, Joan, who was horrified by her own husband's infidelity. "It doesn't mean a thing. You can't let it get to you because you shouldn't take it personally."

In 1962, when a *New York Times* reporter asked her what her husband would do after his presidency, without missing a beat she said, "He'll probably take a job as a headmaster of an exclusive, all-girls prep school."

Still, Jackie considered divorcing her husband once he was out of office. She told U.S. ambassador to the United Nations Adlai Stevenson that she and her sister Lee—unhappily married to a Polish aristocrat—"always talked about divorce as something to look forward to."

And yet her grief was real after the assassination. The photos of her in the bloodstained pink suit on Air Force One, standing next to Lyndon Johnson as he took the oath of office, and her black-draped figure at the funeral suggest stunned disbelief and pain chewing its way through the numbness of shock. Author Truman Capote said, "Their relationship had become an utter farce by the time he became president. I think she fell in love with him again only after the assassination."

Jackie invented the Camelot tale as a gift to her children, the American people, and herself, obliterating adultery, drugs, and lies, creating a new reality—accepted by all—of a brief, shining moment in time with herself as the glorious female lead.

Jackie married Aristotle Onassis in 1968, defying the Kennedy family and the American public who wanted her to remain frozen on the day of the funeral, a beautiful cold statue eternally veiled in black. They soon led separate lives, Onassis dying in 1975. Jackie moved back to New York and became a successful book editor for Doubleday. She enjoyed a relationship with Maurice Tempelsman, her financial adviser, from 1980 until her death from cancer in 1994 at the age of sixty-four. Many Kennedy wives and lovers suffered appalling tragedy, as if infected with a kind of family curse. But Jackie had the strength to pull herself out of the maelstrom and create a new life for herself on her own terms.

10

LYNDON JOHNSON AND HALF THE PEOPLE IN THE WORLD

*W*hile visiting President Lyndon Johnson's ranch in Texas, a female aide was startled in the middle of the night when a man in a nightshirt appeared at the foot of her bed holding a flashlight. She couldn't make out who it was until she heard a familiar Texas drawl. "Move over," the visitor said. "This is your president."

* * *

It is hard for many of us today to understand the attractiveness of Lyndon Johnson to women. When we look at a photo of him as president, we see a rumpled bulldog face, beady, dark eyes, and thinning gray hair. But many women were fascinated by the young Lyndon's dramatic appearance: his coal-black hair and eyebrows and milky white skin. He used his size—six foot four, with long arms and big hands—to dominate other men, standing a bit too close, wrapping his arm around a shoulder, doling out rib-crushing hugs. His appeal lay mostly in his vitality, his energy, an ability to command and entrance no matter how much like a bulldog he grew to resemble. Add to that a spellbinding eloquence that could wrap his listeners into a story and take them wherever Johnson wanted to go.

"It was his animation that made him good-looking," said the sister of one of his long-term mistresses. "He didn't have power, or money, or anything. He just had this personal force—a huge, unique personal force. He just radiated self-confidence." Another recalled, "He had what they call now a charisma. He was dynamic, and he had this piercing look, and he knew exactly where he was going, and what he was going to do next, and he had you sold down the river on whatever he was telling you. And you had no doubts that he was going to do what he said—no doubts at all . . . You felt the power."

It was that personal power that propelled him from a dirt-poor childhood in the hardscrabble Texas hills to the highest office in the land. The Johnsons were a dilapidated family with pretensions of grandeur. His father was a failed businessman and former state representative who drank too much and owed everyone in town money. His mother was a dreamer who read poetry but didn't wash her children's clothing, nor did she always manage to feed her brood of five. The Johnsons were, in short, the town laughingstocks, and it rankled in the breast of little Lyndon, who hated the sneering, the taunts. At the age of ten, hurt and defiant, he told the other boys in the schoolyard, "Someday I'm going to be president of the United States." Naturally, they laughed at him and said they wouldn't vote for him. But most of them probably did.

Lyndon's political career began in 1930 when the twenty-two-year-old attended a political rally for Pat Neff, a former governor running for reelection. When Neff didn't show, Lyndon stepped forward and made a powerful, persuasive speech promoting him. Lyndon could spin a yarn better than anybody. Filled with self-deprecating good ole boy charm, he grabbed listeners by the heartstrings and didn't release them until he was good and ready. A candidate for state legislature in the crowd that night, astonished by Johnson's impromptu speech, hired him to work on his own campaign. A year later, Johnson was hired by newly elected Texas congressman Richard Kleberg as his secretary. Since Kleberg rarely did any work—spending most of his time playing poker, drinking whiskey, and golfing—it was Johnson who tirelessly ran the office and assisted constituents. He soon became known as the most powerful congressional secretary in Washington at the age of twenty-three.

He relied on the same tried-and-true methods to get ahead in Congress as he had in college at Southwest Texas State Normal School, when he had arrived poor and unknown, an utter nobody. He buttered up older female secretaries and the wives of powerful men, complimenting them on their hairstyles and dresses, bursting into rapture at the cakes and pies they brought him. With influential men, he gazed at them in rapt wonder at their wisdom, a "professional son," as some called him. "He would just drink up what they were saying," a friend of his said, "sit at their knees and drink it up, and they would pour out their hearts to him." When the twenty-eight-year-old was elected to Congress in 1937, he played the same role of adoring son with President Roosevelt, who took quite a shine to the young congressman.

With his colleagues, he was a bully, a liar who always had to be the center of attention. His nickname in college was "Bullshit Johnson." "He'd cut your throat to get what he wanted," said an acquaintance. Yet he inspired unswerving loyalty from some. When he arrived in Washington, he had in tow a clique of young men from his Texas university who would have followed him to hell if he'd asked, and he did. He made them work seven days a week, sometimes fourteen or sixteen hours a day, answering every single letter from a constituent the same day it arrived, and paid them a pittance. He even made them take dictation while he sat on the toilet having a bowel movement—an unfortunate habit he continued throughout his life.

FDR's vast new bureaucracies—the Social Security Administration, the Public Works Administration, the Tennessee Valley Authority—meant many thousands of jobs which, in the heart of the Depression, meant food, housing, even life itself. Wheeling, dealing, and forging alliances, Johnson obtained the right to hand out jobs—not great jobs, but any job was manna from heaven in those days: a postal clerk, an elevator operator, a janitor. One recipient said, "Lyndon didn't make you rich, but he got you a job." He built, job by job, a network of support throughout Texas, people who would vote for him, campaign for him, and convince their friends and family members to do the same.

Now that Lyndon was on his way, he needed a charming wife to entertain and socialize with other congressional wives, a woman to continue building that network of support so crucial to politicians. Moreover, he needed a rich wife to fund his campaigns.

He met twenty-two-year-old Lady Bird Taylor, a reporter for the *Daily Texan*, in 1934. Her real name was Claudia, but soon after birth, her African American nurse gazed at her and said, "She's as purty as a lady bird," and the name stuck. Daughter of a wealthy Alabama businessman who had settled in Texas, Lady Bird was five when she lost her mother. She grew up a shy, lonely child, who wandered for hours at a time in nature, particularly enjoying wildflowers, and often disappeared for much of the day with a book. She was not a classic beauty with her long nose and wide mouth, but she had a distinctive attractiveness, with alert, dark eyes under arched black brows, thick, dark hair, and a beautifully shaped face. She paid scant attention to her appearance, wearing dowdy gray clothes and sensible heels, as if she hoped to fade into the background so no one would notice her.

Beneath her fluttering southern belle charm and drab dresses, Bird, as Lyndon usually called her, was shrewd, determined, and ambitious, a proverbial steel magnolia. She had graduated high school at fifteen and received two university degrees in teaching and journalism.

On their first date over breakfast at an Austin café, Lyndon told her he wanted to marry her. "I thought it was some kind of joke," she said. But she was impressed. "I knew I had met something remarkable, but I didn't know quite what . . . I had a queer sort of moth-and-flame feeling." He introduced her to his parents the following day and acted as if they would soon be engaged.

Lyndon pursued Bird with the same relentless drive and ambition he pursued politics, and within two months, she was somewhat surprised to find herself standing with him in front of a justice of the peace, wearing a $2.50 wedding band bought across the street at Sears Roebuck. The next morning, she called a friend and said, "Lyndon and I committed matrimony last night."

The honeymoon lasted only hours. The next day, while visiting a friend, Lyndon rudely told Bird to change her stockings as one had a run in it. It was a sign of things to come. He criticized her frumpy clothes and bought her more fashionable dresses. He made her wear high heels and red lipstick and have her hair and nails done. He insisted she keep her weight down to 113 pounds and, when they were separated for long stretches, as often happened, instructed her to send him the measurements of her waist and hips in every letter. Whatever orders he shouted at her—and there were many—had to be obeyed immediately.

Every evening, Bird laid out his clothes, polished his shoes, filled his cigarette case, and made sure his fountain pens had ink. Every morning she served him breakfast in bed. Her checkbook was available to help him with his next campaign. And when he yelled and shouted at her at polite dinner parties, and other guests winced, the unflappable Bird just smiled, nodded, and did what he asked. His moods swung wildly from high to low and back again, but she was always stable, always calm, always his anchor in the storm. After her husband became a congressman in a 1937 special election, and a senator in 1948, Bird entered the world of competitive political entertaining, where she never said a bad word about anyone, and made them all love her and, by extension, think better of Lyndon. She went behind him with a figurative dustpan and broom, cleaning up the messes he made, comforting the insulted staff, soothing hurt feelings, telling them he didn't mean it, and they should come by for dinner real soon now.

She accepted all of this because, contrary to appearances, she was actually the stronger, Lyndon the weaker. There were days when his nerves and depression were so bad—the Valley of the Black Pig, he came to call it—he could barely get out of bed, and she was there telling him just to put one foot in front of the other. Bird was so strong she didn't mind appearing weak and bullied. It didn't matter. One issue she had not reckoned with when she married him, however, was his rampant infidelity.

His first serious love affair began in 1938, when he took up with twenty-six-year-old Alice Glass, the gorgeous, six-foot-tall, blue-eyed mistress of Charles Marsh, a wealthy newspaper magnate. Marsh, always bouncing around Capitol Hill, was one of those older, powerful men Johnson so expertly cultivated. Johnson met Alice when Marsh invited him and Bird to spend the weekend at Longlea, his Virginia country estate ninety miles outside of Washington. Marsh had built a replica of an eighteenth-century English manor house Alice had admired, setting it on a thousand acres so she wouldn't have to be bothered with hearing the neighbors.

Born and raised in sleepy Marlin, Texas, Alice was a nineteen-year-old secretary in Austin when she met the forty-four-year-old Marsh at a party. They became lovers that night, and he left his wife and three children soon after. A friend said that Marsh "lavished jewels on her—not only a quarter-of-a-million-dollar necklace of perfect emeralds, but earrings of emeralds and diamonds and rubies." Alice's cousin recalled, "The first time she came back to Marlin and walked down the street in her New York clothes and her jewels, women came running out of the shops to stare at her." Another friend said that "when she walked into a restaurant, between those emeralds and her height and that red-gold hair, the place would go completely silent."

"Her blond hair had a red overlay," said Frank Oltorf, a Washington lobbyist. "Usually it was long enough so that she could sit on it, and it shimmered and gleamed like nothing you ever saw . . . There was something about the way she walked and sat that was elegant and aloof. And with her height, and that creamy skin and that incredible hair, she looked like a Viking princess."

"She was a free spirit, very independent, in an era when women weren't that way," said her sister, Mary Louise. She didn't believe in marriage, and she had refused to marry Marsh, even though she had two children while with him, though one, according to Marsh's daughter, had been sired by Alice's interior designer. Outspoken, highly intelligent, and idealistic, she looked up to politicians who tried to help the less fortunate. When she met Johnson, and he regaled her with tales of Texas poverty, and all he was doing to bring jobs and electricity to his district, she thought that she had met a kindred spirit. Looking back, Mary Louise said, "She thought he was a young man who was going to save the world."

Alice also admired what she believed was Johnson's indifference to money. Marsh and his friends almost always spoke of money, how to make it, how to spend it, how to take it from others. "She was just sick of money, money, money," her sister said. We can picture Alice, sitting at her thirty-foot-long dining room table, sipping champagne her butler offered her, as candlelight glinted off those emeralds, just bursting with rage that everyone was discussing a subject as sordid as money.

"Lyndon was the love of Alice's life," Mary Louise said. "My sister was mad for Lyndon—absolutely mad for him." When Marsh was traveling the country to supervise his countless businesses, Lyndon and Alice met in Marsh's Washington, D.C., apartment or at Longlea, where Lyndon repaired on weekends without Bird.

But sometimes Bird was invited. When she was there, Alice Glass's salon of witty, beautiful, rich, and powerful people ignored the lackluster woman sitting in the corner, dark eyes watchful. Alice's cousin Alice Hopkins recalled, "Everybody was trying to be nice to her, but she was just . . . out of place." Even Bird herself agreed. "I remember Alice in a series of long and elegant dresses," she said, "and me in—well, much less elegant."

Did Bird know her husband was having an affair with Alice Glass? Frank Oltorf said, "Oh, I'm sure she did." Alice's sister, Mary Louise, said, "The thing I could never understand was how she stood it. Lyndon would leave her on weekends, weekend after weekend, just leave her home. I wouldn't have stood it for a minute."

While Alice hoped to marry Johnson, they both knew it to be impossible. For one thing, no matter how he treated Bird, he loved her—he absolutely lit up when she entered a room—and needed her as he did no other. Because no other woman could help him get through the Valley of the Black Pig. Surely, he never told Alice Glass about his serious struggles with depression, about those days when he was helpless and trembling in bed with the covers pulled up over his head. He also needed Bird's money for his campaigns—not just her father's money, but the profits she was making on her own. A shrewd businesswoman who counted every penny, she managed three thousand acres of Alabama cotton- and timberland and would, starting in 1943, become immensely wealthy by owning a chain of Texas radio stations. And then there was his political career. It was believed that no divorced man could ever become president, which was Lyndon's lifelong dream.

In late 1939, Charles Marsh discovered the affair and felt doubly betrayed. He had looked on Johnson as a son, had made sure his newspapers wrote glowing articles about him, and had even helped Johnson financially by selling him nineteen acres of prime Austin real estate ripe for development at a below-market price. Marsh yelled and cursed and threw Johnson out. But Johnson came back the next morning and abjectly apologized—we can picture tears glistening in his eyes—and promised to end the relationship. Surprisingly, Marsh forgave him. Marsh's daughter, Antoinette Marsh Haskell, said, "They didn't let her come between them. Men in power like that don't give a damn about women. They were not that important in the end. They treated women like toys. That's just the way it was."

In early 1940, Alice married Charles Marsh but quickly divorced him. The woman who said she didn't believe in marriage ended up marrying six times. "She never got over Lyndon," Alice Hopkins said. After she divorced Marsh, Lyndon visited her again at Longlea. The relationship lasted on and off until the mid-1960s, when he plunged the nation deeper into the Vietnam War. Alice told friends she had burned Johnson's love letters because she didn't want her granddaughter to know she had been to bed with the man responsible for the worst brutalities of the war.

Lyndon's next long-term affair was with a beautiful new California congresswoman, Helen Gahagan Douglas. A Hollywood star and opera singer married to matinee idol Melvyn Douglas, she took up her office in 1944, while her husband was serving in the army. Johnson virtually lived with the tall, curvy blonde, driving with her to work in the morning and walking hand in hand into the Capitol.

It is likely that in 1949 Johnson began an affair with a twenty-four-year-old Texas advertising saleswoman named Madeleine Brown. At least, that is what she later claimed. Brown was a bit of a grifter—in 1989 she was convicted of forging a will. Moreover, she had no love letters from Johnson, had no eyewitnesses who saw them together, and made a good amount of money from the story. But she did have one document no one could explain away.

Cute and petite with dark hair, sparkling, dark eyes, and a dazzling smile, Madeleine claimed she met Johnson, then a powerful senator, at an Austin social event. He pursued her, and they soon found themselves in a hotel bathtub together. "When he closed his eyes and parted my lips with his tongue, I felt as if I were lost in a whirlpool," she wrote in her steamy 1994 tell-all. "With deliberate slowness, he teased and tasted my lips and tongue. Lyndon's lustful kiss blazed through me with the fire of a thousand suns, withering my reserve and melting my resistance . . . He devoured me with a ferocity that turned me into liquid heat. My body simmered from one end to the other. Every inch of my being was eager for his touch."

She continued, "Lyndon was trembling with agonizing anticipation as he rubbed my breasts and began running his hands over the silky terrain of my hips, thighs, and legs. Suddenly he stood up, scooped me into his arms and carried me soaking wet into the bedroom . . . Lyndon was as thrilling in bed as he was in the public forum of politics—energetic, powerful, and commandeering. He explored all the nuances of my body. I felt nothing but wild pleasure as he entered me effortlessly. Together our ecstasy grew like a roaring tide, overpowering us in its intensity until ultimately my moans rose into an ecstatic cry."

According to Brown, one night Johnson showed up at her hotel room with a brown grocery bag that held "a little black whip along with a string of pearls and a funny-looking big peter." Johnson asked, "Madeleine, you ready for something different?" Oh yes, she was. Sadly, Madeleine didn't describe what he did with these items. She wrote that Johnson loved to watch homemade movies of animals mating, and during sex with her he would imitate the animals' bellows. While we might not believe such tales about, say, Dwight Eisenhower, they do have the ring of truth with Lyndon Johnson.

Madeleine claimed that Johnson was the father of her son born in 1950, Steven Brown, and that Johnson paid for her two-bedroom Austin home, maid service, unlimited charge cards, and a new car every two years. Brown claimed she withheld the truth of her son's paternity until she had a heart attack in 1987 and feared she might go to her grave without him knowing. Soon after, Steven Brown filed a $10.5 million patrimony suit against

Johnson's estate but lost the case when he failed to appear in court. He died of cancer in 1990 and left no children upon whom DNA tests could be conducted.

Indeed, the whole story might be suspect except for a letter a Dallas attorney wrote Madeleine Brown soon after Johnson's death in 1973. Jerome Ragsdale promised to "continue with the financial arrangements that Lyndon provided for you and Steve throughout the past." Though Ragsdale was dead by the time Brown first publicly claimed to be Johnson's son in 1987, the letter was genuine, and we can only wonder why the former president of the United States would be making financial arrangements for a woman he had never met and her son.

By 1954, Johnson was having an affair with his secretary, twenty-two-year-old Mary Margaret Wiley, whose desk was right next to his. A meltingly beautiful honey blonde, Mary Margaret was perfectly in tune with Johnson's moods, often knowing what he wanted before he said it. Their closeness during the day extended to after-hours socializing. Naturally, he had to fly his secretary around with him on business trips.

Many speculated that he might divorce Bird, who had given him two daughters, to marry Mary Margaret and have the son he had always longed for. As it happened, in 1962 she married Johnson aide Jack Valenti—later the longtime president of the Motion Picture Association of America. When she had a daughter, Courtenay, a year later, Johnson was so crazy about the curly-haired little girl—he had never shown any extraordinary fondness for his own daughters—that many in the White House assumed he was her father. The crude, foulmouthed president sat in cabinet meetings with the baby on his lap.

At some point in the early years of their marriage, Bird threatened to divorce Johnson if he continued his infidelity, but she soon managed to make peace with it. Perhaps she realized he couldn't stop, and she didn't really want a divorce. Perhaps, too, there was an advantage that Bird was not the sole recipient of her husband's urgent desires. One of the first things she did after their brief honeymoon was to phone her gynecologist for an appointment to make sure she wasn't internally injured.

More than just accepting her husband's other women, Bird went out of her way to be kind to them, complimenting them on their hair and clothing, inviting them to dinner. If Lyndon got out of hand with a woman at a party, she would say gently, "You're wanted over there, Lyndon. You're neglecting some of your friends." She referred to Lucy Mercer Rutherfurd—Franklin Roosevelt's lifelong lover—as nothing more than "a fly on the wedding cake."

On one occasion, a longtime Johnson secretary, Marie Fehmer, accompanied Lady Bird to Johnson's California hotel room, where they found Mary Margaret Wiley's bras and panties strewn around the room. Bird gathered them up in a tidy little heap and "went on her way to be nice" to Mary Margaret, according to Fehmer. On another occasion, when Lady Bird inadvertently opened a box delivered to the Johnson ranch in Texas and found an impossibly tiny lavender bikini, she handed it to her husband and said sweetly, "It must be for one of your lady friends."

In 1974, a year after Lyndon's death, Barbara Walters of the *Today* show asked, "How did you handle your flirt and ladies' man husband?" Bird replied calmly, "Lyndon was a people lover and that certainly did not exclude half the people of the world, women. He got a lot of solace and happiness and inspiration from women." She agreed that Lyndon was "a flirt and a ladies' man."

Then she added, "I hope that I was reasonable. And if all those ladies had some good points that I didn't have, I hope that I had the good sense to try to learn by it."

Though Bird accepted Lyndon's infidelity, voters might not have. In 1939, when his aide Walter Jenkins expressed concern about his playboy reputation, Johnson replied that he paid close attention to constituents' opinions in all matters but two—the car he drove and the women he slept with. He could afford such equanimity. He would be the last U.S. president whose blatant marital infidelities would be concealed by the press. At the time of Jenkins's warning, news organizations had conspired to hide from the American people the fact that their president was a paraplegic and he was sleeping with his secretary. The affairs of a young Texas congressman would have been far less interesting.

Nor was the press remotely interested in Johnson's public urination. "He would piss in the parking lot of the House Office Building," said Wingate Lucas, a representative from Fort Worth. "Well, a lot of fellows did that. I did it. But the rest of us would try to hide behind a car or something. He just didn't care if someone noticed him." Lucas recalled one occasion where Johnson and some men were walking across the parking lot with female secretaries behind them, and "he just stopped and began to take a piss right in front of them." Perhaps it was Johnson's pride in the size of his member that caused such behavior. Lucas recalled, "In the men's bathrooms in the House Office Building, if a colleague came in, Johnson, after he finished urinating, would wave his penis and ask, 'Have you ever seen anything as big as this?'"

In 1948, Johnson became a senator after having, evidently, stuffed the ballot boxes in the highly contested Democratic primary. He became Senate majority whip in 1951, Senate minority leader in 1953, and, when the Democrats returned to a majority in the Senate in 1955, majority leader. Johnson was, quite possibly, the most powerful Senate majority leader ever. Perhaps he learned a lesson from FBI director J. Edgar Hoover, a good friend, who had files on every politician in Washington, D.C. Johnson, too, accumulated files on all his fellow senators. One Johnson biographer wrote, "He could get up every day and learn what their fears, their desires, their wishes, their wants were, and he could then manipulate, dominate, persuade and cajole them."

Johnson's tactics to persuade a senator to vote yea or nay on a bill came to be called "the Treatment." It involved Johnson dominating with his height, leaning over his victim and causing him to lean backward as their noses almost touched. A colleague of Johnson's described it as "an incredible blend of badgering, cajolery, reminders of past favors, promises of future favors, predictions of gloom if something doesn't happen. When that man started to work on you, all of a sudden, you just felt that you were standing under a waterfall and the stuff was pouring on you."

According to two journalists, "The Treatment could last ten minutes or four hours. It came, enveloping its target, at the Johnson Ranch swimming pool, in one of Johnson's offices, in the Senate cloakroom, on the floor of the Senate itself—wherever Johnson might find a fellow Senator within his reach. Its tone could be supplication, accusation, cajolery, exuberance, scorn, tears, complaint and the hint of threat. It was all of these together. It ran the gamut of human emotions. Its velocity was breathtaking, and it was all in one direction . . . The Treatment was an almost hypnotic experience and rendered the target stunned and helpless." Harvard historian Arthur Schlesinger agreed. "After nearly two hours of hypnosis," he wrote about a 1956 meeting with Johnson, "I staggered away in a condition of exhaustion."

Johnson had hoped to win the Democratic nomination for president in 1960 but saw it going to John F. Kennedy instead. When Kennedy—a Catholic from Massachusetts—offered Johnson the vice presidential slot, it was to balance out the ticket. Johnson was a southerner, a Protestant. Kennedy told his aides that Johnson could deliver the South and take "the Catholic flavor off me." Johnson also boasted far more political experience. He was the second most powerful man in the country after President Eisenhower, having served twenty-three years in Congress, nine of them as a Senate leader. Kennedy had less than half the experience, and none of it in leadership.

There was another huge advantage to having Johnson as vice president. It was a position of no power—other than breaking ties in Senate votes and doing whatever errands the president assigned him. And Kennedy wanted to neutralize Johnson's power in Washington. He could be a formidable enemy in the Senate if he didn't agree with the president. By offering Johnson the position, Kennedy could, in one move, both deliver the South and take this powerful piece off the political chessboard.

Johnson knew he would not be electable in eight years and might not even be alive. Though only fifty-two, he looked much older. It is hard to believe that he was only nine years Kennedy's senior. Johnson had smoked a hundred cigarettes a day until his 1955 heart attack and knew he could quite possibly be living on borrowed time. But did he want to lose his Senate position for a job that John Nance Garner, FDR's unhappy vice president from 1933 to 1941, called "not worth a bucket of warm piss"? The nation's first vice president, John Adams, wrote his wife, "My country in its wisdom has contrived for me the most insignificant office that ever the invention of man contrived or his imagination conceived."

Johnson decided he did. "I looked it up," Johnson told journalist Clare Boothe Luce. "One out of every four presidents has died in office. I'm a gamblin' man, darlin', and this is the only chance I got." Johnson also knew what many in Washington did not. That Kennedy was terribly sick, racked with pain from Addison's disease, a potentially fatal illness. "Here was a young whippersnapper," he said of Kennedy, "malaria-ridden and yellah, sickly, sickly . . . Now I admit that he had a good sense of humor and he looked awfully good on that goddamn television screen, and through it all he was a pretty decent fellow, but his growing hold on the American people was simply a mystery to me."

Kennedy, who would have hated to see Johnson succeed him, told his aide Kenny O'Donnell, "I'm forty-three years old. I'm not going to die in office. So the vice-presidency doesn't mean anything."

It was a union of opposites. Kennedy was four inches shorter, leaner, graceful, a handsome man who listened intently, his few words carefully chosen with a clipped Boston accent. Johnson was huge, lumbering, crude, and grizzled; he could spin out a story for hours in his Texas drawl, and the minute someone else began to tell a story he would fall sound asleep. Johnson called Kennedy "sonny boy" and his brother Bobby—whom he despised—"that little shitass." The Kennedy circle called Lyndon and Lady Bird "Uncle Cornpone and his Little Pork Chop." Kennedy thought Johnson was "uncouth and somewhat of an oaf," but told his aides to "literally kiss his ass from one end of Washington to the other" because he was a "very insecure, sensitive man with a huge ego." The relationship was to be one of stiff formality and elaborate courtesy.

Given Johnson's strong support of civil rights, Kennedy appointed him chairman of the President's Committee on Equal

Employment Opportunity. He also became chairman of the National Aeronautics and Space Council, where he helped select Houston for the new $60 million NASA command center, which would be renamed in his honor after his death. But overall, Lyndon's years as vice president were the unhappiest of his life. Kennedy sent him on ridiculous assignments, such as posing with Miss Muffin at the National Retail Bakers Association. To get him out of Washington, Kennedy arranged for him to visit thirty-three countries where he made one hundred and fifty speeches. Johnson saw it as demeaning busywork to keep him away from the seat of power. A colleague called him "thoroughly, visibly and persistently miserable." He was a "frustrated force of nature," said journalist Joe Alsop. His vice presidency was "gilded impotence," crowed that little shitass Bobby.

"I can't stand Johnson's long face," Kennedy told his friend Florida senator George Smathers. "He just comes in with his face all screwed up, never says anything. He looks so sad." Whenever Johnson was asked his opinion, he would say firmly, "I agree with the president." In February 1963, *Time* magazine ran a story on Johnson titled "Seen, Not Heard." "Power has slipped from his grasp," the article stated. At White House meetings, "He is free to speak up, but nobody really has to heed him anymore." Many people felt sorry for him. Harry McPherson, general counsel of the Democratic Policy Committee, recalled, "It was so moving to think of this massive figure, reduced in his eyes and the eyes of others." Sometimes Johnson was so depressed he would go to his Texas ranch and pull the covers over his head.

The Kennedys and their privileged friends laughed at Johnson's Texan accent, his dirt-poor beginnings, and just about everything else about him. The only one of them Johnson liked was Jackie, who "was always nicer to me than anybody in the Kennedy family," he said. "She just made me feel like I was a human be-ing." As for the rest of the snotty lot, Johnson made fun of them right back, telling the majority leader secretary Bobby Baker, "All those Bostons and Harvards . . . didn't know any more about Cap-itol Hill than an old maid does about fuckin'."

For Bird, however, the years of her husband's vice presidency were perhaps the happiest of her life. For one thing, she loved the trips to foreign countries as she had never had the opportunity to travel much before. For another, she delighted in interacting with the press and the public. When Jackie was punishing Kennedy for his infidelity by not showing up at an official event—usually once a week—Bird graciously stepped in with a genuine smile. Jackie told Johnson how much she appreciated Lady Bird's "willingness to assume every burden. She assumed so many for me."

By August 1963, Johnson was wondering if he should even stay on Kennedy's ticket for the 1964 election. Maybe he should retire from politics and live at his ranch, away from Kennedy's snobbery, condescension, and demeaning errands. Then, on No-vember 22, 1963, everything changed during a motorcade ride in Dallas. Suddenly Johnson was president. In the midst of national chaos, Johnson stepped into the role with dignity and somber leadership. He "looked carved in bronze those hours," Lady Bird recalled. "Very stern and very grave." Kennedy's secretary of ag-riculture, Orville Freeman, said, "The frustration seemed gone, he seemed relaxed. The power, the confidence, the assurance of Majority Leader Johnson seemed to be there."

It is an interesting footnote to history that the Constitution makes no provision for what to call a vice president who succeeds a president who dies in office. The first president to die in office was sixty-eight-year-old William Henry Harrison in 1841 from pneumonia contracted during his cold, wet inaugural a month earlier. All agreed that Vice President John Tyler would assume the president's duties, as mandated in the Constitution, but no one knew if he should take the oath of office and become president. Would the Founders have agreed to someone bearing the title of president without having being elected? A son of one of those Founders, former president John Quincy Adams, who hated Tyler, wanted to call him "Mr. Vice-President Acting as President." Many people called him "His Accidency." Tyler insisted on taking the oath and becoming president, a precedent that resulted in the orderly transfer of power on future such occasions.

Under the best of circumstances, the Kennedys would have been a difficult act to follow. But as "Accidencies," the Johnsons had a delicate balancing act with a nation in deep mourning. Lyndon had to show he was following Kennedy's vision for the nation while demonstrating his own able leadership. A week after the assassination, he issued an executive order to rename NASA's Apollo Launch Operations Center and the NASA/Air Force Cape Canaveral launch facilities as the John F. Kennedy Space Center. He pushed hard for Kennedy's Civil Rights Act— which ultimately became law in 1964—against southern politicians vehemently opposed to it by insisting that its passage would be the best way to honor Kennedy's memory. He asked Kennedy's cabinet members to remain in office and even kept that little shit-ass Bobby as attorney general.

Many Kennedy appointees left in the first months, however, unable to stand the contrast of Kennedy elegance with Johnsonian crudity. The new president farted so much his dogs ran under the furniture to hide. If he didn't like his food, he would spit it out—on the plate of the person sitting next to him. He threatened his own Secret Service agents, saying, "If you don't get away from me, I'm gonna shoot out your tires." His language was often crude, redolent of Texas country sayings. For instance, when someone pressed him to fire J. Edgar Hoover, Johnson replied, "If you've got a skunk around, it's better to have him inside the tent pissing out than outside the tent pissing in." Looking out his window, "It's raining as hard as a cat pissing on a flat rock." And, regarding a Republican senator's speech, he scoffed, "Making a speech on economics is a lot like pissing down your leg. It may seem hot to you, but it never does to anyone else." Camelot it was not.

But the public didn't see this side of Johnson. They saw a noble, skilled politician, unexpectedly president under the most tragic circumstances, rising to the position while following in the footsteps of their martyred leader. After only two months in office, Johnson had an 80 percent approval rating. In 1964, he signed legislation for the Civil Rights Act and the largest reduction of income taxes in the nation's history. Johnson was overwhelmingly elected president in November, receiving 486 electoral votes compared to his Republican opponent's 52, a satisfying confirmation of his leadership.

As for Bird, she knew she could never compete with Jackie's beauty and style and didn't even try. It would be months after becoming first lady before she even bought new clothes. Though Bird was trim and attractive, she was seventeen years older than her predecessor, several inches shorter, and lacked her stunning wide-eyed beauty. When a friend commiserated with her that she would inevitably be compared with Jackie, Bird replied in surprise, "Don't feel sorry for me. I still have my Lyndon."

Lady Bird Johnson offered something far more compelling than Hollywood looks: her approach to the job. A first lady, she stated, should always be available to the press and public and never lie. She instructed her press secretary to reach out to journalists, to befriend and cultivate them in the hopes of positive coverage that would reflect well on her husband's administration. Jackie, on the other hand, had despised reporters as threatening her beloved privacy. She had told her press secretary to keep them away with any lie or excuse possible.

As first lady, Lady Bird initiated a program to beautify Washington, D.C., which Jack Kennedy had jokingly called "a city of Southern efficiency and Northern charm." She created the Society for a More Beautiful National Capital, which planted millions of flowers, many of them along roadways around the city. "Where flowers bloom, so does hope," she said. She pushed for the Highway Beautification Act, which limited unsightly billboards across the country and planted wildflowers along highways. Those flowers we see blooming today on the roadside are there because of Bird Johnson's love of nature.

In the #MeToo era, Lyndon Johnson's treatment of female employees and reporters would make us all cringe and beat a path for HR or the nearest lawyer. Johnson let it be known that he only wanted to hire women with "good behinds" so he could "enjoy" their rear ends as they left his office. Calling all his female staffers "honey," he instructed them to get their "hair fixed real pretty" and "get perfumed up." He gave them expensive jewelry and high-heeled shoes and stole kisses.

His ultimate compliment was to tell a woman, "You're just as pretty as a polecat," which must have puzzled many, especially because it was the same thing he told his dogs. Dog keeper Traphes Bryant recalled, "At White House events, he would fix his eye on an attractive woman, cry, 'Come over here! You're the prettiest little thing I ever saw!' and invite them into a private room where they could have a 'serious conversation.'"

One day Johnson told Bryant, "I can't help it. I put a high

mark on beauty. I can't stand an ugly woman around or a fat one who looks like a cow that's gonna step on her own udder."

His bad behavior went beyond crude flirtation. According to some reports, he was having affairs with four of his six White House secretaries. Before he hired one, he would ask around to determine, "Does she shuck her drawers?" Lady Bird walked into the Oval Office one day to find him having sex with a secretary on a couch and quietly walked back out. After that, the president had a buzzer system installed. The Secret Service was to buzz him when the first lady was on her way so he could pull up his pants before she arrived. His official diary records dozens of forty-five-minute sessions in the Oval Office with only one woman present, many of them with a *Washington Star* reporter. He enjoyed numerous evening trysts on the presidential yacht, the *Sequoia*. On Air Force One, he would lock himself in his private compartment with a secretary, even with his wife aboard.

Naturally, the Washington press knew. In 2012, Hal Wingo, who had been a reporter for *Life* fifty years earlier, recalled spending New Year's Eve 1963 with the newly inaugurated Lyndon Johnson and a group of other reporters. Johnson put his hand on Wingo's knee and said, "One more thing, boys. You may see me coming in and out of a few women's bedrooms while I am in the White House, but just remember, that is none of your business." They remembered, and not a peep made it into the papers.

"I've had more women by accident than Kennedy ever had on purpose," Johnson often bragged to his friends. But there was one difference between these two philandering presidents. Most of Kennedy's women were disposable. He used them, often without even getting their names, and tossed them aside. Lyndon formed lasting relationships and truly cared about his women. And, despite his appalling behavior with female staff, he instructed all his cabinet members to promote fifty women each. He made many women ambassadors.

Johnson's domestic accomplishments were significant. He signed into law legislation creating Medicare and Medicaid, the Head Start program, the Civil Rights Act, the Voting Rights Act, and the National Endowment for the Arts. He supported the space program, declared a "War on Poverty," and established several programs to help the disadvantaged. "Our chief weapons," he said, "will be better schools, and better health, and better homes, and better training, and better job opportunities to help more Americans, and especially young Americans, escape from squalor and misery and unemployment." Decrying the Ku Klux Klan as a "hooded society of bigots," he was the first president to arrest and prosecute members of the Klan since Ulysses S. Grant ninety-three years earlier. Author Robert Gilbert wrote that Johnson's national policies were "perhaps as extraordinary as [those] of Franklin D. Roosevelt, making him one of the most effective legislative leaders in American history."

But the war in Vietnam would tarnish his legacy beyond repair. Casualties mounted—by 1967 more than seventy thousand Americans had been killed or wounded—and U.S. involvement in the conflict became immensely unpopular. Johnson lied to the press about what was going on, and reporters on the ground in Vietnam pointed out his "credibility gap." His approval ratings tanked. Anti-war protests started up all over the country—one involved one hundred thousand people at the Pentagon. Whenever Johnson left the White House, he was met with chants of "Hey, hey, LBJ, how many kids did you kill today?"

Johnson was baffled about Vietnam. Should the U.S. withdraw and let the Communists take over Southeast Asia? Or should he stick it out, despite the high cost, and beat them back? He told his press secretary Bill Moyers that he was accustomed to looking "for the light at the end of the tunnel." But in this case, "Hell, we don't even have a tunnel; we don't even know where the tunnel is." The Valley of the Black Pig returned. Many days the president stayed in bed, Bird at his side, coaxing him to eat something from his tray. Only she could cheer him, cajole him, inspire him to stand up and "put one foot in front of the other."

On other occasions he was paranoid, accusing his staff of being in the pay of Communists or Kennedys, accusing them of treason. One day, when reporters bombarded him with questions about why he was intensifying the American commitment in Vietnam, Johnson pulled out his eight-and-a-half-inch penis, waved it at the stunned journalists, and shouted, "This is why!" Which was as good an explanation as any. Not a word about this unusual response made it into the papers.

Finally, Johnson decided not to run for a second full term. "I tried to make it possible for every child of every color to grow up in a nice house, eat a solid breakfast, to attend a decent school and to get a good and lasting job," he told an aide. "But look what I got instead . . . Young people leaving the university, marching in the streets . . . They shot me down. The only difference between the Kennedy assassination and mine is that I am still alive and feeling it."

After retirement from a political career that had lasted thirty-nine years, Johnson grew restless and frustrated. He went back to his five-pack-a-day smoking habit, gained weight, and drank too much. In 1972, he had another heart attack. His heart was so damaged the nation's top heart specialist refused to perform surgery. On the afternoon of January 22, 1973, Johnson felt another heart attack coming on. Bird was out of the house, so he called the Secret Service. They found him moments later, dead at sixty-four, still gripping the phone.

Lady Bird lived thirty-four years after his death. She traveled a great deal, served on various boards, including that of the National Park Service, and became closer to her daughters and grandchildren. She died in 2007 at the age of ninety-four.

The marriage of Lyndon and Lady Bird was an odd love story. Toward the end of Johnson's life, when a friend reminded him that the best thing he ever did was marry Bird, he replied not a day passed that he did not think of that.

Years after Johnson's death, Bird said, "Lyndon pushed me, he drove me, at times he humiliated me, but he made me become someone bigger and better than I would have been." Her calm acceptance of his infidelities was not because she was weak, but because she was strong. As she explained, "I had a great love affair. No matter what, I knew he loved me best."

11

GARY HART AND THE MONKEY BUSINESS THAT CHANGED EVERYTHING

*I*n the first part of 1987, Senator Gary Hart of Colorado was the top contender early in the presidential race, crushing all other candidates for the Democratic nomination by double digits and boasting a similar lead over the presumed Republican candidate, Vice President George H. W. Bush. Widely acknowledged as having the finest political mind in the nation, Hart was so confident of his ascent to the White House, he had already prepared a detailed eight-year action plan.

Yet Hart had a blind spot. He was locked into the JFK-era mentality that a politician's private life had nothing to do with his governing ability. No self-respecting journalist would stoop to cover it, and no reputable news organization would think of publishing it. But Gary Hart learned the hard way that times had changed. After Hart was eviscerated, all other politicians knew they had to take precautions.

★ ★ ★

At 8:40 p.m. on Saturday, May 2, 1987, fifty-year-old Gary Hart steered his date, twenty-nine-year-old sometime model and full-time pharmaceutical rep Donna Rice, out of his Capitol Hill townhome toward his car. They would meet another couple for dinner: his campaign aide, Bill Broadhurst, and Rice's friend, Lynn Armandt.

Though married for twenty-nine years, Hart—with the tawny mane, blue-gray eyes, and chiseled good looks of the Kennedys—had never let that stop him as far as women were concerned. People in Washington political and society circles were well aware of his reputation as a ladies' man.

Hart had connected with the leggy blonde a month earlier when he and Bill Broadhurst spent a weekend in Miami to relax a bit before they officially announced the campaign two weeks later. One evening, Donna Rice and some friends left a disco and strolled along the piers, admiring the yachts. She noticed Gary Hart on an eighty-three-foot chartered yacht called *Monkey Business*, greeted him, and reminded him that they had met at a New Year's Eve party at the Aspen home of singer Don Henley, whom Rice had been dating. Hart invited Rice and Armandt to join him the next day on a cruise to the isle of Bimini, fifty-seven miles away, where Bill Broadhurst would pick up his own yacht from a repair company. They would be back by nightfall. Under a blue sky, the four enjoyed the cruise and, upon landing in Bimini, Armandt took a picture of Hart, wearing a *Monkey Business* T-shirt, sitting against a piling, a smiling Rice in his lap.

But they soon discovered that Broadhurst could not get his vessel out of customs as the office had closed for the day; they would have to wait until it opened the following morning. Later,

Hart and Rice would claim the women had spent the night on the *Monkey Business*, and the men had slept on Broadhurst's yacht. Hart's friend Armandt, in an article for *People* magazine, would claim she woke up in the middle of the night to find that Donna had vanished, and she assumed she was with Hart on the other boat. After the cruise, Hart and Rice spoke frequently, trying to meet up again, and finally arranged to do so in Washington, D.C., the first weekend in May.

Now, as Hart and Rice left his town house and strode toward his car, the senator noticed something strange. On a warm May night, there was a man wearing dark sunglasses and a hooded parka standing in front of Hart's house. Another man, in a jogging suit, was periodically running up and down the block. Fearing something amiss, Hart ditched his dinner plans and guided Rice back inside, where they peered out the windows.

Hart was right to be alarmed. The five men in front of his home were reporters from the *Miami Herald*. The previous Monday, one of them, Tom Fiedler, had received a call from a woman who refused to identify herself, claiming to have proof that Gary Hart was having an affair with a friend of hers. Fiedler had written a story on rumors of Hart's infidelity, which appeared that morning with the headline "Sex Lives Become an Issue for Presidential Hopefuls." In his article, Fiedler reported that as Hart stood in the aisle of his press plane, reporters peppered him with questions about his rumored love affairs. "Anybody want to talk about ideas?" Hart had asked. They didn't.

The tipster on the phone, who had seen Fiedler's story, told him about two women she refused to name who had been on Hart's cruise to Bimini. She told him about numerous calls Hart had made to the blonde, who was flying to Washington on Friday to spend the weekend with him at his home. Fiedler mulled over the issue. No news organization had ever undertaken a stakeout of a presidential candidate's home to sniff out a sexual affair. The sex, he decided, wasn't important. But if a leading presidential candidate was a liar and a hypocrite, voters should know. Only two weeks earlier, Hart had promised to hold himself to the "very highest possible standards of integrity and ethics." Even though Hart had been talking about integrity in public office—contrasting himself with corrupt Reagan administration officials then embroiled in the Iran-Contra Affair—could the senator claim to be an ethical leader if he lied not only to his wife but to the American public?

Given the hypocrisy angle, Fiedler decided to pursue the story. He assigned a reporter, Jim McGee, to get on the Friday flight that Hart's as-yet-unnamed girlfriend was taking from Miami and stake out the senator's house. The following morning, McGee called in that Hart had left the house the evening before with the blonde, returned two hours later with another couple—evidently after eating dinner out—and no one had left the house all night. Fiedler himself got on a plane and assigned a photographer and editor to meet him near Hart's home.

Whatever misgivings Fiedler had on the plane vanished when he read an advance copy of the *New York Times* set to publish Monday, May 3, provided as a courtesy to other major news organizations. When *Times* reporter E. J. Dionne had pressed Hart on rumors of his infidelities, Hart had snapped, "Follow me around. I don't care. I'm serious. If anybody wants to put a tail on me, go ahead. They'd be very bored."

Hart had *invited* the press to do exactly what Fiedler and his team were doing.

Peering out from his town house at the men below, Hart considered calling the police but thought it would sound stupid to complain that people were standing in front of his home. Instead, he called Broadhurst, who brought dinner over with Armandt and discussed strategy. According to Armandt's subsequent account of that evening in *People*, everyone agreed to deny that Rice had spent the night there. They would say they were planning to talk about possible campaign jobs for the women over dinner. Broadhurst took the two women out the back door and departed.

Angry now, Hart put on a white sweatshirt with a hoodie and got into his car, hoping the reporters would follow him, which they did. When he wrote down the license number of the reporters' car, they realized there was no point in evasion anymore. They trailed him down an alley between the rows of town houses and saw him leaning against a brick wall, sulkily waiting.

"Good evening, Senator," McGee began, "I'm a reporter from the *Miami Herald*. We'd like to talk to you." He then asked about the young woman in Hart's house. Hart denied there was a woman in his house. When McGee asked him about his relationship with the woman, Hart denied that, too. McGee asked about all the phone calls he had made to the woman. Hart claimed they involved discussions about fundraising. When McGee pointed out that they had seen Hart and the woman enter the town house earlier, Hart declared he was being set up.

The reporters continued to pepper Hart with questions about his blond companion, questions he answered evasively. He didn't remember any yachting trip in Miami. Then Fiedler asked, "Have you had sex with the woman in the town house?"

Hart replied, "The answer is no. I'm not going to get into all that."

He walked toward his home and, as the photographer started taking pictures, he spun around to face them, resulting in an unfortunate photo: the leading presidential contender in a hoodie, cornered, guilty, turning away. Hart would later say that he knew, at that moment, something had irrevocably changed, and he felt nothing so much as sadness. The old rules no longer applied. The mainstream media had, at that moment, gone tabloid. A door sealed for nine decades had opened, and he was the first person to hurtle through into the vicious howling maws of the press.

Blazing across the Monday edition of the *Herald* was the headline "Miami Woman Is Linked to Hart" with the photo of Hart in his hoodie. The same morning, the *Times* ran the E. J. Dionne interview with Hart's taunting dare to follow him around.

The *Herald* piece began: "Gary Hart, the Democratic presidential candidate who has dismissed allegations of womanizing, spent Friday night and most of Saturday in his Capitol Hill townhouse with a young woman who flew from Miami to meet him," adding "Hart has denied any impropriety." The article stated that *Herald* reporters had witnessed Hart and the blonde leave his house, return two hours later, and not reemerge until the following evening.

The Hart campaign fought back. Broadhurst claimed to have been in the house Friday night with Armandt and to have taken the two women out the back door to the alley around midnight. They spent the night in his home in spare bedrooms, he said. They returned to the Hart house Saturday evening by the alley door. The *Herald* reporters admitted they had only watched the front door.

With reporters thronging his town house, Hart issued a statement.

Recent accusations about Senator Hart's personal life are preposterous and inaccurate in their entirety. They have taken a casual acquaintance and a simple dinner with three friends and political supporters and attempted to make a story where there is none. The system, when reduced to hiding in bushes, peaking in windows, and personal harassment, has clearly run amok. Senator Hart accepts the scrutiny that comes with his leadership role in the Democratic Party and the country. But scrutiny and questions of character are one thing; character assassinations are entirely another. Those who cover politics have some duty of self-restraint; here the boundaries of journalistic ethics have clearly been crossed.

On Monday, Rice was devastated to learn that her name had been leaked to the press. She gave a hasty press conference in which she denied having a sexual relationship with Hart.

Meanwhile, at the *Washington Post*, the reporter covering the Hart campaign, Paul Taylor, met with editor Ben Bradlee and others to discuss a question that had, in their lifetimes, never been considered by a major newspaper. Taylor, in his own book about the 1988 campaign, *See How They Run: Electing the President in an Age of Mediaocracy*, summed it up as follows:

If a candidate for president is believed to be a womanizer but there's no suggestion that his sexual activities have ever interfered with his public duties, is it even worth investigating, much less publishing? Is there a statute of limitations, or is screwing around in the past tense just as newsworthy as in the present? Is a series of one-night stands more reportable than a single long-term extramarital affair? Does it matter if a candidate has an open-marriage understanding with his spouse?

Is Hart a special case, or if we begin looking into his mating habits, must we do the same with everyone else running for president?

Bradlee, who had known of JFK's countless affairs, including one with Bradlee's own sister-in-law, Mary Meyer, and never written a word about them, decided that times had changed. Hart's sex life had already become a major issue in his campaign for president. The *Post* would cover it. News organizations across the country followed suit.

At a news conference in New Hampshire, Hart said that a man's character should be measured by his fifteen years of public service, not by a single weekend.

The *Washington Post*'s Paul Taylor asked him what later became known as "the Question." "Senator," he began, "in your remarks yesterday you raised the issue of morality, and you raised the issue of truthfulness. Let me ask you what you mean when you talk about morality, and let me be very specific. I have a series of questions about it. When you said you did nothing immoral, did you mean that you had no sexual relationship with Donna Rice last weekend or at any other time that you were with her?"

"That is correct. That's correct," Hart replied.

"Do you believe that adultery is immoral?

"Yes."

"Have you ever committed adultery?" Those in the room couldn't believe what Taylor had just asked. No reporter had ever asked a presidential candidate anything like that. Seconds ticked by like hours.

Finally, Hart said, "Ahhh, I do not think that's a fair question."

"Have you ever committed adultery?" Taylor persisted.

"I do not know—I'm not going to get into a theological definition of what constitutes adultery. In some people's minds, it's people being married and having relationships with other people, so . . ."

"Can I ask you," Taylor pressed, "whether you and your wife have an understanding about whether or not you can have relationships, you can have sexual encounters with—"

"My inclination is to say no, you can't ask me that question. But the answer is no, we don't have any such understanding. We have an understanding of faithfulness, fidelity, and loyalty."

Hart then jumped into a supporter's car and barreled out of there.

After the fiasco of the New Hampshire press conference, Hart learned there was a second woman, a Washington resident, who had confirmed an affair with him. He knew his campaign would tank under another such story. On May 8, just five days after the Donna Rice story broke, he suspended his campaign.

On *Nightline* in September, Hart, interviewed by Ted Koppel, was the first politician to admit on national television that he had committed adultery. But he wouldn't say if it had been with Donna Rice.

"The question should have never been asked," he said, "and I shouldn't have to answer it."

Despite the negative coverage, most Americans didn't care about Hart's adultery. According to a *Time* magazine poll taken at the time, 67 percent disapproved of the press reporting on a candidate's sex life, and 60 percent believed that Hart's relationship with Rice was irrelevant to the presidency. If he had emulated the actions of Alexander Hamilton or Grover Cleveland and admitted his mistakes, he could have remained in the race and possibly become the Democratic nominee. But Hart refused to apologize for what he vehemently believed was nobody's damned business but his and his wife's. His anger seemed like arrogance to many, and his obfuscation was just plain irritating. His haughty, holier-than-thou lectures on responsible journalism offended voters when he was the one caught cheating on his wife. How could they forgive him if he didn't confess, didn't apologize? It was like sitting in a theater, watching the wrong ending to a play. It was unsatisfying. The play's flawed hero—Hart—had proved to be unlikable, stony, with no desire for redemption.

Moreover, the American public didn't like being lied to. What was a fifty-year-old man doing spending the night on a boat on an island with a twenty-nine-year-old blonde? Why did he spend the weekend with her? Did he really expect them to believe they were discussing fundraising all that time before she had left through the back alley? Not bloody likely. And why did these meetings occur when his wife was thousands of miles away, back at the ranch? The American people might be able to embrace adulterers, but not liars and hypocrites. Soon after the story came out, *Time* magazine conducted a poll asking Americans what they disliked more in a politician: engaging in extramarital sex or lying to the public. Sixty-nine percent responded that they disliked being lied to, while only 7 percent said they minded the extramarital sex more.

With Hart's affair the biggest story in the country, Lynn Armandt decided to cash in. She sold the iconic photo of Donna Rice sitting on Hart's lap to the *National Enquirer* for $75,000—it made the cover and would define him the rest of his life—and sold her story to *People* magazine for $150,000. Donna Rice lost her job and turned down a million-dollar offer to pose nude for *Playboy*.

In December, Hart returned to the race, hoping the scandal had died down. It hadn't. He was fodder for raunchy late-night television jokes. *Late Night* host David Letterman quipped, "In, out, in, out, isn't that what got him in trouble in the first place?" Another popular joke was: "Who do you want to be president? Answer: In my heart I want Bush, but in my bush I want Hart." Issues of character—a candidate's sex life—were suddenly fair game for journalists and the public alike. Hart's results were so bad in New Hampshire and on Super Tuesday, he withdrew from the race.

It is no wonder that Hart was caught completely unawares by the full-scale press assault. After all, it had been 103 years since journalists tore into a presidential candidate—Grover Cleveland—for sexual wrongdoing. What happened? By 1987, the history of political sex scandal coverage had come full circle: from the muckraking rags of the eighteenth and nineteenth centuries screaming out headlines about Hamilton's adultery, Thomas Jefferson's enslaved mistress, and Grover Cleveland's illegitimate child, to the dignified, sedate press of the first decades of the twentieth century, right back into shrill muckraking.

Several factors contributed to the profound shift. For one thing, social mores had changed by the late eighties. The *Mad Men* era—when chain-smoking executives slapped their secretaries on the butt and enjoyed three-martini lunches—was over. Adultery, which had been seen as men's prerogative for centuries, was less tolerated. For another thing, high political office was no longer a source of awe so much as it was of disgust due to the government's lies and policies concerning the Vietnam War and the resulting carnage.

In 1969, journalists who protected the bad behavior of the

Kennedy men had no choice but to report Teddy Kennedy's catastrophic car accident in Chappaquiddick. The drunken Massachusetts senator had careened off a bridge, swum to safety, and pretended it never happened while his female companion, a twenty-nine-year-old campaign worker named Mary Jo Kopechne, trapped in the car, slowly drowned over a period of several hours.

Then there was journalistic guilt for not reporting something they probably should have, something which may have saved the young woman's life. Only a few months before Chappaquiddick, Teddy Kennedy had staggered onto a plane full of reporters in Anchorage, Alaska, clearly intoxicated and swigging from a silver flask. He threw a dinner roll at a network correspondent and tossed a pillow at a flight attendant. He lurched down the aisle holding a cup of boiling hot coffee, frightening a woman holding a newborn. A *Newsweek* reporter wrote his editor that Kennedy was "an accident waiting to happen." No one on that plane full of journalists wrote a word about it to the public.

Perhaps most importantly, during the Watergate scandal of the early 1970s, Bob Woodward and Carl Bernstein of the *Washington Post* exposed a corrupt president, further tarnishing the image of the office. Journalists were no longer buddies with the chief executive, hiding his weaknesses in the hopes of a news scoop or an invitation to a great party. They were adversaries *searching* for weaknesses, hoping to be the next Woodward or Bernstein. They were heroes, exposing corruption, hypocrisy, and lies. Journalism schools were flooded with eager students.

After the floodgates were opened, the press covered the next political sex scandal relentlessly—that of sixty-five-year-old, married Congressman Wilbur Mills of Arkansas, one of the most powerful members of Congress, who at 2:00 a.m. on October 9,

1974, was stopped near the Tidal Basin by D.C. Park Police for speeding and driving without his headlights on. Both Mills and his passenger, a thirty-eight-year-old stripper who went by the name of Fanne Foxe, the Argentine Firecracker, were heavily intoxicated and had been beaten brutally in the face, evidently by each other. Much to the officers' surprise, the Firecracker got out of the car and leaped into the water, where one officer jumped in after her and the other threw the two of them a spare tire to climb onto. Given Mills's status, the police declined to pursue the matter. But the press got wind of it and unearthed stories of the congressman's devastating alcoholism, discovering he had spent half his time in Congress in a drunken daze and couldn't remember what had happened in most of his meetings. He was stripped of his chairmanship of the House Ways and Means Committee, his reputation demolished.

No politicians were immune to the new journalism, even a martyred president. The dam around Jack Kennedy's reputation started to crack in 1975 when the Senate Committee on Intelligence Operations, led by Senator Frank Church of Idaho, was looking into an early 1960s CIA plot to hire Chicago mobster Sam Giancana to assassinate Fidel Castro. The Church Committee, as it was called, discovered that Giancana and Kennedy had shared the same girlfriend, Judith Campbell, for eighteen months, that she telephoned Kennedy at the White House seventy times during a fifty-four-week period in 1961 and early 1962, and that many of those calls came from Giancana's home. Sam Giancana was deposed to testify, but he was gunned down in his kitchen while frying sausages the day before he was due to appear. No one knew if the murder was a mob hit or a CIA assassination. The committee left Judith's relationship with the president out of the final report, concluding that the late president's sex life was nobody's business. Perhaps it was no coincidence that the committee member who pushed hardest to keep it out was none other than young Senator Gary Hart of Colorado.

In 1975, Hart didn't see that times were changing after Vietnam, Chappaquiddick, and Watergate; the Kennedy–mob connection story leaked and made national headlines. On December 29, *Time* magazine published an article with the headline "Scandals: JFK and the Mobsters' Moll." Companion articles described "Jack Kennedy's Other Women," detailing Kennedy's countless adulteries in the White House. The same year, Traphes Bryant published his book, *Dog Days at the White House*, in which he recalled Kennedy's orgies. Judith Campbell herself wrote a memoir of her affair with the president in 1977. All the stories of bad Kennedy behavior, dammed up for so many years, came tumbling forth. The gloves were off, the knives were out, and the syrupy nostalgia for Camelot had turned to ash.

In 1976, the *Washington Post* broke the story that sixty-five-year-old Congressman Wayne Hays of Ohio kept a gorgeous, thirty-three-year-old blond mistress named Elizabeth Ray on his staff on the taxpayer dime who couldn't type or file or even take phone messages. The FBI and the House Oversight Committee began investigations, and Hays resigned from office.

The media also began reporting the off-color jokes and statements of prominent politicians. In 1976, Agriculture Secretary Earl Butz said to entertainers Sonny Bono and Pat Boone and former White House counsel John Dean, "I'll tell you what coloreds want. It's three things: first a tight pussy; second, loose shoes; and third, a warm place to shit, that's all." Shocked, John Dean reported the story to the press, and Butz was forced to resign amid general outrage.

Perhaps because he did not drive drunk with a stripper, or

keep a girlfriend who did no work on a public payroll, or share a girlfriend with Al Capone's successor, or make lewd and racist remarks, Gary Hart expected better treatment from this disturbing, dangerous new crop of journalists. Moreover, since well before he was born, the press had never unearthed the illicit sex life of a living president or presidential candidate, and Hart naively thought he was safe. But he was, in fact, rather like the first victim of a serial killer, knocked off balance and taken by surprise. Those adulterous politicians who followed in his footsteps, including a young governor from Arkansas, would be prepared for investigations into their sexual foibles.

In Hart's speech announcing his withdrawal from the race in May, he said,

> In public life, some things may be interesting, but that doesn't necessarily mean they're important . . . We're all going to have to seriously question the system for selecting our national leaders that reduces the press of this nation to hunters and presidential candidates to being hunted, that has reporters in bushes, false and inaccurate stories printed, photographers peeking in our windows, swarms of helicopters hovering over our roofs, and my very strong wife close to tears because she can't even get into her own house at night without being harassed. And then after all that, ponderous pundits wonder in mock seriousness why some of the best people in this country choose not to run for higher office . . . We'd all better do something to make this system work, or we're all going to be soon rephrasing Jefferson to say, I tremble for my country when I think we may, in fact, get the kind of leaders we deserve.

There is a recent twist to this decades-old story. Throughout the scandal, Hart whined that he had been set up. He sounded childish and petulant; a naughty little boy caught with his hand in the cookie jar. At first it seemed that Lynn Armandt had set the sting in motion because she and a friend of hers, Dana Weems, were jealous of Donna Rice. It was Weems, after all, who had called the *Miami Herald*, Armandt straining to listen at her side. But Hart may have been right, and there may have been something far more sinister at work than a pair of catty, envious women.

In 1991, forty-year-old Lee Atwater, who had been the campaign manager for George H. W. Bush in the 1988 election, knew he was dying of an inoperable brain tumor. A savvy political operative, he had numerous confessions and apologies to make before he died, numerous requests for forgiveness. He told Raymond Strother, an aide to Hart, that he had set up Hart by bribing Broadhurst. It was Broadhurst, he said, who arranged for the women to come on the cruise to Bimini, to rent the yacht with the most memorable name, to make sure he showed up too late to get his yacht out of customs, and to plan in advance with Armandt and Rice to take the picture as proof. As for the rest, Broadhurst just needed to step back and let Hart be Hart.

Shocked by the confession, Strother opted to let sleeping dogs lie and keep this information to himself. Atwater died soon after his confession, and Broadhurst died in 2017. But then, a few months later, Strother was diagnosed with possibly fatal prostate cancer and had his own confession to make. He met face-to-face with Gary Hart and told him the story. Hart had always thought someone had set him up for a fall; he had even said he was being set up to the *Miami Herald* reporters who confronted him in front of his town house the night that shattered everything. There was no proof, of course, and he didn't know *who* had set him up. But now, with the Lee Atwater story, it must have all suddenly made sense: Atwater had booted him out of the race in disgrace, clearing the path for George Bush to win.

In retrospect, it was most likely a loss for the nation. We can only imagine the country's trajectory if Hart had become president. "A scandal to me," he said, "is a child living in poverty. An elderly person without medicine. Unemployed workers. Those are scandals. People's sex lives or their personal lives are scandals only in the sense of tabloid journalism, but not in the sense of ethics. They're not bribery. They're not some under-the-table exchange of money, buying votes. Those, I suppose, would be real political scandals."

Donna Rice briefly modeled for No Excuses jeans and kept refusing to answer questions about what had happened between her and Gary Hart. She disappeared from public view for seven years, during which she reconnected with her evangelistic Christian faith.

In 1994, she married a tech entrepreneur in the Washington, D.C., area and raised three stepchildren. The same year, now Donna Rice Hughes, she began working for a nonprofit organization, Enough Is Enough, whose mission is to protect children online, and has been president and CEO since 2002. On the organization's website, she wrote about the Hart scandal, "I have chosen to remain silent, for the most part, about this devastating turning point in my life. Rather than exploit the situation for my own gain, I chose the high road and sought to use my pain to help others. By the grace of God, I found healing and restoration and eventually came full circle . . . I encourage others to seek the high road, as I did, and find hope and purpose in the midst of their life's storms."

After his failed presidential campaign, Hart resumed his law practice and was appointed by President Bill Clinton to lead a commission to study homeland security. In 2014, President Barack Obama named him U.S. special envoy to Northern Ireland, a position he held for three years. Hart is now eighty-three, retired, and still married to the same woman. And yet, he will forever be trapped in amber, sitting on a pier piling, a grinning blonde on his lap.

12

BILL CLINTON DID NOT HAVE SEX WITH THAT WOMAN

*O*nly a few U.S. presidents can boast of statements so memorable they define both their legacy and an era. Franklin Roosevelt said, "We have nothing to fear but fear itself." John F. Kennedy said, "Ask not what your country can do for you, but what you can do for your country." Richard Nixon emphatically stated, "I am not a crook." And Bill Clinton insisted, "I did not have sexual relations with that woman—Miss Lewinsky."

★ ★ ★

According to her 2003 memoir, *Living History*, on the morning of Saturday, August 15, 1998, Hillary Clinton was awakened by her husband, President Bill Clinton, pacing agitatedly next to her bed. Bill, it seemed, had a little confession to make. Though he had denied for months to special prosecutors that he had had a sexual relationship with former White House intern Monica Lewinsky, well, that wasn't exactly the truth. Not that he had lied—because blow jobs aren't really sex, everyone knows that—but still, Hillary recalled, he "told me for the first time that the situation was much more serious than he had previously acknowledged. He now realized he would have to testify that there had been an inappropriate intimacy. He told me that what happened between them had been brief and sporadic." In all likelihood, the only reason Bill fessed up was that the FBI had DNA evidence of the affair. Otherwise, it's safe to say Bill would have denied it until he was blue in the face.

"I could hardly breathe," Hillary continued. "Gulping for air, I started crying and yelling at him, 'What do you mean? What are you saying? Why did you lie to me?' I was furious and getting more so by the second. He just stood there saying over and over again, 'I'm sorry. I'm so sorry. I was trying to protect you and [their eighteen-year-old daughter] Chelsea.'" According to Hillary's account, until that morning she'd believed that he was being unfairly attacked. In January, she had even told Matt Lauer of NBC that the whole story was ginned up by "a vast right-wing conspiracy."

Now, upon hearing the truth, Hillary maintained, "I was dumbfounded, heartbroken and outraged that I'd believed him at all." Yes, she was shocked, *shocked*, to find that Bill had been at it with a girl because such behavior was so very unlike him.

The fact is that Hillary Rodham knew Bill was a philanderer well before she married him. They met at Yale Law School in 1971 and immediately became an item, though they were an odd couple from the get-go. Bill was handsome, personable, and funny, a back-slapping good ole Arkansas boy, always flying by the seat of his pants and coming out on top. Hillary, from Chicago, was chilly, calculating, painstakingly prepared, and frumpy. A creature of the mind, she gave no heed to her appearance. She had good features but wore no makeup to bring them out and had thick glasses and limp brown hair in no particular style. Long, unflattering granny dresses hid her figure. According to Jerry

Oppenheimer's 2000 book, *State of a Union: Inside the Complex Marriage of Bill and Hillary Clinton*, when Bill's childhood friend Paul Fray met Hillary, his reaction was, "My God, Bill Clinton, you son of a bitch—you could have any damn woman on the face of the earth, and you brought one that looks like the south end of a mule going north?"

Oppenheimer wrote that Bill leaped to Hillary's defense. "He told me she was the smartest woman he'd ever met," Paul said, "brilliant beyond compare." When Bill's mother, Virginia, first met Hillary, she, too, was unimpressed by the looks, and even more so by the aloofness that hinted of sneering superiority. "I want you to know that I've had it up to here with beauty queens," Bill raged. "I have to have somebody I can talk to. Do you understand that?" And to a woman he'd dated, who asked him what on earth it was about Hillary that fascinated him so, he replied, "She challenges me, every moment of every day, intellectually. She makes me a better person. She gets me started, kicks my butt, and makes me do the things I've got to do."

And, in fact, their differences held them together, like two puzzle pieces of vastly different shapes, interlocking perfectly. Both were highly intelligent and politically ambitious, but she had the cold calculation to maneuver him into political office, while he had the overwhelming charm. Because getting into office—*getting into the White House*—was the goal of their relationship. Both had dreamed of it since childhood. Both had chosen their postgraduate education, their internships and volunteer work for political campaigns based on that single goal. According to Gail Sheehy, author of the 1999 *Hillary's Choice*, Hillary had already dumped one boyfriend for lack of ambition. David Rupert, whom Hillary dated when they both worked as summer interns in Congress, told Sheehy Hillary lost interest in him because he never "stated a burning desire to be president. I believe that was a need for her in a partner."

And because the White House was Hillary's goal, the regular rules of a relationship didn't necessarily apply. According to Oppenheimer, they came to an agreement: Bill could carouse with women all he wanted as long as it didn't rise to the level of interfering with their political future. That would be the only betrayal of significance.

After graduating Yale in 1973, Hillary went to Washington, D.C., where she joined the impeachment inquiry staff of the House Judiciary Committee during the Watergate investigation. Bill went to Little Rock, where he taught law at the University of Arkansas. He ran for the U.S. House of Representatives in 1974, lost narrowly, ran in 1976 for Arkansas attorney general and won.

Though Hillary would periodically swoop into Little Rock to visit Bill, he was dating other women, including one in particular, Marla Crider, a winsome, dark-haired, twenty-one-year-old political science major at the University of Arkansas who volunteered on his first campaign. Marla told Jerry Oppenheimer that one day Bill told her to stop by his house and pick up some things she would need for the campaign trail. He also asked her to retrieve some papers from his desk. On the desk she saw an open letter, clearly meant for her to read. According to her recollection, it went like this:

Dear Bill,

I still do not understand why you do the things you do to hurt me. You left me in tears and not knowing what our relationship was all about. I know all your little girls are around there, if that's what it is, you will outgrow this. They will not be with you when

you need them. They are not the ones who can help you achieve
your goals. If this is about your feelings for Marla, this too shall
pass. Let me remind you it always does. Remember what we
talked about. Remember the goals we've set for ourselves. You
keep trying to stray away from the plan we've put together. Take
some time, think about it, and call me when you're ready.

Hillary

Though Bill had clearly maneuvered Marla into reading Hillary's letter, she didn't understand it. She knew Hillary was possessive of Bill, giving Marla the evil eye during her brief visits. But other than the first couple of lines, this wasn't a letter of love and jealousy, doubt and heartbreak. It was a letter about goals, about a plan. Love, fidelity, and trust were not the main focus of their relationship. There was something else, something Bill wanted Marla to understand.

Looking back years later, Marla said that Hillary "decided the most important thing was that political partnership, that goal they'd set, rather than taking care of their personal life, or being confident, or having a trustworthy relationship. I'm just amazed, as a woman, at her thought process. To be so smart and allow that to happen . . . to go for politics over personal life and love and happiness."

Nightclub singer Gennifer Flowers alleged in her 1995 memoir *Passion and Betrayal* that she had had a twelve-year affair with Bill. She wrote, "Hillary never tried to put a stop to my relationship with Bill. In fact, he told me that after he hung up from talking with me one night, she walked into the room and asked, 'How's Gennifer?' He looked at her carefully and replied, 'Just fine.' And that was the end of it . . . In retrospect, I can see that Bill and Hillary's political career was undoubtedly more important to her than her husband's faithfulness. But back then I couldn't imagine why she would close her eyes to his fooling around."

After Nixon's resignation in August 1974, Hillary gave up the chance for a lucrative job at a D.C. law firm and joined Bill, where she taught at the University of Arkansas and then accepted a position at the Rose Law Firm. She made no effort to adapt to her new environment. She didn't bleach her hair and tease it high, or slather on makeup, or wear more stylish clothing. She didn't try to acquire a bit of southern charm or learn how to bake peach pie. Instead, she was brusque, impatient, giving the impression of disdaining those she spoke to, of not having the time to bother with them. After Bill and Hillary married in 1975, she even kept her maiden name, a shocking break from tradition for the time and place.

In 1978, Bill was elected governor of Arkansas—the youngest governor in the country at thirty-two—a position he held for twelve nonconsecutive years (1979–1981 and 1983–1992). Their only child, Chelsea, was born in 1980. Some, who just didn't understand the dynamics of the Clinton marriage, called it an immaculate conception or the result of artificial insemination. Yet, over the years, there was never any doubt that the Clintons were devoted parents; even their most hostile political opponents agreed to that. Despite hectic schedules, they were there at the soccer games and ballet recitals. They drove their daughter to math programs, music lessons, and slumber parties.

When Bill lost the 1981 governor's race, Hillary realized she needed to make some changes. She took his name—she was now Hillary Rodham Clinton—and did a full-body makeover. With shorter blond hair, tasteful makeup, contact lenses, and more becoming clothing, she was quite attractive and far more appealing to southern voters with strong ideas of how women should look.

As soon as Bill started running for public office, he was more of a babe magnet than ever before. On the campaign trail, women handed him their phone numbers on slips of paper. One campaign aide said every day some twenty-five women would show up at campaign headquarters looking for him. He would later tell Monica Lewinsky that he had slept with hundreds of women before he ran for president.

Bill loved the story of Lyndon Johnson having sex in the Oval Office, and the legendary tales of Kennedy's endless harem of starlets and secretaries. His friend U.S. Senator J. William Fulbright of Arkansas admonished him, "Bill, if you're going to idolize the womanizing side of Jack Kennedy, you're gonna end up turning out that way yourself. You don't need to be putting yourself in that kind of jeopardy. Don't idolize someone who does things that are wrong."

Rumors percolated, mostly in right-wing quarters years later, about Hillary having an affair of her own. At the Rose Law Firm, she developed a close friendship with another lawyer named Vince Foster. Handsome with thick graying hair, courteous and thoughtful, he was married with three children. Vince and Hillary ate lunch together most days, often having a drink after work. Those who suspected an affair couldn't blame Hillary for seeking a little solace outside her own marriage, given Bill's reputation. Others thought she couldn't be having an affair with Foster because she was a lesbian; given her lifelong disinterest in makeup and clothing until political expediency required a trip to the hair salon, Hillary had to be gay.

By 1987, Bill was ready to toss his hat in the ring and run for president. But those plans crumbled after Gary Hart's political meltdown in May of that year. As one of Bill's state troopers said, "Governor, you're gonna make Gary Hart look like a damned saint."

"Yeah," Bill replied. "I do, don't I?"

In his memoir, Clinton wrote, "After the Hart affair, those of us who had not led perfect lives had no way of knowing what the press's standards of disclosure were." By the time he did run, four years after *Monkey Business*, he had a better idea than Hart how to navigate the media onslaught.

For one thing, Clinton learned that it was better to address the issue right off the bat. Republican consultant Eddie Mahe told the *New York Times*, "The press has collectively made a decision that when any information is presented to them and documented, they will publish it. So the new rule on these things is you'd better talk about it, and you'd better talk about it first." When confronted with proof of his infidelity, Gary Hart had hemmed and hawed, obfuscated and denied, and chastised the media for even asking about his private life. By the late eighties, with the rise of cable TV talk shows like *Oprah*, voters wanted gut-wrenching honesty—or what passed for it—along with an apology.

On October 3, 1991, Bill Clinton announced his plans to run for president. His youth, vitality, eloquence, and charm all helped him become the early front-runner in a lackluster field of Democrats. He addressed his infidelity issue with members of the national political press at an off-the-record event in Washington. There had been problems in his marriage, he admitted, but that was in the past. He and Hillary had worked them out and were committed to each other. Bill must have hoped that was all that would be required. It was not.

In February 1992, on the eve of the New Hampshire primary, Bill's long-term mistress, Gennifer Flowers, appeared in the tabloid *Star*, describing their relationship in an article with the headline, "My 12-Year Affair with Bill Clinton." Denial wasn't an option for Bill; Gennifer had recordings of their phone conversations indicating they'd had a relationship. History seemed to be repeating itself. This looked like *Monkey Business*, Part Two.

According to Flowers, their affair began in 1977 when he was the twenty-nine-year-old Arkansas attorney general and she a twenty-seven-year-old reporter for a local Little Rock TV station. "I can still remember the way he had of staring at me," she wrote in her 1995 autobiography. "He did more than just mentally undress me, he was visually seducing me, and he made sure I knew it. He was turning me upside down and inside out just by looking at me, and when he looked away, I almost felt as though we had just made love. I was breathless and more than a little uneasy."

When they ended up making jubilant love in her bed, it was the start of a twelve-year love affair. "As a lover, Bill was great," she wrote. "Though not particularly well-endowed, his desire to please was astounding. He was determined to satisfy me, and boy, did he! I thought my head would explode with the pleasure . . . His stamina amazed me. We made love over and over that night, and he never seemed to run out of energy." In 1977, she wrote, she realized she was pregnant with his child and he gave her money for an abortion.

He suggested she take an apartment not far from the governor's mansion so he could jog over in the morning and spend half an hour in the sack. His driver, waiting outside, would drop him off a block from the governor's mansion, where he would start jogging again and arrive red-faced and sweaty, with an excellent excuse for jumping into the shower immediately. Though their affair had ended in 1989 when she began dating a single man, Gennifer and Bill remained on friendly terms.

As soon as Bill announced his candidacy, reporters came to Little Rock, determined to dig up dirt on him, and soon heard about Flowers. They called her at work and at home and stalked her. She was ambushed by cameramen and lost her nightclub job. But something more sinister was at work than an overzealous press. Her mother got death threats, evidently from Clinton supporters, while Gennifer received a lot of heavy-breathing hang-up calls. Her apartment was ransacked, after which she made recordings of her conversations with Bill.

When Gennifer spoke to Bill about the break-ins and mysterious phone calls, he told her it was Republican harassment and to just deny, deny, deny. But now she wondered if Bill himself was behind it, or at least a group of his wealthy and powerful supporters determined to see him become president. Her neighbor in her apartment building, a lawyer named Gary Johnson, had set up a video camera in the hallway for security purposes with a clear view of Gennifer's door. When rumors got around that Bill had had an affair with her, Johnson let it be known he had videotapes of the governor entering her apartment with his own key. One day, some men forced their way into his apartment, beat him severely, and left him for dead. When he regained consciousness, the videos were missing.

Flowers said that she sold her story to the *Star* as a means of self-defense. It would be out there once and for all; there would be no need to threaten her and her mother or to ransack her apartment.

But Gennifer didn't count on the Clintons' ruthless counterattacks. When the Flowers story broke, Hillary was campaigning for her husband in South Dakota. Gail Sheehy, covering Hillary for *Vanity Fair*, heard her on her phone talking to campaign aides. Hillary was furious, Sheehy said. "Not anger at Bill, but at Flowers, the press and Republicans."

Sheehy heard Hillary ask, "Who's tracking down all the research on Gennifer?"

The research involved a ruthless private investigator named Jack Palladino whose job it was, as he wrote in a memo, to disparage Gennifer's "character and veracity until she is destroyed beyond all recognition . . . Every acquaintance, employer, and past lover should be located and interviewed." Any unflattering information was given to Betsey Wright, Bill's former chief of staff in Arkansas, who was made responsible for dealing with "bimbo eruptions," as she called accusations of infidelity. Wright would release the information to the press. Gennifer Flowers, Wright said in an interview with *Penthouse*, was a liar, out for money, and guilty of "résumé hype, attempted blackmail, manufacturing a self-styled affair with Clinton to salvage a flopola singing career."

It was a brutal response that would be replayed some two dozen times over the next eight years as women came forward with stories about sex with Bill Clinton. Wright's job turned out to be a kind of bimbo whack-a-mole, standing vigilant with a mallet ready to hammer the women back into the holes they popped out of.

The Clinton campaign took their attack a step further by accusing President George H. W. Bush of having a twelve-year affair with his own Jennifer, his aide Jennifer Fitzgerald, who had joined his staff in 1974 when she was forty-two. The divorcée had served as Bush's gatekeeper for his two terms as vice president under Ronald Reagan. *People* magazine reported that in 1984, Ambassador Louis Fields allowed the two to stay at his Geneva home during an official trip while Barbara Bush was off promoting a book on their dog. "It became clear [they] were romantically involved," Fields said, adding that the relationship of the vice president and Fitzgerald made him "very uncomfortable."

An acquaintance of both Bush and Fitzgerald told the London *Times* in 2004 that Jennifer Fitzgerald "wasn't just another woman. She was a woman who came to exert enormous influence over George for many, many years . . . She became, in essence, his other wife . . . his office wife." The acquaintance added that Barbara Bush put up with the relationship mainly because her husband never humiliated her. Yet, as Barbara wrote in her diary, "His eyes really glaze over when you mention her name. She is just what he wants, he says, and says the hell with it all." Friends said Fitzgerald could be charming—but only to Bush. She was so rude to others that many valued staff members quit rather than work with her.

Rumors about Bush and Fitzgerald had bounced around Washington for years and even made a few fairly discreet headlines. The *Washington Post* had the best one: "Fitzgerald has served President-elect Bush in a variety of positions." Now Hillary brought the rumors front and center to media attention.

During Bush's August 11, 1992, press conference with Israeli prime minister Yitzhak Rabin, a CNN reporter asked the president about a front-page *New York Post* story on Fitzgerald titled "The Bush Affair." "I'm not going to take any sleazy questions like that from CNN," the president snapped. "I'm very disappointed that you would ask such a question of me, and I will not respond to it. I think it's—I am outraged. But, nevertheless, in this kind of screwy climate that we're in, why, I expect it. But I don't like it, and I'm not going to respond other than to say it's a lie." When NBC's Stone Phillips asked him about the affair, Bush retorted, "You're perpetuating the sleaze by even asking the question, to say nothing of asking in the Oval Office." Bush clearly thought he was living in a pre–*Monkey Business* world.

The story ended up withering away. Short and stern-faced, her blond hair lacquered into a French twist, the prickly Fitzgerald didn't seem to be the kind of femme fatale capable of turning a president's head. Buttoned-up, plump, and now sixty, she was an uninteresting target of media attention compared to the sexy bleached-blond lounge singer Gennifer Flowers and her audio-tapes.

The twin Clinton strategy of accusing their political opponents of engaging in adultery and disparaging Bill's women would not be enough. If the Clintons learned how not to address the infidelity issue from Gary Hart, perhaps they also learned some pointers from Alexander Hamilton, who made a gut-wrenching public confession of his affair with Maria Reynolds in his hundred-page pamphlet. Two hundred years later, Bill Clinton would choose television as his confessional. Bill and Hillary appeared on *60 Minutes* right after the 1992 Super Bowl, the most watched program in the world.

Bill's confession lacked something that Hamilton's had: the full truth. He denied having an affair with Gennifer Flowers. But, looking chastened and remorseful, he said, "I have acknowledged wrongdoing. I have acknowledged causing pain in my marriage. I think most Americans who are watching this tonight will know what we're saying. They'll get it, and they'll feel we've been more than candid. And I think what the press has to decide is: Are we going to engage in a game of 'gotcha'?" Hillary asked whether people who had experienced marital difficulties should be prevented from running for public office. The two of them looked like a typical married couple who had had problems over the years. An ABC News poll found that 80 percent of those surveyed thought Bill Clinton should stay in the race.

Ironically, the Gennifer Flowers scandal helped Bill Clinton win the Democratic nomination. Primary voters saw that he had the skill, grace, and media savvy to parry attacks by the Republican machine. While it is usually difficult to unseat an incumbent president, Clinton's candidacy was aided and abetted by the U.S. economy, which had fallen into a recession. On November 3, 1992, Clinton received 370 delegates, Bush 168.

If the Clintons believed the scandals were behind them, they were dead wrong. In May 1993, it was Travelgate. Soon after taking office, Clinton had fired seven employees of the White House Travel Office, which he was fully entitled to do as any of his staff could be dismissed at his pleasure. But his political opponents claimed he had sacked efficient career employees to hire his friends and supporters.

In July, Vince Foster, Hillary's good friend from the Rose Law Firm in Little Rock, shot himself in a Virginia park. A sensitive, gentlemanly soul, Foster had come to Washington to work as deputy White House counsel. But almost immediately he disliked his new life. For one thing, Hillary no longer had time for him. "It's just not the same," he told Webb Hubbell, White House liaison to the Department of Justice, another Clinton associate from Little Rock. "She's so busy that we don't ever have any time to talk."

Attacked by the media for botched Justice Department nominations and his handling of Travelgate, Foster soon slipped into a deep depression. In a note, found torn to pieces in the bottom of his briefcase after his death, he wrote, "The WSJ [*Wall Street Journal*] editors lie without consequence . . . I was not meant for the job or the spotlight of public life in Washington. Here, ruining people is considered sport." Although the FBI, the park police, the independent counsel, and two congressional investigations found his death to be suicide, according to conspiracy theories, Hillary had had him murdered.

Another scandal, called the Whitewater controversy, resulted in an investigation into purported illegal activities of the Clintons and another couple, the McDougals, with regards to a failed Arkansas real estate deal. The McDougals were convicted of financial crimes, but the Clintons were never charged.

In December, it was Troopergate, news articles reporting allegations by four Arkansas state troopers that Clinton had forced them to help with his romantic assignations. They claimed Clinton sent them to scout out attractive women, obtain their phone numbers, arrange hotel rooms, drive him there and back, deliver gifts to the women afterward, and lie to Hillary about where he was. One trooper estimated that Clinton had been intimate with hundreds of women. "There would hardly be an opportunity he would let slip to have sex," he said. Bill denied the allegations. It turned out that Troopergate was orchestrated and, in some cases, financially supported by Clinton's political enemies, yet there was never proof that the men were lying. In 1996, the scandal du jour was Filegate—improper access to hundreds of security clearance documents without the individuals' permission, which Clinton explained away as a "bureaucratic snafu."

But there were political successes along with the scandals. On November 30, 1993, Clinton signed into law the Brady Bill, which mandated federal background checks on people who purchase firearms in the United States. He also expanded the earned income tax credit, a subsidy for low-income workers. In 1994, he implemented a directive known as "Don't Ask, Don't Tell," which allowed gay men and women to serve in the armed services as long as they didn't discuss their sexual orientation, which was considered a huge stride forward at the time. In 1997 he proposed—and signed—legislation to create the State Children's Health Insurance Program (SCHIP), which helped pay for medical care for children from low-income families.

Despite Bill Clinton's political achievements, the largest scandal by far, the one that would define his presidency, was Monica Lewinsky. That morning in August 1998, according to Hillary, Bill finally told her the truth after months of vehement denials. He had lied to her, lied to the American people and, most dangerous of all, lied to the independent counsel, Ken Starr.

The affair had started when Monica, a recent twenty-two-year-old college graduate, began working as a White House intern in the summer of 1995. Aimless, smarting from the ending of an affair with her married former high school drama teacher, she thought this position, arranged by an influential family friend, would look good on her résumé. But when she first caught sight of the charismatic Bill Clinton in person, she shifted her obsession to him, arriving for White House ceremonies hours early to have a place up front to catch his eye. At one such event, she was successful. The president not only noticed the voluptuous brunette with a toothy grin and lustrous shoulder-length hair, he gave her "the full Bill Clinton," as she said, and her description is quite similar to that of Gennifer Flowers. "It was this look, it's the way he flirts with women . . . We shared an intense but brief sexual exchange. He undressed me with his eyes."

According to Lewinsky's testimony in the Starr Report, on the evening of November 15, 1995, Monica walked past the inner office of the West Wing and saw the president alone. She lifted the back of her jacket to flash the straps of her thong panties and a sizable amount of firm, round buttock. A few minutes later, Clinton summoned her into his study, and they kissed. Two days later, Lewinsky gave him oral sex as he spoke on the phone with two congressmen. But he never allowed her to bring him to climax and finished himself off over a wastepaper basket. Perhaps he was afraid that DNA might be used as evidence—and rightly so, as events would prove. Or perhaps he had convinced himself that sex wasn't sex without orgasm, and the orgasm he achieved all by himself, so that was actually masturbation, not sex. On one occasion, however, Clinton left two small spots on Monica's navy blue Gap dress. Over the course of a year and a half, during which Lewinsky went from intern to full-time employee, the two engaged in physical encounters nine times—during one he inserted a cigar in her vagina and then put it in his mouth—and in phone sex fifteen times.

The relationship wasn't just sex. "We enjoyed talking with each other and being with each other," Lewinsky said. "We were very affectionate. We would tell jokes. We would talk about our childhoods, talk about current events . . . I think back on it and he always made me smile when I was with him. He was sunshine." A good friend of Bill's told author Jerry Oppenheimer, "I know how he is with women. But she was different. He was literally hooked on her and pursued her with the same level of adolescent obsession that she pursued him. He desperately needed to be loved—I'm not talking just about sex, but a caring kind of love, and Monica probably more than any other woman—except his mother—filled that need. Certainly Hillary never did. From things he has said since, I truly believe that Bill would have run off with that girl if he had the chance, if things had been different." Caught up in the euphoria of secret, forbidden assignations, Bill even suggested he might divorce Hillary after he left the White House. Overjoyed, Monica boasted to a friend that one day she might become the second Mrs. Clinton.

In April 1996, concerned Secret Service agents informed Deputy Chief of Staff Evelyn Lieberman that Monica was spending too much time with the president. Lieberman immediately transferred her to a job at the Pentagon. Monica was devastated at being so distant from her lover, though she did make a few White House visits.

Soon, Clinton's passion for Monica ebbed, rather like helium leaking out of a balloon until all you have left is a limp, sagging memory of better times. He wanted to end the relationship but he feared she would blab if he did. As long as they had a relationship, he believed she would keep quiet about it. Bill promised to find Monica a great job and asked Washington power broker Vernon Jordan to help. By January 1998, Jordan had an exciting job lined up for Monica at Revlon in New York.

Unfortunately for Clinton, Monica couldn't keep her mouth shut even though he was still stringing her along. At the Pentagon, she befriended Linda Tripp, who had worked at the White House for George H. W. Bush and then briefly for Clinton, whom she despised. She was, in fact, planning to write a tell-all book about Bill's sexual dalliances and even had a literary agent, Lucianne Goldberg. When Monica began confiding in Linda about her affair with the president, including details of their sexual encounters, Linda notified her agent, who suggested she tape-record the calls. It was Linda who instructed Monica to put that navy blue dress in the freezer to preserve the DNA.

Linda heard that lawyers for a woman named Paula Jones, who were suing Bill Clinton for sexual harassment, were looking for other women who had worked as his subordinates and been subjected to romantic overtures. Paula's run-in with Clinton occurred on May 8, 1991, at an event in Little Rock's Excelsior Hotel, when Governor Clinton asked a state trooper to invite the twenty-five-year-old, $6.35-an-hour state document examiner to come up to his room. According to Jones, when she arrived, Clinton "began pulling me over like he has done this a million times and grabs me and pulls me over to him to the windowsill and tries to kiss me and just didn't ask me or nothing." Then the governor pulled his pants down, sat down and asked, "Would you kiss it for me?" Paula uttered the immortal words, "I'm not that kind of girl!" and fled.

In 1994, with Clinton now president, Jones filed a lawsuit against Clinton for sexual harassment, as she had been a state employee when he, her ultimate boss as governor, pressed for sex. She wanted $700,000. To prove she was no liar, she said she could identify an unusual bend in his penis. In an affidavit that is considered one of the strangest legal documents ever, she stated that Bill's penis was "five to five and one-half inches, or less, in length . . . a circumference of the approximate size of a quarter, or perhaps very slightly larger" and "was bent or crooked from Mr. Clinton's right to left."

The main question was whether a civil suit could go ahead against a sitting president. For two hundred years, such suits had been dismissed, as judges presumed national security depended on a president completely focused on protecting the nation. But by the time Jones filed her suit, the Cold War and America's arch-enemy, the Soviet Union, were no more. Perhaps the president could handle some distraction without the country going up in smoke. In January 1997, the Supreme Court unanimously ruled that Jones's suit could proceed. The *New York Post* trumpeted the headline "Grin and Bare It" for an article that suggested the best method of proving Jones had seen the president's penis would be for the president to drop his pants in court. Those in the court-room could study it to see how bent it actually was.

Tripp told Jones's lawyers that her friend—and we use that term loosely—Monica Lewinsky had confided that she had been having an affair with the president for some eighteen months while she was a federal employee. The lawyers subpoenaed Mon-ica, and on January 7, 1998, she signed an affidavit under penalty of perjury that she had never engaged in sexual relations with the president. Foiled and bursting with venom at the thought of losing her book deal, Tripp turned over the tapes of her phone conversations with Monica to Independent Special Counsel Ken Starr, who had been looking into the Whitewater controversy but had the prerogative to investigate any suspicious matters that came his way. Now Starr turned a gimlet eye on Monica Lewinsky. On January 16, Starr wired Tripp for a meeting with Monica and prosecutors listened to their conversation. Minutes later, they swooped in, took her into custody, and told her she could either cooperate or go to jail for twenty-five years for perjury, obstruction of justice, and several other charges.

The following day, January 17, 1998, Bill Clinton was deposed under oath in the Paula Jones case. He didn't remember Jones, he said. He certainly never showed her his penis in a hotel room. He did know Monica but had never had a sexual relationship with her, couldn't even remember being alone with her.

Meanwhile, rumors of the Clinton-Lewinsky affair had reached the press. The same day as Clinton's deposition, the internet news site the Drudge Report first published the story about the affair and, over the next few days, stories about blow jobs in the White House, presidential perjury, and a cushy job in the private sector as a bribe for silence.

What to do? Clinton did what most men do in such a situation: deny, deny, deny. On January 26, he marched into the Roosevelt Room of the White House, looked straight into a TV camera, and said the words that would define his presidency. "I did not have sexual relations with that woman—Miss Lewinsky."

On April 1, 1998, a federal judge dismissed Paula Jones's sexual harassment suit, finding that Clinton's conduct did not constitute sexual assault. Jones's lawyers appealed the dismissal. Given the newer, bigger, and more dangerous mess of Monica Lewinsky, however, Clinton didn't wait for the appeal decision and settled with Jones for $850,000—$150,000 more than she had asked for in her lawsuit—with no acknowledgment of wrongdoing. Costly as it was, he had whacked that mole.

But other moles had popped up during the Paula Jones case. On March 18, 1998, Dallas lawyer Dolly Kyle Browning, who had attended high school with Clinton, testified that they had had an affair starting in the mid-1970s which lasted until January 1992. According to Browning, her own brother, who worked for the Clinton campaign, said, "We think you should deny the story," and, "If you cooperate with the media, we will destroy you."

Fifty-one-year-old White House volunteer aide Kathleen Willey had also been subpoenaed by Paula Jones's lawyers. On March 15, 1998, she went public with her story, telling *60 Minutes* that Clinton had sexually assaulted her on November 29, 1993, in the Oval Office. She had met with him to discuss some personal and professional issues, she said, when he grabbed her crotch and rubbed up against her. In a deposition, Clinton denied Willey's story but did finally admit he'd had sex with Gennifer Flowers. But only once. In 1977. It seems that Bill Clinton couldn't help but lie even when he was telling the truth.

Bill's most important testimony occurred on August 17 when he appeared before a grand jury on a closed-circuit television feed from the White House and conceded that he'd had "inappropriate intimate physical contact" with Monica Lewinsky. But he stubbornly insisted it had not actually been sex as defined by the judge in the Paula Jones deposition, so he had not really perjured himself. The judge had defined sex—and many of us may wonder why he had felt the need to do so—as "contact with the genitalia, anus, groin, breast, or buttocks of any person with an intent to arouse or gratify the sexual desire of any person." Clinton argued that if a woman was performing oral sex on him, he was actually not in contact with her genitalia, anus, groin, breast, or buttocks, but with her lips.

That night, Clinton curtly told the nation, "I know that my public comments and my silence about this matter gave a false impression. I misled people including even my own wife. I deeply regret that." The American public was unimpressed. They wanted breast-beating drama, streaming tears, agonized sobs, guilt, and remorse, not this tight-lipped pseudo-apology. They wanted a poignant performance. They would get it on September 11, when Clinton tried again at a prayer breakfast. "I have sinned," he lamented. The voice cracked. The eyes overflowed with tears. The audience found it far more satisfying.

The same day, Starr released a 452-page report full of disgusting details: the cigar-cum-tampon, the ejaculating into the trashcan, the blow job while he was talking to members of Congress on the phone. The press was horrified. More than sixty-five major newspapers demanded he resign. Worse for Clinton, Starr's findings reported that he had discovered "substantial and credible information that President William Jefferson Clinton committed acts that may constitute grounds for impeachment."

On December 19, the House of Representatives voted to impeach Clinton on two charges of perjury and obstruction of justice. On February 12, 1999, the Senate, however, acquitted him of perjury with a vote of 55 to 45, and of obstruction of justice by 50 to 50.

Oddly, impeachment only served to beef up Clinton's approval ratings. His highest Gallup score ever—73 percent—occurred the week of the impeachment. A *Washington Post* poll found that even though a majority of Americans believed Clinton had lied under oath, the lies didn't bother them as they had only been about sex, and almost everybody lied about sex. If he had lied, say, about stealing taxpayer dollars and putting them in an offshore bank account, it is likely they would have felt quite differently.

The majority of Americans also believed that Clinton was a victim of a political conspiracy. A man playing around with a girlfriend was far less objectionable than a political group plotting to take an opponent down by any means, no matter how ridiculous. Starr's investigation smacked of sexual McCarthyism; his investigation was a kind of House Committee on Unpious Activities, where old white men shrieked with outrage as they examined semen stains under a magnifying glass, but also experienced a prurient thrill.

Time magazine named Bill Clinton and independent counsel Kenneth Starr its 1998 Persons of the Year. Columnist Michael Kinsley wrote, "The most significant political story of the year is that most citizens don't seem to think it's significant that the President had oral sex with a 22-year-old intern. Yes, yes, and he lied about it. Under oath. Blah blah blah. They still don't care. Rarely has such an unexpected popular consensus been so clear. And rarely has such a clear consensus been so unexpected."

Clinton's sex life was unimportant compared to the sky-high stock market, record job creation, low inflation, higher household incomes, a federal budget surplus, reduced crime, and the lowest welfare rolls in thirty years. Gary Langer of ABC News summed up how most Americans felt about Bill Clinton: "You can't trust him, he's got weak morals and ethics—and he's done a heck of a good job."

During the impeachment, the *Los Angeles Times*, which had supported Clinton in the past, declared, "The picture of Clinton that now emerges is that of a middle-aged man with a pathetic inability to control his sexual fantasies." No one could deny that, but it didn't necessarily mean he was a bad president. In fact, Clinton's sexual behavior came to be seen as part and parcel of his political brilliance. The energy, the drive, the impish charm, and the insatiable love of life seemed irrevocably interwoven with his skill for foreign relations and handling of the U.S. economy. A dried-out old stick of a president surely would not have been so successful at governing. Personal morality, Americans of the 1990s figured out, had little to do with leadership capability. It was as if the American public were becoming French.

Many Americans were also disturbed by the hypocrisy angle of the impeachment. How many of those lantern-jawed hanging judges in Congress and the independent counsel's office had had a little sex on the side themselves? Larry Flynt, the publisher of *Hustler* magazine, was determined to find out. In October 1998, as the House initiated impeachment proceedings, he placed an $85,000 full-page ad in the *Washington Post* offering a $1 million reward to anyone who could provide "documentary evidence of illicit sexual relations" involving any senators, congressmen, or other high-ranking government officials. "I feel the people who are going to be sitting in judgment who have not been truthful about similar activities in their own lives should recuse themselves," Flynt said. "What we are talking about is hypocrisy in its highest form."

"That's some very easy money," said one veteran House staffer interviewed by the *Washington Post*, and he was right. More than two thousand calls came into the hotline. Evidence arrived showing that Congressman Henry Hyde, the House leader on impeachment, had been unfaithful to his wife with a hairdresser back in the 1960s. Flynt released transcripts from the 1985 divorce case of Congressman Bob Barr—one of the House managers who presented the Clinton case to the Senate—in which he refused to answer questions about cheating on his second wife with the woman who would become his third. Congressman Bob Livingston, the powerful chairman of the House Appropriations Committee, had had numerous affairs, including one with an employee. When Livingston accused Flynt of being a "bottom feeder," the publisher replied, "Well, that's right. But look what I found when I got down there." As a result of Flynt's inquiry, Livingston resigned from Congress in March 1999. Bill Clinton quipped, "The interesting thing was, Larry Flynt turned out to be a better guy than Ken Starr."

Even after Flynt's stunt, proof of more hypocrisy came rolling in. In 2007, Senator Larry Craig, who had spoken harshly against Clinton's crimes, was accused of soliciting sex from a male undercover cop in an airport men's room. In 2015, Dennis Hastert, who had replaced Newt Gingrich as speaker of the House, pled guilty to charges of illegally structuring cash withdrawals to make blackmail payments to young men he had molested decades earlier while working as a high school wrestling coach.

Two months after Clinton was acquitted, just as things were finally settling down, the most serious accusation of all arose. On February 24, 1999, Juanita Broaddrick told NBC's *Dateline* that Clinton had raped her in 1978 when she was a thirty-five-year-old volunteer on his gubernatorial campaign. She had arranged to meet him in a hotel coffee shop, but Clinton suggested they meet for coffee in her hotel room to avoid the throng of journalists in the hotel lobby. There, she said, he raped her so violently he left her bloody. Her friend Norma Rogers, who shared the hotel room with Broaddrick, said she found her in bed with torn panty hose and a bleeding, swollen lip. Rogers stated that Broaddrick described the rape to her, as did three other friends of Broaddrick's. Yet in 1997, when Juanita was deposed in the Paula Jones case, she denied having any sexual contact with Clinton. A year later, when Ken Starr questioned her, she told the truth, she said, as she was terrified of the harsher criminal penalties for lying to the independent counsel. Yet she ended up as only a footnote in Starr's final report.

By the time her story came out, Americans were exhausted by the Lewinsky scandal, the Starr Report, and the impeachment. Broaddrick's allegation was far worse than the others, as she claimed rape, but still. Broaddrick had no proof to bring a lawsuit against Clinton and had muddied the waters by denying the assault in her original deposition. Scandal fatigue caused most Americans to insert their fingers in their ears, close their eyes, and stick out their tongues. Broaddrick ended up self-publishing her book, *You'd Better Put Some Ice on That: How I Survived Being Raped by Bill Clinton*, in 2019.

The most recent accuser of Bill Clinton behaving badly was Leslie Millwee, who in 2016 came forward to accuse him of sexually assaulting her three times in a small editing room in 1980 when she was working as a reporter at an Arkansas television station. According to Millwee, Governor Clinton came up to her on each occasion, groped her breasts and, on the second and third assaults, rubbed himself against her until he climaxed.

In 2017, public opinion veered in another direction with the #MeToo movement. Unwanted groping, rubbing, and touching was now defined as sexual assault. It was time to reexamine Clinton's bad behavior, even his consensual relationship with Monica Lewinsky.

Lewinsky had been twenty-two when the affair began, an adult, but barely. Most of us with a few more years on us, looking at twenty-two-year-olds, see them as big children with functioning reproductive organs. And who among us hasn't done something illegal, immoral, or just plain idiotic at twenty-two? Luckily for us, our poor judgment was not at the center of a presidential impeachment inquiry, resulting in the global sliming of our names for all time to come. Blushing furiously as we remember foolhardy choices, we can raise a toast to the good fortune of our own obscurity.

In contrast to Lewinsky's youth, Clinton had been forty-nine, her superior in the workplace, and the most important man in the country, arguably in the world. After he left office, he remained an A-list celebrity, earning fortunes in speaking fees, campaigning for Democratic candidates, going to all the best parties. Little if any slime stuck to him, but then again, Teflon skin is usually a male attribute. Lewinsky, reduced to a punchline and a semen-stained dress, struggled to find work and a relationship. Fleeing the U.S., she obtained her Master of Science degree in Social Psychology at the London School of Economics in 2006 but had difficulty getting a job due to her notoriety.

In 2014, she reemerged from a long hibernation to discuss the scandal in an essay in *Vanity Fair* and began to speak out against cyberbullying. "When news of my affair with Bill Clinton broke," she wrote, "I was arguably the most humiliated person in the world. Thanks to the Drudge Report, I was also possibly the first person whose global humiliation was driven by the Internet." In 2105 she joined the anti-bullying organization Bystander Revolution as an ambassador and strategic adviser.

In a March 2018 *Vanity Fair* essay, Lewinsky shifted her position from four years earlier when she had accepted full responsibility for her actions. Now, in the light of #MeToo, she saw her relationship with the president as replete with "inappropriate abuse of authority, station, and privilege . . . Now, at 44, I'm beginning (just beginning) to consider the implications of the power differentials that were so vast between a president and a White House intern. I'm beginning to entertain the notion that in such a circumstance the idea of consent might well be rendered moot."

A few months later, when Bill Clinton was asked in an interview if he owed Lewinsky an apology, he said he did not. Hillary Clinton said Bill had not abused his power as Lewinsky had been an adult.

"What feels more important to me than whether I am *owed* or *deserving* of a personal apology is my belief that Bill Clinton should want to apologize," Lewinsky said. "I'm less disappointed *by* him and more disappointed *for* him. He would be a better man for it . . . and we, in turn, a better society."

In the 2020 Hulu documentary series *Hillary*, Bill finally apologized to Monica, sort of. "I feel terrible about the fact that Monica Lewinsky's life was defined by it, unfairly, I think," he said. "Over the years I watched her try to get a normal life back. But you gotta decide how to define normal." His final remark seemed to indicate she should just accept the spectacular public derailment of her life, suck it up, and move on.

Oddly, Clinton blamed his decision to pursue the affair on the stress of office. "Here's something that will take your mind off it for a while," he explained. "Things I did to manage my anxiety for years." It seems he did indeed emulate his hero, JFK, who used unseemly sex to prevent stress headaches.

Most Democrats stood by the Clintons despite Bill's numerous sex scandals and Hillary's rather chilling reaction to them. But when the Clintons' supporters excoriated another candidate trailing a long list of similar allegations, including rape, Republicans called them out on hypocrisy. That candidate's name was Donald Trump.

13

DONALD TRUMP CAN DO ANYTHING

*O*n October 7, 2016, the *Washington Post* and NBC News released an audio tape of Republican presidential nominee Donald Trump bragging back in 2005 to *Access Hollywood* coanchor Billy Bush about groping and kissing unsuspecting women. "And when you're a star," he said, "they let you do it. You can do anything. Grab them by the pussy. You can do anything."

Such a revelation would have quickly tanked any other candidate, but not Donald, who has enjoyed one of the most highly improbable lives in the history of mankind.

★ ★ ★

Most single-name celebrities are entertainers or athletes: Adele, Shaq, Oprah. Trump was a single-name celebrity real estate developer, the world's most shameless and successful self-promoter, a barking Ringling Bros. and Barnum & Bailey ringmaster, whose blustering hyperbole praised the greatest, most spectacular, most amazing show on earth, with himself as the only act. He was, by turns, brash, irritable, childish, deceitful, and a marketing

genius. A man whose over-the-top buildings combined Buckingham Place with Caesar's Palace. And, since 2017, a man whose
presidential power has put hubris syndrome on the world stage.

Born in 1946 in Queens, New York, Donald was the son of
Fred Trump, a successful real estate developer. Though Donald
dutifully graduated from the Wharton School of the University
of Pennsylvania with a degree in economics, as his father wished,
he was itching to run his own real estate business. Fred Trump
had focused on developing Queens and Coney Island, eventually
building some 27,000 apartments and rowhouses in the New York
area for the working class in the postwar housing shortage. Young
Donald gazed across the river at Manhattan, where glittering sky-
scrapers rose above a city devastated by crime and tottering on
the brink of bankruptcy. "I'm basically an optimist," he wrote in
The Art of the Deal, "and frankly, I saw the city's trouble as a great
opportunity for me. Because I grew up in Queens, I believed,
perhaps to an irrational degree, that Manhattan was always going
to be the best place to live—the center of the world."

He started off in 1978 by buying the run-down Commodore
Hotel, next to Grand Central Terminal, refurbishing it, and re-
naming it the Grand Hyatt. The same year he began building
Trump Tower, a fifty-eight-story, mixed-use building in Mid-
town, which opened in 1983. He acquired the Plaza Hotel in 1988
for $400 million and spent another $50 million renovating it.
Then came Atlantic City casinos: Trump Plaza, Trump's Castle,
the Trump Taj Mahal, for hundreds of millions of dollars each.
Trump was always betting big while rolling the dice, acquiring
properties in a real-life Monopoly game. He started developing
resorts and golf courses in countries around the world, and li-
censed his name for a variety of products: hotels, wine, menswear,
vodka, steaks, water, deodorant, eyeglasses, coffee, mattresses,

home furnishings, adult learning courses, and a board game, most of which did not last long. His real estate projects bounced in and out of bankruptcy restructuring, and several times he was forced to give up his interest to those who'd assumed his debt. Often, Father Fred came through, pledging his own equity toward his son's success. Undaunted by bankruptcy, undeterred by investor takeovers, and unembarrassed at accepting his father's help when he was in his thirties, Donald Trump proclaimed himself a giant success and moved on to the next big deal. According to a Gallup poll conducted in December 1988, he was the tenth most admired man in America.

Trump's mind-set has always been a rather simple one: the world is composed of winners and losers, and he wants to be a winner every single time. If he admitted defeat—even a single, minor mistake—he would be a loser. He also has a rather negative view of his fellow humans. In a 1981 article in *People*, he said, "Man is the most vicious of all animals, and life is a series of battles ending in victory or defeat. You just can't let people make a sucker out of you." And in a 2011 speech at the National Achievers Congress in Sydney, Australia, he said, "When a person screws you, you screw them back ten times harder!"

In 1977, Trump married a blond, six-foot-tall Czech model named Ivana Zelnickova, three years his junior. His marriage proposal was unique: "If you don't marry me, you'll ruin your life." Ivana agreed that she did not want to ruin her life. They had three children: Donald Jr. in 1977, Ivanka in 1981, and Eric in 1984. Trump has always made it clear who was boss in his marriages. He and Ivana never had "tremendous fights" because, he said, "ultimately, Ivana does exactly what I tell her to do." Though Ivana often acquiesced to his bidding, she was no Stepford wife and played an active role in her husband's businesses as vice president for interior design. Her projects included the Trump Tower, the Plaza Hotel, and the Trump Plaza Hotel and Casino in Atlantic City, supervising a budget of tens of millions of dollars for each property.

Perhaps he sent his wife to Atlantic City in 1985 for personal rather than business reasons. That same year, Trump began an affair with a twenty-two-year-old, five-foot-eight model from Georgia named Marla Maples, stashing her on his yacht and at his various hotels. He'd lost interest in Ivana—and told her so— even though she bought herself bigger breasts, wider cheekbones, a softer face, and fuller lips to please him, emerging from her bandages looking a lot like a young Brigitte Bardot. But her efforts were futile. Marla boasted something unattainable to Ivana— youth—and somewhat resembled her idol, Farrah Fawcett, with a wild mane of feathery blond locks.

Donald bemoaned to Marla the state of his loveless marriage for years and promised he would get a divorce one day soon—as most unfaithful married men do. Finally, Marla grew sick of waiting. In December 1989, she marched up to Ivana, Donald, and the three kids at a restaurant in Aspen, where they had been enjoying a ski vacation, and said, "I'm Marla and I love your husband. Do you?" Specific accounts differ, but Ivana told her something like "You bitch, leave my husband alone," followed by a string of Slavic profanities.

The ski-slope face-off soon made the headlines. It was the perfect tabloid story in that era of excess, a time of huge hair and linebacker shoulder pads and record Wall Street numbers. It was a real-life version of one of the biggest TV shows of the eighties— *Dynasty*, where money was no object and the ex-wife and the current wife and the mistress all bitch-slapped each other in public to the cheers of onlookers. As the Trumps' marriage quickly crumbled, New York tabloids slavered after the story, splashing photos and headlines of the love triangle on their covers for months.

The average man would be horrified by a public confrontation between his wife and his mistress—in front of the children, no less—and its breathless coverage in the New York papers, but not Donald Trump. He reveled in it. There he was for all to see, the object of lustful desire of two beautiful blondes fighting over him. The infamous *New York Post* headline "Marla Boasts to Her Friends: Best Sex I've Ever Had" was one that Trump himself convinced the paper to run, according to Jill Brooke, a *Post* reporter.

He scoured the papers every day, pleased that his divorce was getting far more coverage than the high-profile split of director Steven Spielberg and actress Amy Irving, and claimed the press increased his casino profits. "A divorce is never a pleasant thing," he explained, and indeed, his elder son didn't speak to him for a year, "but from a business standpoint, it's had a very positive effect." In a 1991 interview with *Esquire* magazine, he said, "You know it doesn't really matter what they write as long as you've got a young and beautiful piece of ass."

It is curious that of the two dozen or so accusations women have made against Trump for sexual assault, unwanted kissing, and dressing-room leering, the very first one came from his wife, and it was nothing less than an accusation of rape. In a divorce deposition obtained by Harry Hurt, author of the 1993 *Lost Tycoon: The Many Lives of Donald J. Trump*, Ivana stated under oath that she had recommended a cosmetic surgeon to treat her husband's bald spot, and he came home furious because the procedure was not only painful, but ineffective. According to Hurt, Ivana stated that he pinned back her arms, yanked handfuls of hair from her scalp so she, too, would have a sore bald spot, tore off her clothes, and raped her. The following morning, Ivana awoke sore and bruised, and gazed at clumps of her hair all over the bed. As she examined her own bald spots in the mirror, Trump glared at her and asked casually, "Does it hurt?" She told several friends about it soon after.

Once she reached a generous divorce settlement, however, and signed a gag order, she changed her tune. Her lawyers insisted that new editions of Hurt's book include a statement from Ivana on the flyleaf. "During a deposition given by me in connection with my matrimonial case, I stated that my husband had raped me," the statement said. "On one occasion during 1989, Mr. Trump and I had marital relations in which he behaved very differently toward me than he had during our marriage. As a woman, I felt violated, as the love and tenderness which he normally exhibited towards me, was absent. I referred to this as a 'rape' but I do not want my words to be interpreted in a literal or criminal sense." Trump denied the rape, but perhaps he was more concerned about the allegations of scalp surgery. His hair was so naturally thick, he never would have needed such a thing.

But if the story of the angry, balding rapist faded away, the fable of the celebrity playboy was just getting started. Now that he was getting divorced, beautiful women would only burnish his brand, the brand of a regular guy—setting aside for the moment that his father was worth hundreds of millions of dollars—who worked hard and obtained amazing success. *You too*, he was saying, in what was perhaps the world's most brilliant marketing ploy, *could be like me if you stay in my hotels and buy my wine and fly my airline and wear my ties.* He gave consumers—for a price—the cachet of Trump fabulousness, dreams of a life of private jets and Bond girls and gilded penthouse apartments.

When in 1991 a reporter from *People* magazine named Sue

Carswell called Trump's office to confirm or refute the rumor that he had dumped Marla Maples for Italian model and future first lady of France Carla Bruni, she quickly got a return call from a man who identified himself as Trump's publicist, John Miller. Miller confirmed that Trump had dumped Marla and had numerous beautiful women hoping he would pick them as his next girlfriend, including Bruni. "Important, beautiful women call him all the time," Miller said. He listed several names, including Madonna. "He mentioned basically every hot woman in Hollywood," Carswell said. Miller told her, "Actresses just call to see if they can go out with him and things." He boasted that in addition to living with Marla, Trump had "three other girlfriends." For her part, Bruni denied dating Trump, calling him "the king of Tacky" and "obviously a lunatic."

John Miller sounded eerily similar to Trump himself. When Carswell called Marla and played the tape, she began to cry and confirmed John Miller was none other than Trump. Sometimes Trump said he was John Barron, a vice president of the Trump Organization, when he called major newspapers and magazines to tell journalists how dozens of gorgeous women were panting to go to bed with Trump.

In January 1993, an event occurred that would lead to the second sexual assault allegation made against Trump. According to a lawsuit filed four years later, a woman named Jill Harth and her boyfriend George Houraney dined with Trump at his opulent Florida estate, Mar-a-Lago, to celebrate a business deal. During the meal, Harth got more than she bargained for when Trump tried to slip his hands between her legs. After dinner, Trump gave her a tour of the mansion and, in his daughter Ivanka's bedroom, Harth claimed in a 2016 interview with the *Guardian*, "He pushed me up against the wall, and had his hands all over me and tried to get up my dress again, and I had to physically say, 'What are you doing? Stop it.' It was a shocking thing to have him do this because he knew I was with George, he knew they were in the next room. And how could he be doing this when I'm there for business?"

She and George, who had planned to spend the night, left. After Jill and George became engaged, Trump began to stalk her, Harth stated in her suit claiming sexual assault and relentless sexual harassment. New York tabloids trumpeted the suit, but it was withdrawn after George Houraney settled with Trump for an undisclosed amount in a lawsuit that claimed Trump had backed out of a business deal.

Marla Maples traveled frequently with Donald, perhaps to keep her eye on him, and always packed a wedding dress, just in case he changed his mind and decided to marry her on the spot. "You've got to be prepared," she explained. She was supposed to be on the pill but, curiously, got pregnant anyway. When relating the story to Howard Stern, Trump said he asked her, "What are we going to do about this?" which seemed to indicate abortion was an option. But it was not an option for Marla, who in October 1993 gave birth to his daughter Tiffany—named after the jewelry store—and still he didn't marry her. Circumstances, however, pushed the reluctant groom toward the altar. Trump's reputation for instability—financial and personal—would reduce the price of his casino stock offering early in 1994. But a newly married man, settled down with an infant, would likely increase his revenue. The final shove came on December 7, 1993; a mass shooting on the Long Island Rail Road made Trump realize that "life is short," as he later explained it, so they might as well get married. Perhaps it's not surprising Marla cooked up a lavish wedding with a thousand of their closest friends in the Grand Ballroom of the Plaza in just days, because she was prepared.

Delighted as Marla was with the nuptials, Trump was less so. "I was bored when she was walking down the aisle," Trump later said. "I kept thinking, 'What the hell am I doing here?'"

O. J. Simpson was among the guests watching the radiant bride come down the aisle. "I think everybody in the country believes if *their* relationship can work, then anyone's relationship can work," he said, six months before he was charged with stabbing his wife and a friend of hers to death in her front yard.

Ivana was a strong-minded, independent woman, which is why she quickly divorced her husband once she realized he was a philanderer. She had held important positions in the Trump Organization, made her own schedule, and spoke her mind. Not so Marla, a delicate southern belle who let Trump run the show. Maureen Orth of *Vanity Fair* wrote, "Getting to know Marla Maples is akin to pressing your thumb on an aerosol can and watching mountains of Reddi-wip flow out."

Marla knew she didn't fit into Trump World. "Once we started going out in public, an image was expected," she recalled. "The hair and makeup and the designer dresses, and you become a caricature of yourself. And I think what he loved about me the most was that I wasn't part of that world. But once we were together publicly, he wanted to change me into that social animal . . . Putting on gowns and going out hosting events and having Harry Winston put jewelry on my hands was always uncomfortable for me—that was me playing a role. I felt that's what the job called for." Indeed, her primary job as Trump's wife was to make men jealous of Trump.

Marla did what she was told, but it wasn't enough. A little

more than a year after the wedding, in an interview with *Vanity Fair* in 1995, Trump looked back on his bachelor days between wives with longing. "I had been in Europe fucking every model in the world. My life was wild," he lamented. As could be expected, while Marla stayed home with the baby, Trump resumed his playboy ways, traveling around the world in his private jet with gorgeous models. Marla grew lonely and sad.

She had signed a prenup capping her divorce settlement at a measly $1 million if they separated within five years, with another million for a house and $100,000 a year child support for Tiffany that would end when she turned twenty-one or before that if, oddly enough, she joined the army or the Peace Corps. But Trump dumped Marla well before the deadline. At 4:00 a.m. on April 16, 1996, police caught her with Trump's bodyguard, a thirty-five-year-old hunk named Spencer Wagner, under a lifeguard stand on a beach not far from Mar-a-Lago while Trump was out of town. The *National Enquirer* crowed, "Shock for Trump! Marla Caught with Hunk/Cops Interrupt Late Night Beach Frolic."

Trump and Marla both denied the story. She and the bodyguard had gone for a walk, they said—as many people do at 4:00 a.m.—and when she had to pee, the only place offering a modicum of privacy was under the lifeguard stand. But Trump was livid. This time the screaming tabloid headlines weren't burnishing his image but tarnishing it. This time *he* was the cuckold, the dupe, the fool, while his sexy young wife was making love in the sand with a younger, buffer, more handsome man. Serving her with divorce papers immediately would have validated the story. It is stunning that a man known for impatience and outbursts of anger didn't fire the bodyguard until four months later. He bided his time even longer with Marla, informing her of the divorce a year later by leaving a copy of the *New York Post* outside their bedroom door with the headline "Donald Is Divorcing Marla."

Under the terms of their prenuptial agreement and divorce settlement, Maples is bound by a confidentiality agreement regarding their marriage which has rendered her as mute as a zombie whose mouth has been filled up with salt and whose lips have been sewn together. She got a contract from HarperCollins in 2001 for her memoirs, to be called *All That Glitters Is Not Gold*. But the book was never published. At the time, Trump refused to comment whether he invoked the confidentiality agreement to scotch the deal. Either way, her story, such as it is, looks lost to history.

Trump was overjoyed to be a bachelor again, to publicly surround himself with beautiful women. In his bestselling 1997 memoir, *Trump: The Art of the Comeback*, he recalled—or, more likely, invented—stories of women wild to have sex with him. "If I told the real stories of my experiences with women," he wrote, "often seemingly very happily married and important women, this book would be a guaranteed bestseller (which it will be anyway!)" He told of a certain "lady of great social pedigree and wealth," whose husband was also at the dinner table. "All of a sudden, I felt her hand on my knee, then on my leg. She started petting me in all different ways." Then, in language from a 1940s film noir starring Bette Davis, language no woman in real life would *ever* utter, she cried, "Donald, I don't care. I just don't care. I have to have you, and I have to have you now." When Trump gave a limo ride to another "truly great-looking and sexy" wealthy woman who was about to get married, "within five seconds after the door closed, she would be jumping on top of me wanting to get screwed."

In 1998, Trump arrived at New York's Kit Kat Club with a

beautiful Norwegian heiress named Celina Midelfart as his date. There he spotted twenty-eight-year-old Slovenian model Melania Knauss. At five foot eleven, slender and shapely with wide cheekbones, catlike blue eyes, and a tumble of gleaming brown hair, she enchanted him immediately. "She's incredible," he told a friend. "I want this woman." While Midelfart powdered her nose, Trump asked Melania for her phone number. Having seen Trump with a date, she turned him down, but he persisted. They married in a million-dollar ceremony in 2005. A year later, they had a son, Barron. Trump's older children called Melania "the Portrait" because she was beautiful and spoke so little. Indeed, each of Trump's wives has grown more silent than the one before.

In 2003, Trump began filming *The Apprentice*, a reality TV show in which aspiring businesspeople competed for a one-year, $250,000 contract at one of Trump's companies. Trump proved a natural; easy to work with, fascinating to watch, memorizing direction so well the crew often needed only one take. It was he who came up with the famous line, "You're fired!" Over fourteen seasons, the show made Trump a household name nationally, paving the way for his entry onto the political stage.

Trump had long been interested in politics and in 1987 took out several full-page ads in major newspapers promoting a reduced budget deficit, peace in Central America, nuclear disarmament with the Soviet Union, and renegotiating the money the U.S. spent supporting global organizations. He changed his party several times, from Republican to Reform to Democrat back to Republican. Starting in 2010, he helped fuel the Obama "birther" movement, the false belief that President Barack Obama had been born in Kenya, not Hawaii, and was therefore constitutionally prohibited from becoming president. The theory was trumpeted by the *National Enquirer*, owned by Trump's good friend David Pecker, and appealed to many Americans who didn't like Obama.

After Obama released his long-form birth certificate on April 27, 2011, Trump put a self-congratulatory spin on the fact that he had been wrong. "I am really honored, and I am really proud, that I was able to do something that nobody else could do," he said.

On June 16, 2015, a Republican again, Trump announced his candidacy for president at Trump Tower in Manhattan. He was one of seventeen candidates vying for the 2016 Republican nomination; the largest presidential field in American history. Political analysts scoffed at Trump's campaign. *Chicago Tribune* columnist Clarence Page wrote, "Let's not treat Donald Trump like a serious candidate. He's a marketing genius, and that's what he's doing." CNN political analyst Jeffrey Toobin said, "Donald Trump is engaging in one of his fictional presidential campaigns." Yet this darkest of dark horse candidates quickly rose to the top of opinion polls. On May 3, 2016, he became the presumptive Republican nominee.

Why did he run for president? Was it because he reveled in publicity? Was it to sell Trump-branded consumer products—those that hadn't gone bankrupt—and Trump hotel rooms and Trump condos? Was he planning on having his own Fox News TV show, the *Trump Hour*, after he dropped out of the race? Did he actually think he could win running against Republican favorites like Ted Cruz, Jeb Bush, and Marco Rubio? Journalist Michael Wolff, who interviewed numerous people involved with Trump's campaign for his book *Fire and Fury: Inside the Trump White House*, offers us insight into this question: Trump didn't really want or expect to win. "Losing would work out for everybody," he reportedly said. "Losing was winning." Because, according to Wolff, "Once he lost, Trump would be both insanely famous and a martyr to Crooked Hillary. His daughter Ivanka and son-in-law Jared would be international celebrities . . . Melania Trump, who had been assured by her husband that he wouldn't become president, could return to inconspicuously lunching."

When Trump threw his hat in the ring, there had been only two allegations of sexual misconduct, that of Ivana in 1990, which she recanted after her divorce settlement, and the sexual harassment lawsuit of Jill Harth in 1996, which she dropped when her boyfriend's lawsuit was settled. Now that his name was everywhere, however, new reports surfaced. In May 2016, the *New York Times* reported allegations by Temple Taggart McDowell, who had been twenty-one and Miss Utah USA in 1997. McDowell accused Trump, who owned the pageant, of kissing and embracing her in such an alarming manner that one of the pageant chaperones told her not to remain in a room alone with him.

Also in May, Bridget Sullivan, who was crowned Miss New Hampshire 2000, spoke publicly about how Trump came into the Miss USA pageant changing room while the contestants were naked, ostensibly to wish them good luck. "The time that he walked through the dressing rooms was really shocking. We were all naked," she told BuzzFeed in May 2016. Mariah Billado, Miss Vermont Teen USA 1997, said, "I remember putting on my dress really quick, because I was like, 'Oh my God, there's a man in here.'" Trump, she recalled, said something like, "Don't worry, ladies, I've seen it all before." Billado said she brought the matter to the attention of Trump's daughter Ivanka, who responded, "Yeah, he does that." Another contestant, Victoria Hughes, Miss New Mexico Teen USA, agreed that Trump marched into their dressing room, where the youngest contestant was fifteen.

In June, former Miss Washington Cassandra Searles posted a photo on Facebook of several Miss USA contestants from 2013, Trump grinning in the center. "This one guy treated us like cattle," she wrote. "I forgot to mention that guy will be running to become the next President of the United States . . . He probably doesn't want me telling the story about that time he continually grabbed my ass and invited me to his hotel room."

In October, Tasha Dixon, Miss Arizona USA 2001, told a CBS affiliate in Los Angeles that in 2001, Trump "just came strolling right in. There was no second to put a robe on or any sort of clothing or anything. Some girls were topless, other girls were naked." The same month, Ninni Laaksonen, Miss Finland 2006, claimed that Trump squeezed her rear end after posing for a photo before an appearance on the *Late Show with David Letterman* that year. "Trump stood right next to me and suddenly he squeezed my butt. He really grabbed my butt. I don't think anybody saw it but I flinched and thought: 'What is happening?'"

Trump's 2016 campaign team denied the pageant contestants' allegations, though they seemed to be substantiated by a 2005 interview Trump gave to radio host Howard Stern in which he talked about going backstage at pageants when the contestants were changing clothes. "No men are anywhere," Trump said, "and I'm allowed to go in, because I'm the owner of the pageant and therefore I'm inspecting it . . . 'Is everyone OK?' You know, they're standing there with no clothes. 'Is everybody OK?' And you see these incredible looking women, and so I sort of get away with things like that. But no, I've been very good."

The pageant contestants' accusations seemed like a mere hiccup in the campaign. Because one faux pas followed the other. Trump mocked a handicapped reporter, twisting his arms and hands. He called many Mexican immigrants rapists, criminals, and drug dealers. He attacked Senator John McCain's record as a prisoner of war, while Trump got a draft deferral four times due to bone spurs in his feet. He encouraged his supporters at rallies to knock the crap out of hecklers. Bizarrely, he even suggested Ted Cruz's father was involved in the assassination of John F. Kennedy. He said he could shoot somebody on Fifth Avenue and get away with it. His supporters ate it up as yet more proof that he had the strength to stand up for them, to change things.

And then, on October 7, came the release of the pussy tape, more politely called the *Access Hollywood* tape. In the tumultuous aftermath of the tape's release, Trump declared he had never sexually assaulted anyone and called the conversation mere "locker room talk." Political pundits believed that Trump's candidacy was toast.

In the second presidential debate on October 9, CNN anchor Anderson Cooper asked Trump if he understood that he had bragged about sexually assaulting women. Trump denied he had ever grabbed women, repeating that his statement was merely "locker room talk." Anderson asked him three times whether he had ever kissed or groped any woman without her consent. Finally, Trump said, "No, I have not."

As seventy-four-year-old Jessica Leeds watched the debate, her anger rose. The next day, she informed the *New York Times* about an experience she had had on a flight in 1980 from the Midwest to New York, when she was seated next to Trump. According to Leeds, about forty-five minutes after takeoff, Trump raised the armrest and began touching her breasts and trying to slip his hand up her skirt. "He was like an octopus," she said. "His hands were everywhere. It was an assault."

In 1980, Leeds was a slender thirty-eight-year-old with tousled short brown hair and a wide white grin. In 2016, she was still trim and attractive, with short white hair and round black glasses. But Trump indicated that her current appearance—rather than any other reservations he might have had—was proof that he had never sexually assaulted her. "Believe me—she would not be my first choice," Trump told a rally of cackling supporters. "That I can tell you."

Other women watching the debate had the same reaction as Leeds and told similar stories, resulting in an avalanche of sexual assault accusations over the next week. Kristin Anderson stated that in the early 1990s, when she was a young, aspiring model, Trump sexually assaulted her in a New York nightclub. They were sitting next to each other—she recognized him—when she felt his hand slide between her legs and touch her private parts through her underpants.

Cathy Heller claimed that Trump had grabbed and kissed her against her will back in 1997, when the forty-four-year-old and her family attended a Mother's Day brunch at the Mar-a-Lago estate. Karena Virginia, a New York–area yoga instructor, said Trump approached her outside the 1998 U.S. Open tennis tournament in New York. While the twenty-seven-year-old was awaiting a car service, he made unseemly comments about her appearance, grabbed her arm, and groped her breast. "Don't you know who I am?" he asked. She said she blamed herself for years for wearing a dress that was too short.

Mindy McGillivray said that Trump grabbed her rear end when she was twenty-three and working as a photographer's assistant at a 2003 event at Mar-a-Lago. The photographer corroborated that she had told him, "Donald just grabbed my ass!" Rachel Crooks, a secretary who worked in Trump's building, was twenty-two and first met Trump in 2005 outside an elevator at Trump Tower in New York City. He shook her hand, she said, and kissed her on the cheeks and then on the lips. "It was so inappropriate," Crooks recalled in an interview. "I was so upset that he thought I was so insignificant that he could do that."

Natasha Stoynoff, a writer for *People* magazine, said Trump inappropriately touched her in 2005 when she was at Mar-a-Lago for an interview timed to be published on the first anniversary of his marriage to Melania. Stoynoff, forty at the time of the encounter, claimed that he pushed her against a wall and forced his tongue into her mouth. "We're going to have an affair, I'm telling you," he said. *People* produced six witnesses who corroborated that Stoynoff had told them about the event soon afterward. Jennifer Murphy, a twenty-six-year-old contestant on the fourth season of *The Apprentice*, claimed that Trump kissed her on the lips after a job interview in 2005.

Adult film star Jessica Drake said Trump kissed her and two other women without their consent in 2006 in his suite at a golf tournament in Lake Tahoe. "When we entered the room, he grabbed each of us tightly in a hug and kissed each one of us without asking permission," said Drake, who was thirty-two at the time of the alleged assault. According to Drake, Trump offered her $10,000 to sleep with him, which she turned down.

Summer Zervos, a contestant in her early thirties on the fifth season of *The Apprentice*, which had filmed in 2005, met with Trump in 2007 in his suite at the Beverly Hills Hotel to discuss a job. She claimed that Trump kissed her open-mouthed, groped her breasts, and thrust his genitals against her. In January 2017, Trump publicly called Zervos a liar. In response, she sued him for defamation, though only for damages of three thousand dollars, a sign that the suit is not about getting rich but about clearing her name. Amid legal scrambling, appeals, hearings, and objections, the case crawls forward.

Lisa Boyne claimed that when she was twenty-five, in 1996, she attended a dinner with Trump, modeling agent John Casablancas, and five or six models, where Trump made the models walk across the table, looked under their skirts, and noted whether they were wearing underwear.

Many Trump supporters wondered aloud why none of these women reported the events earlier. Maybe not the quick kiss on the mouth—inappropriate as that is—but the breast, butt, and genital groping. Were these women paid by the Hillary Clinton campaign to come forward weeks before the presidential election? Were they Clinton supporters? In fact, the accusers held a variety of political affiliations from right-wing Republicans to Democrats who gave the maximum legal amount to Hillary Clinton's campaign.

One accusation that came in early 2019 seemed to validate Trump supporters' suspicions. A former Trump campaign employee named Alva Johnson filed a lawsuit against him alleging gender and pay discrimination against women and African Americans, as well as claiming that he had forcibly kissed her at a rally in Florida in August 2016. Cellphone video surfaced showing Trump giving her a peck on the cheek as she smiled broadly. The judge dismissed the suit, calling it "a political lawsuit."

A more damning accusation surfaced in June 2019 when advice columnist E. Jean Carroll accused Trump of raping her in a Bergdorf Goodman dressing room in 1995 or 1996, when she was fifty-two. She claimed she ran into him at the store's entrance, and he said, "Hey, you're that Advice Lady!" He then asked her for advice on buying a present for "a girl." The two went to the lingerie department where, Carroll claimed, Trump asked her to try on a see-through bodysuit. Inside the dressing room, Carroll alleges that Trump lunged at her, pushed her against the wall, causing her to hit her head "quite badly," placed his mouth on her lips, and reached under her coatdress and pulled down her tights. Carroll recalled, "The next moment, still wearing correct business attire, shirt, tie, suit jacket, overcoat, he opens the overcoat, unzips his pants, and, forcing his fingers around my private area, then thrusts his penis halfway—or completely, I'm not certain—inside me. It turns into a colossal struggle."

She said she escaped from the dressing room and left the store, the whole incident having lasted no more than three minutes. Carroll said she never reported the incident to the police, but that she confided in two friends soon thereafter. One told Carroll that she had been raped and must report it to the police. The other advised, "Tell no one. Forget it! He has 200 lawyers. He'll bury you." Carroll's friends confirmed those conversations to *New York* magazine and ABC News. Trump denied the rape, accusing her of lying to sell her upcoming book, and adding, "She's not my type."

Even if some of the allegations are true, why would Donald Trump grope unknown women and force them to kiss him? Why would he think it was okay to stick his fingers up the underwear of a stranger sitting next to him on a plane or on a barstool? Is it because with his wealth and fame—and the power that comes with them—he can? In terms of self-discipline and emotional development, is he like a naughty six-year-old who can't help himself grabbing a fistful of birthday cake before the party? Does he act wholly on impulse? He sees a nice pair of breasts or buttocks and, without giving it much consideration, marches up and squeezes them? Trump himself seems to confirm it. In *The Art of the Deal*, he wrote, "When I look at myself in the first grade and I look at myself now, I'm basically the same. The temperament is not that different."

The hashtag #WhyWomenDontReport started trending on Twitter in response to the Trump campaign's statements that the accusers were lying. Many women tweeted that they waited months and even years to report a sexual assault, often until other women came forward to accuse the same perpetrator. Many worried that no one would believe them or that a powerful man would make their lives miserable. In Trump's case, the women, like E. Jean Carroll, feared his battery of threatening lawyers would sue them into bankruptcy. They also worried—and were right to do so, as events proved—that they would be accused of lying to get attention and money.

Trump vehemently denied all the claims and called the allegations "a conspiracy against you, the American people." A vast, left-wing conspiracy, no doubt. In the third presidential debate of 2016, Trump said, "I think they want either fame or her [Hillary's] campaign did it and I think it's her campaign."

While we will probably never know exactly what happened between Trump and his many accusers, there are other clues to Trump's outlook on women in general. In the 1990s, he tried to get *Playboy* to do a spread called "The Girls of Trump," and encouraged those he considered his best-looking female employees to pose for the magazine nude or at least topless.

"Women have one of the great acts of all time," he wrote in his 1997 book, *The Art of the Comeback*. "The smart ones act very feminine and needy, but inside they are real killers . . . I have seen women manipulate men with just a twitch of their eye—or perhaps another body part . . ."

In a 1992 story that appeared in *New York* magazine, writer Marie Brenner claimed that Trump said, "Women, you have to treat 'em like shit." Trump was so furious at Brenner for writing that he treated women poorly, that the next time he saw her at a social event, he poured a glass of wine down her back. When asked about Brenner's statement, Trump responded, "I didn't say that. The woman's a liar, extremely unattractive, lots of problems because of her looks."

Then, in 1994, in a *Primetime Live* interview, Trump made a statement oddly similar to what Marie Brenner reported: "I tell friends who treat their wives magnificently, get treated like crap in return, 'Be rougher and you'll see a different relationship.'"

Even before the release of the pussy tape and the resulting onslaught of women coming forward alleging sexual assault, most reputable pollsters and pundits had never expected Trump to win. And yet, he did, on November 8, 2016, winning 304 electoral votes to Hillary Clinton's 227. He lost the popular vote—the fifth elected president to do so—by nearly three million votes, 65,853,514 votes (48.18 percent) to 62,984,828 votes (46.09 percent). It was an election between two candidates who both had more baggage than LAX. And yet, after the pussy tape, how could he have won? What happened?

Sick and tired of career politicians, many voters saw Trump as a no-nonsense businessman who would straighten out the country, hiring the best people, making the U.S. more prosperous than ever before, bringing his brand of sweet success to the entire nation. The economy had left many behind. A large segment of the American population wanted a change, a breath of fresh air, someone to shake up Washington, not someone like Hillary Clinton, who had been in a scandal-plagued White House twenty years before, albeit as first lady. They wanted a man who they saw as having common sense to take them back to a safer time where they understood the world and fit seamlessly into it, before good blue-collar jobs drained away to other countries; before men married men and women could marry women; before people could change the gender on their driver's licenses based on how they identified rather than what was on their birth certificates. Many saw Trump's rhetoric—crude, insulting, and self-aggrandizing—as proof that he was the one to take on the establishment and shake things up. They had been hurting, picked on, scorned, and Donald Trump seemed to be the only politician who understood, the only one who stood with them and vowed to fight for them.

Those election experts who consigned Trump's campaign to the rubbish heap because of his history with women failed to consider his historic persona. While most American male politicians cultivate an image as pious, churchgoing family men, Trump never made the slightest attempt to do so. On the contrary, long before the election, Donald Trump had carefully crafted an image more akin to that of Hugh Hefner, surrounded by adoring, long-legged Playmates in skimpy clothing, though his own costume was a business suit and tie instead of a satin bathrobe.

In other words, Trump's supporters, who had lifted him out of a crowded field of experienced Republican candidates, knew he was no monk and didn't care. Of course, the allegations of sexual assault were clearly far more disturbing than consensual affairs, and most registered voters believed them. A poll showed that only 14 percent believed Trump innocent, while 68 percent believed he was guilty, and the rest weren't sure. It turns out, many who believed him guilty still voted for him. And many of those were evangelical Christians, who had been so horrified to have a Slick Willie Clinton soiling the dignity of the White House yet didn't much care about a "grab them by the pussy" Donald Trump. A poll conducted by the nonpartisan Public Religion Research Institute taken right after the *Access Hollywood* tape release found that 72 percent of white evangelicals believed a politician could be immoral in his private life and still govern well. In 2011, the same poll had the figure at only 30 percent.

What had happened in only five years? For one thing, conservatives found a candidate whose policies they could rally behind, and policy has always been far more powerfully attractive to voters than personal sanctitude. Trump's victory had something in common with Grover Cleveland's in 1884. When a pastor asked, "Do the American people want a common libertine for their president?" the answer was yes, as long as he would reduce taxes.

Second, Trump supporters likely found solace in the fact that his sex stories, consensual and otherwise, had all taken place years before the 2016 election. There had been no examples of bad behavior since then that anyone had heard of. Perhaps he had changed. Once Trump was ensconced in the White House—one that initially leaked like a sieve—there were no stories of naked women running around with "breasts swinging," as in JFK's day, or of interns doing strange things with cigars in the Oval Office, as during Bill Clinton's tenure.

And lastly, it is likely that the 24/7 coverage of scandal—sex, lies, and the bad behavior of governors, senators, and congressmen—has inured us to it all. Just to mention a few scandals leading up to the 2016 election: In 2007, North Carolina senator John Edwards impregnated a campaign employee while his wife was dying of breast cancer, denied it, enlisted his friend in a cover-up, and finally admitted it. In 2008, Elliott Spitzer, the New York governor tough on prostitution, resigned after investigators discovered he had spent as much as $80,000 on prostitutes. Mark Sanford, the married governor of South Carolina, seemed to have disappeared from the planet for six days in 2009, his aides unable to locate him. When he reemerged, he held a press conference to explain that he had fallen in love with a woman in Argentina.

In 2011, New York Democratic congressman Anthony Weiner tweeted photos of his private parts, lied about it, told the truth, found redemption with his wife and the American public, and then did it again, this time with a minor, earning himself a prison sentence. We are exhausted. Numb. Desensitized. We are now a very hard nation to shock, and sexual assault claims have become business as usual. When E. Jean Carroll accused the president of the United States of rape in June 2019, most newspapers didn't put it on their front page, and it was mentioned on only one of the many Sunday morning talk shows.

As for Trump's supporters, a *USA Today* Trump voter panel reported respondents as collectively shrugging about the sex and the lies. "We're human. We all sin," said one. "And he tried to cover it up." "We know he's no angel, and he didn't become a multi-billionaire because he's a nice guy," said another. "I got over the shock of presidential affairs after Kennedy and Clinton."

Given the national prostration regarding political sex stories, when two women Trump had slept with a decade earlier seemed ready to sell their stories shortly before the 2016 election, he should have simply let the tawdry tales unspool. Trump's lawyer and fixer, Michael Cohen, arranged to pay both for their silence.

Karen McDougal, the 1998 *Playboy* Playmate of the Year, first met Trump at the Playboy Mansion in June 2006 when he was filming an episode of *Celebrity Apprentice*. He was stunned by the gorgeous, blue-eyed brunette, and they soon began an affair. Trump would arrange for her to meet him at various hotels or in his homes. Karen told Anderson Cooper of CNN that she loved Trump and "He always told me he loved me." But Karen felt guilty about her affair with a married man and after ten torrid months called it off. "The excitement took over for a while, but I started feeling so bad about myself. . . . It was tearing me apart in the long run. I knew I needed to get out," she said.

Some of Trump's behavior made it easier for Karen to leave. For instance, when she mentioned her mother's disapproval of him, Trump scoffed, "What, that old hag?" even though Trump and Karen's mother were quite close in age. On another occasion, as Karen and a female friend rode in a limo with Trump, her friend mentioned she was dating an African American man. Multiple sources said that Trump said the friend liked "the big black dick." Then he started talking about her good looks and breast size. The friend was outraged, McDougal horrified. The affair was over.

As Trump continued to beat down his opponents for the Republican nomination, a friend of Karen's began posting about the affair on social media. Karen, who would have preferred the story to remain secret, decided that since it was going to come out, she might as well tell it herself to make sure it was, at least, accurate. And, of course, there would be money involved.

On August 16, 2016, she signed a $150,000 contract with AMI, the parent company of the *National Enquirer*, whose CEO, David Pecker, was a close friend of Trump's. AMI agreed to publish one hundred columns written by McDougal on fitness and put her on at least two covers. The contract also stipulated that she would never discuss her relationship with Donald Trump. There's a term for this kind of contract: "catch and kill."

McDougal was delighted with the deal. She had never wanted to tank Trump's chance at the presidency—she had truly cared for him and was a devout Republican—and she was excited about rebranding herself from nude model to fitness guru. But AMI did not live up to its side of the bargain, putting her on only one cover and publishing only a handful of columns.

In March 2018, McDougal filed a lawsuit against AMI in Los Angeles Superior Court, aiming to invalidate the nondisclosure agreement. A month later, just four days after the FBI raided Michael Cohen's homes and office looking for evidence of bank fraud, wire fraud, and campaign finance violations and seizing 3.7 million documents including emails, AMI settled with McDougal, which allowed her to speak about the alleged affair. In the years since her entanglement with Trump, she has returned to her roots and faith. "I'm going to church. I'm involved in ministry," she said. The White House has denied her story.

The other woman paid to keep her mouth shut about Trump in the weeks leading up to the election was Stormy Daniels, a buxom blonde, blue-eyed porn star with an intelligent face whose real name is Stephanie Clifford. According to Stormy, she had met Trump at a celebrity golf tournament in Lake Tahoe in 2006, where they had a one-night stand. In October 2016, she signed a contract for $130,000, in return for which she agreed never to discuss her affair with Trump. Yet the *Wall Street Journal* got hold of the story, resulting in denials by Michael Cohen and Donald Trump that they had paid her. Although Trump never admitted to the affair, he eventually said he'd repaid Cohen from his personal account, not the campaign account.

Though Michael Cohen is currently serving a three-year jail term, Trump's culpability remains debatable. Did he pay Stormy "for the principal purpose of influencing an election," as Cohen's lawyer claimed? If so, that would be a campaign finance violation. Or did he silence the women to save himself personal embarrassment with his wife and family, which would not have been breaking the law?

In March 2018, Stormy Daniels sued to break her nondisclosure agreement, claiming it was invalid because Trump himself had never signed it. But in September of that year, Trump's lawyers stated he would not enforce the agreement, nor would he dispute Stormy's claim that it was invalid. Naturally, she wrote a book, including the only description we have of sex with Donald Trump.

Having accepted an invitation to dinner at his penthouse suite, Stormy found Trump was not at all suggestive or vulgar, and pleasant company initially. Then he talked and talked about himself, bragging and boasting while her stomach grumbled in rage at the absence of the promised dinner. When he showed her a magazine—it might have been *Forbes*—with his face on the cover, she finally lost her temper.

"Are you so insecure that you have to brag about yourself or are you just a fucking asshole? Which is it?" she asked. "Someone should take that magazine and spank you."

"You wouldn't," he said quietly. She ordered him to drop his pants and bend over—which, oddly enough, he did—and swatted him a couple of times. As he stood to pull up his pants, he said, "I like you. You remind me of my daughter." His daughter, he explained, was smart, beautiful, and a woman to be reckoned with. Trump then offered to get Stormy a role on his hit show *The Apprentice*.

Three hours after she had arrived, still with no food in sight—she went to attend a call of nature. When she emerged from the bathroom, she was shocked to find him sitting on the bed, waiting for her, wearing only his briefs, an undershirt, and socks. "I sighed inwardly," she recalled. The ever-practical Stormy figured sex was just the price she had to pay to get on his show. And it might help to finally get her dinner.

"I was lying down on the bed with him on top of me, naked," she wrote. "I was just there, my head on the pillow. There was no foreplay and it was one position. Missionary. We kissed, and his hard, darting tongue pushed in and out of my mouth. *He's even a terrible kisser.*"

Her description certainly dampens our expectations that sex with a man dynamic enough to win the U.S. presidency would rock our world, but it gets worse. "I lay there as he fumbled his dick into me," she continued. "I was surprised he didn't even mention a condom. I didn't have one with me anyway because I wasn't meeting him for sex . . . He was a little verbal, but nothing dirty. 'That's great,' he said. 'That's great. Oh, you're so beautiful.' I certainly didn't do any kind of performance. I just kind of lay there . . ." She added that during the sex act, she replayed the past three hours in her mind to figure out how she had gotten herself in that position. We can picture her frowning up at the ceiling as she went over events, paying no more attention to Trump thrusting and groaning over her than if she had been having a manicure.

With the frankness that only a porn star could muster, Stormy described his private parts. "The world is waiting to hear about his penis," she wrote, which might be the only lie in her entire autobiography. "I am sorry to report that it is not freakishly small. It is smaller than average—below the true average, not the porn average. I didn't take out a measuring stick." She added that it had a "huge mushroom head like a toadstool." The sex, she said, lasted two or three minutes and, after his orgasm, he rolled off her, sighed, and said, "We're so good together, honey bunch."

Stormy didn't agree, saying that it might have been "the least impressive sex" she'd ever had. Though Trump pursued her, and she met him a couple of times over the course of the next year to discuss her appearance on *The Apprentice*—which never came to fruition—there was no sex. Stormy never wanted to see that mushroom of his again.

It is possible that the payoffs to Karen McDougal and Stormy Daniels were just the tip of the iceberg. Michael Wolff reported a comment made by Steve Bannon, CEO of Trump's campaign, regarding Marc Kasowitz, another of Trump's longtime fixer attorneys. "Kasowitz has gotten him out of all kinds of jams," Bannon allegedly said. "Kasowitz on the campaign—what did we have, a hundred women? Kasowitz took care of all of them."

The Trump of decades ago—the funny, irreverent, boisterous showman—has taken on a darker, angrier tone since he became president. While narcissistic personality disorder and hubris syndrome have some common symptoms, it is fair to say he has slipped into the latter, especially in August 2019 when he said he was the "second coming of God" and "the Chosen One." Hubris syndrome symptoms include using power for self-glorification; an almost obsessive focus on personal image; contempt for others; excessive self-confidence; refusal to listen to the advice of others; refusal to admit even minor mistakes; loss of contact with reality; reckless and impulsive actions; and incompetence due to supreme overconfidence, leading to inattention to details.

Trump's three wives have had very different reactions to his infidelity. Outspoken, independent Ivana divorced his ass and got a large settlement. She went on to become the queen of the home-shopping channels, making millions hawking her clothing, skincare products, and jewelry. A successful, globe-trotting entrepreneur and tabloid fixture, she married twice after her divorce from Trump. The second one was to a man twenty-three years her junior, and neither marriage lasted much more than a year. She has houses around the world and often chooses to stay in Saint-Tropez with a handsome young lover. In her seventies, she is often seen tottering around in a miniskirt and four-inch heels, still sporting her signature blond beehive, a small dog in tow.

Sweet little Reddi-wip Marla had an affair of own. Dumped with chump change, she moved with Tiffany to California to escape the screaming tabloids of New York City. She ditched her glass slippers, which had pinched rather severely, lived modestly, and never remarried. Her Trump trauma awakened an interest in spirituality; she goes to church, keeps Shabbat, eats kosher, explores her past lives, and does a lot of yoga. Her primary focus, however, has been raising her daughter, which is just as well because Tiffany grew up without her father—reportedly seeing him only four times between his separation from Marla in 1997 and the start of his campaign in 2015. Indeed, Tiffany was treated by Trump something like the bastard child of an eighteenth-century English duke. In August 2019, Trump's personal assistant, Madeleine Westerhout, lost her job after she told reporters the president didn't like being photographed with Tiffany because he thought she was fat and joked that he couldn't pick her out of a crowd.

A joyless sphinx, Melania appears at his side now and then for official functions, though she reportedly spends much of her time at her parents' house in Potomac, Maryland, with her son, Barron, whose school is nearby. When staying at the White House, she sleeps in a separate bedroom. This is not so unusual; all U.S. presidents and their wives have separate White House bedrooms, though whether they choose to sleep separately or together is up to them. Former White House aide Omarosa Manigault Newman wrote that Melania plans to divorce Trump as soon as he leaves the White House. Formerly sparkling and animated, Melania looks as if she has gazed on cursed, snake-headed Medusa—and perhaps, in a way, she has—and her face is slowly turning to stone.

Certainly, Melania wasn't happy when Donald won the election. She valued, above all things, her privacy and that of her son. According to Michael Wolff, when returns began to show that Trump would, in fact, win, Melania, sitting on the couch, began to cry. She didn't even move to the White House from New York for six months after the inauguration, saying she wanted Barron to finish the school year.

Reports indicated that Melania was "blindsided" and "furious" about her husband's affairs with McDougal and Daniels, according to anonymous sources who spoke with the *New York Times*. These reports make us scratch our collective head. It smacks of Hillary Clinton claiming to be shocked by Bill's diddling the intern. Though perhaps Melania was surprised that her husband had had unprotected sex with a porn star. That would pretty much shock even the most hardened betrayed wife.

But unlike Hillary Clinton, Melania didn't spring into action to defend her husband and attack his accusers. On the contrary, she canceled several public appearances with him and drove to his 2018 State of the Union address separately. "It is not a concern and focus of mine," she sniffed, when asked about press reports of Trump's infidelities. "I'm a mother and a First Lady and I have much more important things to think about and to do."

Even before Stormy's story took the nation by storm, Melania wasn't all that thrilled with Donald. Perhaps her feelings are best summed up in the hand swat seen round the world, that unforgettable moment on May 22, 2017, when the first couple deplaned Air Force One at Ben Gurion Airport in Tel Aviv and, walking down the red carpet, the president reached out for his wife's hand. With a disdainful flick of the wrist, she pushed him away in a small gesture that screamed, *Don't you even touch my fingers.*

FROM OOH-LA-LA TO BUNGA BUNGA: THE POLITICAL SEX SCANDALS OF OTHER NATIONS

*I*n Europe, because love affairs between married people are considered normal, fewer stories of presidential adultery make it out of the bedroom and into the public eye
compared to the puritanical republic of the United States. The
French, weaned on stories of riotous kings and fragrant royal mistresses, are titillated by modern scandals, to be sure, but almost
never horrified. Their reaction to the love affairs of their political
leaders is a smirk, in between a swig of espresso and a puff of a
cigarette. According to a 2006 survey in the popular newspaper
Le Figaro, only 17 percent of French voters would vote against a
candidate for president if he'd had an affair.

In France, a lusty sex life is seen as evidence of good health.
They want their leaders to be virile, bold, and radiantly confident. The Latin root of the word "impotent" literally means "lack
of power," and in the French view, the limp penis of a president
or prime minister might signify he cannot effectively run the

country. Such beliefs were epitomized by poor Louis XVI, unable to make love to his luscious young wife, Marie Antoinette, for seven years after marriage. Cartoonists portrayed him as a giant flaccid penis with one testicle—his head—lying helpless and inert on the ground. Seen as impotent in bed and on the throne, he was guillotined in 1793, and no French leader wants to follow in his footsteps. On the other hand, many Americans might see a limp presidential penis as a bonus.

In the 1990s, while many Americans expressed disgust at Bill Clinton's unending stories of adulterous dalliances, a top French politician, Christine Boutin, said, "He loves women, this man? It is a sign of good health!" The French were utterly baffled by the Lewinsky scandal, which they called Le Zippergate. French journalist Anne-Elisabeth Moutet wrote, "It looked pretty ridiculous to Europeans, who asked, 'Why doesn't he have a normal relationship with a nice, elegant, clever mistress who won't talk?' We do not talk about politicians' private lives. President François Mitterrand had lots of mistresses, and two regular mistresses, and every journalist in town, myself included, knew all about them, and we had the telephone numbers and we knew about the kids and everything. And we never wrote it. It was perfectly understood that nobody will back you up. The public will hate you to kingdom come. Do not talk about politicians' love lives." She added, "Besides, the French like their leaders to have a sex drive."

In 1992, when Bill Clinton's adulteries dominated his campaign, a reporter asked French politicians whether they had ever betrayed their wives, apparently the first time in French history that a member of the press had ever done so. One senator said, "This concept doesn't make any sense to me." A minister of health replied, "Betrayed, no. Had various relationships, yes." Another senator boasted, "I adore women. I have been a very, very, very big womanizer." A leading national politician said, "No. But I just got married two days ago."

In January 2018, iconic actress Catherine Deneuve and more than a hundred other well-known Frenchwomen in entertainment, business, and academia signed a letter to the newspaper *Le Monde* newspaper denouncing the #MeToo movement for hampering the fine art of seduction in the workplace. The movement, they claimed, repressed the sexual freedom of men who only tried to touch a knee, steal a kiss, or speak about pornographic matters at a business dinner, as well as the sexual freedom of women who might like it.

The most shocking story of a French president and his mistress is that of Félix Faure who, in 1895 at the age of fifty-four, began an affair with a twenty-five-year-old society hostess, Marguerite Steinheil. Though Marguerite was not beautiful—she had heavy features and no neck—she was dazzlingly sexy. Society meant everything to her, and she reveled in the swirl of balls and concerts, of revolving lovers and bitter feuds. She wrote, "This is Parisian life. And when you have tasted its exquisite poison you cannot do without it." To earn money to keep up her social pretensions, she convinced her numerous wealthy lovers to buy paintings from her artist husband, the timid, feeble Adolphe Steinheil. Out of guilt, many did.

Marguerite visited the presidential palace once or twice a week, where she and Faure closeted themselves in his office behind locked doors to work on his memoirs, as she explained. On one such occasion in 1899, the president had an unusual reaction to her tender ministrations. He cried out in pain rather than passion and locked his hands into rigid fists in her hair, an iron grip from which Marguerite could not extricate herself. She screamed for the guards, who broke down the door and, summing up the situation, grabbed a pair of scissors and cut off the hair on the top of her head to free her.

As the palace descended into an uproar and the first lady made her way rapidly to her moribund husband, Marguerite threw on her clothes and, sporting an unattractive new hairstyle, raced from the palace. Unfortunately, in her haste she had forgotten her corset, which the first lady found on the floor. A French newspaper reported, "Félix Faure passed away in good health, indeed from the excess of good health." It can also be said that he was one of the few political leaders who came and went at the same time.

Oddly, the fact that President Faure died while receiving oral sex from Marguerite enhanced her reputation greatly in Parisian society. Many suitors, believing she could drive men so wild their hearts stopped, bravely wanted to give it a try, especially after her hair grew back. One of her lovers, Aristide Briand, became prime minister in 1909. Others included rich industrialists, the Prince of Wales, and the king of Cambodia.

Most French presidents have continued to embody the tradition of Gallic lustiness. In 1974, President Valéry Giscard d'Estaing, having told his Secret Service agents to clear off, was driving a Ferrari on the Champs-Élysées at 5:00 a.m. when he collided with a milk truck. Clearly, the president had been returning from a romantic tryst. The police were called, the milk bottles swept up, and when the story appeared in the press, d'Estaing's poll ratings soared.

It shocks American sensibilities to imagine the future president of France, François Mitterrand, his wife, Danielle, and her lover, Jean Balenci, companionably dipping croissants into their café au lait at their communal Paris home and reading *Le Figaro*. We cannot picture, for instance, Bill and Hillary Clinton inviting Monica Lewinsky to live with them and the three buttering their toast together at breakfast. Or Stormy Daniels passing a bowl of scrambled eggs to Melania Trump. But such a situation seems perfectly reasonable to the French, and in Mitterrand's case, it lasted for many years.

Though Mitterrand was faithful to none, he fell deeply in love with one, a love that would last until death. In 1964 at the age of forty-seven, he began an affair with twenty-year-old Anne Pingeot, who became his lifelong companion and gave him a daughter, Mazarine, ten years later.

On November 3, 1994, the magazine *Paris Match* published a photo spread showing President Mitterrand and his secret daughter, then twenty, leaving a restaurant together. The French public was outraged—not at their president for having a second family, but at the press for invading his privacy, and closed ranks behind the old fellow. Many journalists agreed, calling it a sign of creeping Anglo-Saxon puritanism infecting French joie de vivre. "It's a pity I don't have one or two more daughters in reserve," Mitterrand said wryly. "It would have helped me climb back further in the opinion polls."

When Mitterrand was dying of cancer in 1995, the seventy-nine-year-old instructed his bodyguards to drop him off at the apartment of a pretty, young brunette who had just turned twenty. Sometimes he had her picked up and taken to the presidential palace to spend the night. His staff believed it was another secret daughter. It was not.

He did, however, have a secret son in Sweden with a journalist named Christine Forsne, with whom he had a thirteen-year relationship ending only when he became fatally ill in 1994. The son, Hravn, was born in 1988, when Mitterrand was an impressive seventy-two years old. Hravn revealed the identity of his father in 2014 when he ran for public office.

Mitterrand's successor, Jacques Chirac, was just as much a philanderer, though with less aplomb. The night of August 30–31, 1997, when Diana, Princess of Wales, died in a car accident in a Paris tunnel, Chirac had gone AWOL. No one—not his wife, not his security detail—had any idea where he was, and the British prime minister was desperately trying to reach him. At least President D'Estaing, twenty years earlier, had had the foresight to leave a note with his whereabouts in a sealed letter on his presidential desk so that security could contact him if nuclear war broke out. But Jacques Chirac often just wandered off without a trace. Having spent the night with a well-known Italian actress, he reappeared at seven o'clock in the morning—nearly seven hours after Diana's accident—to a presidential palace plunged into crisis.

Chirac's wife, Bernadette, put on a brave face when asked about her husband's countless love affairs. "He's a handsome man, and very charming, very gay. Girls are always galloping by," she said in a 2002 interview. When, in 2006, a reporter from the French magazine *L'Express* asked her if she suffered from her husband's reputation as a serial seducer, she replied, "No, I'm rather proud of it! It is necessary for a politician to be able to seduce."

Yet according to Chirac's chauffeur of twenty-five years, Jean-Claude Laumond, in private Bernadette was far less understanding. After depositing the president at a mistress's apartment, Laumond would return to the presidential palace, see the curtains of Bernadette's window twitch, and glimpse her disapproving face staring out at him. Then she would throw the window open and yell for all the world to hear, "And my husband, Monsieur Laumond, where is he?"

Despite his reputation as a ladies' man, Chirac was not a satisfying lover. His women friends—journalists, government employees, actresses—called him, "Chirac, three minutes shower included."

Italy, home of the prototypical Latin lover, has an unbroken tradition of virile leaders going back to ancient times. In 49 BCE, Julius Caesar's legions marched from Gaul to Rome singing,

> *Home we bring our bald whoremonger;*
> *Romans, lock your wives away!*
> *All the bags of gold you lent him*
> *Went his Gallic tarts to pay.*

It was a boast. Fast-forward two thousand years and Italians elected a thirty-six-year-old porn star to Parliament. Ilona Staller, known as La Cicciolina, won the 1987 election, according to the Italian press, because voters "appreciated her revealing talent and biological actions." To forestall the Gulf War breaking out, the congresswoman generously offered to have sex with Iraqi leader Saddam Hussein in return for peace. Ironically, the American press reported on Staller's background far more often than their Italian counterparts, which didn't find her election all that odd.

The multibillionaire media tycoon Silvio Berlusconi, prime minister of Italy for nine years between 1994 and 2011, entered politics not to help the nation but to avoid going to jail. His empire of television stations and newspapers was so corrupt that he needed the protection of high political office and, when he got it, immediately set about passing laws to protect himself. Out of thirty-two criminal cases against him, he was convicted in only one, and that was after he left office.

As prime minister, Berlusconi had much in common with Donald Trump. His skin a preternatural shade of orange, his scalp a mass of hair plugs, he had never held any public office before running for prime minister. He committed an unending stream of jaw-dropping social and diplomatic gaffes, befriending Russian president Vladimir Putin and calling German Chancellor Angela Merkel "an unfuckable lard-arse." With federal prosecutors hard on his trail pretty much all the time, he decried their investigations as a "witch hunt." At a Holocaust memorial ceremony in Milan, at the spot from which thousands of Italian Jews were sent to death camps, he said that Mussolini hadn't been all that bad and had done some "good things." One Italian journalist moaned, "What else could he have done? Snore? Fart noisily during the minutes of silence? Piss in the corner?"

Berlusconi's romantic life was even more colorful than his political one, though there are no reports of any women actually falling in love with him. His partners were in it for the cash, lots of it. In 2011 alone, he had handed out $15 million to those who indulged in his orgies, most of them held in his private palace on the island of Sardinia. His bodyguards and female employees pimped for him, inviting attractive young women to his parties, promising them three thousand euros each. Those whom he slept with—often as many as a dozen in one night—received twice as much. He also promised them jobs as weather girls on the many television stations he owned or high-level political jobs. A topless model and dancer on one of his TV shows became equal opportunities minister. His buxom dental hygienist who performed explicit lesbian floorshows in a naughty nun's costume became a regional councilor. An eighteen-year-old girlfriend said in an interview that she wanted to become an underwear model, a showgirl, or a member of Parliament, whatever Berlusconi decided. One journalist called Berlusconi's regime a "tartocracy."

He was the epitome of the *uomo forte*, the charismatic strong man considered single-handedly capable of leading the nation to greatness. Berlusconi's unending stream of amatory escapades—

such as keeping highly paid harems of very young women in his island palace well into his seventies and holding extreme lap-dancing competitions he called "bunga bunga"—served not to detract from his popularity but to increase it. Even his affairs with seventeen-year-old prostitutes failed to rattle Italian voters who, according to opinion polls, believed it to be a private matter.

Berlusconi routinely boasted about his sexual prowess publicly, saying it was "better to be passionate about beautiful women than to be gay." In 2011, he joked that pollsters asked women if they would have sex with him. "Thirty percent said yes," he explained, "while seventy percent replied, 'What, again?'"

In one conversation recorded by government investigators seeking evidence of the prime minister's financial corruption, Berlusconi told a friend about a party the night before. "I had a queue outside my door, there were eleven of them. I only managed to do eight of them, I couldn't manage any more. You just can't get around to all of them. But this morning I feel great, I'm pleased with my stamina." As any man in his seventies should be.

Considering the constant stream of scandal Berlusconi trailed in his wake, his continued popularity—he was elected three times—may surprise us. But stories of his romantic dalliances just made him more likable to many, and even corruption stories didn't upset many voters, who supported him for not bothering to collect their taxes.

Losing support in Parliament, Berlusconi resigned in October 2011, as large crowds sang the hallelujah chorus from George Frideric Handel's *Messiah* outside Rome's Parliament building. In 2013, he received a four-year prison sentence for tax fraud but was exempt from incarceration because he was over seventy. Instead, he was sentenced to serve food in old age homes where he was the most popular server ever. Because of his conviction, he was barred from running for public office for six years. In July 2019, at the age of eighty-three, he ran for European Parliament. And won.

It is likely that Berlusconi's wife, Veronica Lario, never expected him to be faithful. After all, their relationship began in 1980 when the married Berlusconi saw her topless in a stage play. With sublime dignity, Veronica put up with his infidelities and unexplained absences. Then, in 2009, she discovered that he had been sleeping with underaged girls. On May 3, 2009, she published a letter in *La Repubblica* newspaper informing him of her decision to seek a divorce. "I cannot stay with a man who frequents minors," she wrote. "I've tried to help my husband; I've implored those he's with to change things, as you would with a person who's not well. But it was useless. Now I say 'enough.'"

Knowledge of the love affairs of Great Britain's prime ministers has, for the most part, evaporated due to upper-crust discretion. William Ewart Gladstone, who served as British prime minister for twelve years at different times between 1868 and 1894, said that he had known twelve British prime ministers, and all but one were adulterers. We are not certain where he put himself on that list as nothing is known of most of these affairs. True, adultery among Britain's elite was rampant at the time—even among women, once they had given their husbands an heir and a spare, as long as it didn't become public knowledge. Journalists refused to cover their leaders' love lives, unless, ending up in divorce court, they were already a matter of public record.

The love affair of the fifty-seven-year-old Prime Minister William Lamb, 2nd Viscount Melbourne, and the novelist, twenty-eight-year-old Caroline Norton, exploded into the press in 1836 because it was the centerpiece of a public trial. Caroline's husband, the Honorable George Norton, sued Melbourne for "criminal conversation" with Norton's wife, demanding ten thousand pounds (close to a million pounds in today's money) for depriving him of her body. According to contemporary descriptions of Caroline's beauty, it was worth every penny.

Melbourne called on Caroline Norton three or four times a week when her husband was at work. During the visits, she would lock the parlor door and instruct her servants not to disturb her. Servants testified that, on rare occasions when the door was not locked, they had entered to find Mrs. Norton on her knees in front of Melbourne or lying on the floor with "her clothes in a position to expose her person."

After much tawdry testimony, the jury found the prime minister not guilty. Though it seemed clear he was guilty as sin, the jurors believed that Melbourne's political enemies had manipulated the scandal to remove him from office, and they weren't going to be used as pawns in such a scheme. He remained prime minister, his reputation burnished rather than tarnished by dallying with a famous beauty thirty years his junior. (We can only assume he would have been pleased to see Rufus Sewell's devastatingly rakish portrayal of him in ITV's *Victoria* series.) But Caroline Norton's reputation was ruined. Her husband confiscated their three young sons, refusing to grant her visitation. For decades, she campaigned tirelessly to bring about legislation to protect the legal rights of separated and divorced mothers.

British Prime Minister David Lloyd George, a Welshman by birth, guided the nation through much of World War I. Dubbed "the Welsh goat" for his relentless pursuit of women, he usually had discreet affairs with married society ladies, much to the consternation of his wife, Margaret. He fathered so many illegitimate children that one day his son Dick ventured into a pub and saw a man who could have been his twin. The two realized they were brothers. Lloyd George's daughter Olwen thought it wasn't entirely his fault. She said, "Many of his friends felt he should be protected against women; they flocked round him and often threw themselves at him."

In 1913, at the age of fifty, Lloyd George began an affair with his private secretary, twenty-five-year-old Frances Stevenson. When his wife left one of their many residences by one door, Frances would be coming in another, like something out of a French farce. After having two abortions, Frances had his daughter in 1929 at the age of forty and pretended she had adopted an orphan. In 1943, two years after Lloyd George's wife died, Frances finally married him after waiting thirty years. The dashing groom was eighty, and Frances was relegated to nursing him for the remaining eighteen months of his life. While one might wonder if it was worth the wait, Frances did seem quite satisfied that she had outlasted the wife and gotten him in the end.

True to form, the British press reported on various lawsuits against Lloyd George over the years naming him corespondent in adultery cases—all of which he successfully defended. But journalists refused to publish anything on Frances Stevenson who, everyone in government circles knew, was a kind of second wife. It would have been unworthy of English gentlemen to tarnish the reputation of the public servant who had steered Britain through the perils of a world war.

Most Australians, too, believe that a politician's sex life should remain private, and journalists Down Under have followed that lead. But in 2018, the married, fifty-year-old Deputy Prime Minister Barnaby Joyce resigned over a relationship with his thirty-three-year-old press secretary, whom he had impregnated. Joyce admitted he was the father of the unborn child and had been having a relationship with the woman.

In the #MeToo era, it wasn't Joyce's extramarital affair that led to his resignation but the fact that the woman in question worked for him, and their relationship could be seen as sexual harassment on the job. Prime Minister Malcolm Turnbull introduced a rule prohibiting sexual relations between ministers and their staff, which social media immediately dubbed the "bonk ban." Now Australia is wrestling with the ethics of exposing the sex lives of politicians.

"It licenses the press to investigate politicians' private lives," said the director of an Australian think tank, the Center for Independent Studies. "It's an invasion of privacy."

Japan has long had the tradition of the *uwaki mono*—the frivolous womanizer—which sounds like a bad thing to us but was seen as a good thing by them. In 1952, during a public forum, an opponent accused political party leader Bukichi Miki of keeping four mistresses. "I must strive for accuracy," Miki retorted angrily. "I will go ahead and correct the mathematical errors of the aforementioned weak candidate right now. It was said that I have four mistresses, but actually I have five. Confusing four with five ought to be considered shameful even for a first grader . . . However, all these women have now become old maids and aren't of use to me anymore. Even so, Bukichi Miki could never do something so inhumane as abandon them! Even today I care for them all." The crowd roared with laughter, applauding Miki's generosity, and Miki's party won the election.

It was a lack of generosity that toppled sixty-six-year-old Prime Minister Sosuke Uno in 1989. Uno resigned from office after only sixty-nine days due to a sex scandal with a geisha. His crime was not the sex—no one cared about that—but his stinginess. Though Uno was one of Japan's wealthiest politicians, he had only given his thirty-five-year-old lover, Mitsuko Nakanishi, about $2,300 a month over their five-month affair—meager indeed for a geisha—and no traditional goodbye present when he dumped her. Incensed at the injustice, when Uno was suddenly appointed prime minister four years later, the geisha contacted a Japanese magazine because, she said, "A man who treats women so shabbily shouldn't be allowed to lead a nation."

Many Japanese citizens, however, felt the scandal unworthy of press coverage. As one politician said on TV, "What's below the navel isn't personal character."

CONCLUSION

*W*ith regards to political sex scandals, Americans have historically gasped in outrage as the cultural descendants of Puritans are bound to do. But then we forgave Alexander Hamilton, who had done so much for the economy and told the truth about his affair, and Thomas Jefferson, who doubled the size of the nation. And we voted for rapist Grover Cleveland, who saved the taxpayers a boatload of money. True, we were upset at Gary Hart's lies more than his affair. But these days we don't even care about the lies anymore. Bill Clinton had a 73 percent approval rating the week he was impeached for lying about sex. Compared to the constant chaos of all his other scandals involving the coronavirus, national security, and the Constitution, Trump's lies about sex are trivial.

Still, some illicit affairs are more dignified than others. There is a difference between Woodrow Wilson's years'-long relationship with Mary Peck and JFK's three-whore-a-day habit. Between FDR's thirty-year affair with the love of his life, Lucy Mercer Rutherfurd, and Trump grabbing unsuspecting women by the genitals.

There is also a difference—at the moment—between how

Democrats and Republicans treat sex scandals. Democrat Al Franken, a senator since 2009 and a comedian before that, was forced to resign by his fellow Democrats in 2017 after several women came forward with various allegations of inappropriate touching and kissing. Perhaps most damning, during a 2006 USO tour Franken was photographed appearing to place his hands above a woman's breasts while she was asleep wearing body armor and a helmet. In his resignation speech, Franken pointed out that President Trump remained in office despite his grab-'em-by-the-pussy tape and accusations of sexual assault, and that the Republican Party supported accused child molester Roy Moore in his 2017 Senate campaign. This is, of course, the polar opposite of 1998, when Republicans were aghast at Bill Clinton's disgraceful amatory antics while Democrats shook their heads at all the uproar over a little sex and several unproven allegations.

Given that so many men who seek high office suffer from hubris syndrome, bipolar disorder, narcissistic personality disorder, and a superfluity of testosterone, it is likely many of them will continue to seek sex on the side, in ways both dignified and sordid. Perhaps a Trump voter best summed up the likelihood of change during an interview in 2016 after the release of the *Access Hollywood* tape. "That's what powerful men do," he said.

But what about powerful women? In November 2018, 121 women won House and Senate seats, a record number. It is quite difficult to unearth sex scandals involving female politicians, which could be rooted in the fact that, according to political science experts, such as University of Washington professor Amanda Clayton, women become politicians in order to *do something*—get behind a cause such as good schools or gun control—while men become politicians in order to *be somebody*, which is where the hubris and narcissism kick in, often trailing naked women in their wake. Most likely, as the number of female politicians increases, the number of sex scandals will decrease.

Because, quite frankly, it is inconceivable that U.S. speaker of the House of Representatives Nancy Pelosi, German chancellor Angela Merkel, former British prime minister Theresa May, or a future female U.S. president would have sex with interns and porn stars, or brag about grabbing unsuspecting men's penises, or tweet images of their nether regions to minors. In other words, girls won't be boys.

Which, certainly, will be a good thing.

BIBLIOGRAPHY

Alford, Mimi. *Once Upon a Secret: My Affair with President John F. Kennedy and Its Aftermath.* New York: Random House, 2012.

Ambrose, Stephen. *Eisenhower: Soldier, General of the Army, President-Elect, 1890–1952.* Volume I. New York: Simon & Schuster, 1983.

Anthony, Carl Sferrazza. *Florence Harding: The First Lady, the Jazz Age, and the Death of America's Most Scandalous President.* New York: William Morrow, 1998.

Atkinson, Diane. *The Criminal Conversation of Mrs. Norton: Victorian England's "Scandal of the Century" and the Fallen Socialite Who Changed Women's Lives Forever.* Chicago: Chicago Review Press, 2012.

Bai, Matt. *All the Truth Is Out: The Week Politics Went Tabloid.* New York: Vintage, 2014.

Benes, Ross. *The Sex Effect: Baring Our Complicated Relationship with Sex.* Naperville, IL: Sourcebooks, 2017.

Bly, Nellie. *The Kennedy Men: Three Generations of Sex, Scandal and Secrets.* New York: Kensington, 1996.

Britton, Nan. *The President's Daughter.* New York: Elizabeth Ann Guild, 1927.

Brown, Madeleine Duncan. *Texas in the Morning: The Love Story of Madeleine Brown and President Lyndon Baines Johnson.* Baltimore: Conservatory Press, 1997.

Bryant, Traphes. *Dog Days at the White House: The Outrageous Memoirs of the Presidential Kennel Keeper.* New York: Macmillan, 1975.

Burleigh, Nina. *Golden Handcuffs: The Secret History of Trump's Women.* New York: Simon & Schuster, 2018.

Caro, Robert A. *The Years of Lyndon Johnson: Master of the Senate.* New York: Alfred A. Knopf, 2002.

———. *The Years of Lyndon Johnson: Means of Ascent.* New York: Alfred A. Knopf, 1990.

———. *The Years of Lyndon Johnson: Passage of Power.* New York: Alfred A. Knopf, 2012.

———. *The Years of Lyndon Johnson: The Path to Power.* New York: Alfred A. Knopf, 1982.

Caroli, Betty Boyd. *Lady Bird and Lyndon: The Hidden Story of a Marriage that Made a President.* New York: Simon & Schuster, 2015.

Cawthorne, Nigel. *Sex Lives of the U.S. Presidents.* London: Prion, 1996.

Chernow, Ron. *Alexander Hamilton.* New York: Penguin, 2004.

Daniels, Stormy. *Full Disclosure.* New York: St. Martin's Press, 2018.

Day, Michael. *Being Berlusconi: The Rise & Fall from Cosa Nostra to Bunga Bunga.* New York: Palgrave Macmillan, 2015.

Deloire, Christophe, and Christophe Dubois. *Sexus Politicus.* Paris: Albin Michel, 2006.

Flowers, Gennifer. *Passion and Betrayal.* Del Mar, CA: Emery Dalton, 1995.

Flynt, Larry, and David Eisenbach. *One Nation Under Sex: How the Private Lives of Presidents, First Ladies, and Their Lovers Changed the Course of American History.* New York: Palgrave Macmillan, 2011.

Gordon-Reed, Annette. *The Hemingses of Monticello: An American Family.* New York: W. W. Norton, 2008.

Hague, Ffion. *The Pain and the Privilege: The Women in Lloyd George's Life.* London: Harper Perennial, 2008.

Holt, Marilyn Irvin. *Mamie Doud Eisenhower: The General's First Lady.* Wichita, KS: University Press of Kansas, 2007.

Hunter, Rielle. *What Really Happened: John Edwards, Our Daughter, and Me.* Dallas, TX: Benbella Books, 2012.

Kaminski, John P., editor. *Jefferson in Love: The Love Letters Between Thomas Jefferson & Maria Cosway.* Madison, WI: Madison House, 1999.

Kranish, Michael, and Marc Fisher. *Trump Revealed: The Definitive Biography of the 45th President.* New York: Scribner, 2016.

Lachman, Charles. *A Secret Life: The Lies and Scandals of President Grover Cleveland.* New York: Skyhorse, 2012.

Laumond, Jean-Claude. *Vingt-Cinq Ans Avec Lui.* Paris: Ramsay, 2001.

Longford, Ruth. *Frances, Countess Lloyd-George: More Than a Mistress*. London: Gracewing, 1996.

Means, Gaston B., and May Dixon Thacker. *The Strange Death of President Harding*. New York: Gold Label, 1930.

Miller, Kristie. *Ellen and Edith: Woodrow Wilson's First Ladies*. Wichita, KS: University Press of Kansas, 2014.

Morgan, Kay Summersby. *Past Forgetting: My Love Affair with Dwight D. Eisenhower*. New York: Simon & Schuster, 1976.

Oppenheimer, Jerry. *State of a Union: Inside the Complex Marriage of Bill and Hillary Clinton*. New York: HarperCollins, 2000.

Owen, David. *In Sickness and in Power: Illness in Heads of Government during the Last 100 Years*. London: Methuen, 2008.

Parks, Lillian Rogers, and Frances Spatz Leighton. *My Thirty Years Backstairs at the White House*. Bronx, NY: Ishi Press International, 2009.

Persico, Joseph E. *Franklin & Lucy: President Roosevelt, Mrs. Rutherfurd, and the Other Remarkable Women in His Life*. New York: Random House, 2008.

Phillips-Schrock, Patrick. *The White House: An Illustrated Architectural History*. Jefferson, NC: McFarland, 2013.

Quinn, Susan. *Eleanor and Hick: The Love Affair That Shaped a First Lady*. New York: Penguin Random House, 2016.

Robenalt, James David. *The Harding Affair: Love and Espionage During the Great War*. New York: St. Martin's Press, 2009.

Ross, Shelley. *Fall from Grace: Sex, Scandal, and Corruption in American Politics from 1702 to the Present*. New York: Ballantine, 1988.

Sciacca, Tony. *Kennedy and His Women*. New York: Manor Books, 1976.

Sheehy, Gail. *Hillary's Choice*. New York: Penguin Random House, 1999.

Short, Philip. *Mitterrand: A Study in Ambiguity*. London: Bodley Head, 2013.

Sloan, Sam. *Mafia Moll: The Judith Exner Story, The Life of the Mistress of John F. Kennedy*. Bronx, NY: Ishi Press International, 2008.

Smith, Jean Edward. *Eisenhower in War and Peace*. New York: Random House, 2013.

Smith, Kathryn. *The Gatekeeper: Missy LeHand, FDR, and the Untold Story of the Partnership that Defined a Presidency*. New York: Touchstone, 2016.

Smith, Sally Bedell. *Grace and Power: The Private World of the Kennedy White House.* New York: Random House, 2004.

Taylor, A. J. P., editor. *My Darling Pussy: The Letters of Lloyd George and Frances Stevenson 1913–41.* London: Weidenfeld and Nicolson, 1975.

Von Post, Gunilla. *Love, Jack.* New York: Crown, 1997.

Witcover, Jules. *The American Vice Presidency: From Irrelevance to Power.* Washington, D.C.: Smithsonian Books, 2014.